# 40 Algorithms Every Programmer Should Know

Hone your problem-solving skills by learning different
algorithms and their implementation in Python

**Imran Ahmad**

**BIRMINGHAM - MUMBAI**

# 40 Algorithms Every Programmer Should Know

**Commissioning Editor:** Kunal Chaudhari
**Acquisition Editor:** Karan Gupta
**Content Development Editor:** Pathikrit Roy
**Senior Editor:** Rohit Singh
**Technical Editor:** Pradeep Sahu
**Copy Editor:** Safis Editing
**Project Coordinator:** Francy Puthiry
**Proofreader:** Safis Editing
**Indexer:** Rekha Nair
**Production Designer:** Nilesh Mohite

First published: June 2020

Production reference: 1120620

Published by Packt Publishing Ltd.
Livery Place
35 Livery Street
Birmingham
B3 2PB, UK.

ISBN 978-1-78980-121-7

www.packt.com

*To my father, Inayatullah Khan, who still keeps motivating me to keep learning
and exploring new horizons.*

`Packt.com`

Subscribe to our online digital library for full access to over 7,000 books and videos, as well as industry leading tools to help you plan your personal development and advance your career. For more information, please visit our website.

## Why subscribe?

- Spend less time learning and more time coding with practical eBooks and Videos from over 4,000 industry professionals

- Improve your learning with Skill Plans built especially for you

- Get a free eBook or video every month

- Fully searchable for easy access to vital information

- Copy and paste, print, and bookmark content

Did you know that Packt offers eBook versions of every book published, with PDF and ePub files available? You can upgrade to the eBook version at `www.packt.com` and as a print book customer, you are entitled to a discount on the eBook copy. Get in touch with us at `customercare@packtpub.com` for more details.

At `www.packt.com`, you can also read a collection of free technical articles, sign up for a range of free newsletters, and receive exclusive discounts and offers on Packt books and eBooks.

# Contributors

## About the author

**Imran Ahmad** is a certified Google instructor and has been teaching for Google and Learning Tree for a number of years. The topics Imran teaches include Python, machine learning, algorithms, big data, and deep learning. In his PhD, he proposed a new linear programming-based algorithm called ATSRA, which can be used to optimally assign resources in a cloud computing environment. For the last 4 years, Imran has been working on a high-profile machine learning project at the advanced analytics lab of the Canadian Federal Government. The project is to develop machine learning algorithms that can automate the process of immigration. Imran is currently working on developing algorithms to use GPUs optimally to train complex machine learning models.

# About the reviewer

**Benjamin Baka** is a full-stack software developer and is passionate about cutting-edge technologies and elegant programming techniques. He has 10 years of experience in different technologies, from C++, Java, and Ruby to Python and Qt. Some of the projects he's working on can be found on his GitHub page. He is currently working on exciting technologies for mPedigree.

# Packt is searching for authors like you

If you're interested in becoming an author for Packt, please visit `authors.packtpub.com` and apply today. We have worked with thousands of developers and tech professionals, just like you, to help them share their insight with the global tech community. You can make a general application, apply for a specific hot topic that we are recruiting an author for, or submit your own idea.

# Table of Contents

# Preface

Algorithms have always played an important role both in the science and practice of computing. This book focuses on utilizing these algorithms to solve real-world problems. To get the most out of these algorithms, a deeper understanding of their logic and mathematics is imperative. You'll start with an introduction to algorithms and explore various algorithm design techniques. Moving on, you'll learn about linear programming, page ranking, and graphs, and even work with machine learning algorithms, understanding the math and logic behind them. This book also contains case studies, such as weather prediction, tweet clustering, and movie recommendation engines, that will show you how to apply these algorithms optimally. As you complete this book, you will become confident in using algorithms for solving real-world computational problems.

## Who this book is for

This book is for the serious programmer! Whether you are an experienced programmer looking to gain a deeper understanding of the math behind the algorithms or have limited programming or data science knowledge and want to learn more about how you can take advantage of these battle-tested algorithms to improve the way you design and write code, you'll find this book useful. Experience with Python programming is a must, although knowledge of data science is helpful but not necessary.

## What this book covers

Chapter 1, *Overview of Algorithms*, summarizes the fundamentals of algorithms. It starts with a section on the basic concepts needed to understand the working of different algorithms. It summarizes how people started using algorithms to mathematically formulate certain classes of problems. It also mentions the limitations of different algorithms. The next section explains the various ways to specify the logic of an algorithm. As Python is used in this book to write the algorithms, how to set up the environment in order to run the examples is explained next. Then, the various ways in which an algorithm's performance can be quantified and compared against other algorithms are discussed. Finally, this chapter discusses various ways in which a particular implementation of an algorithm can be validated.

Chapter 2, *Data Structures Used in Algorithms*, focuses on algorithms' need for necessary in-memory data structures that can hold the temporary data. Algorithms can be data-intensive, compute-intensive, or both. But for all different types of algorithms, choosing the right data structures is essential for their optimal implementation. Many algorithms have recursive and iterative logic and require specialized data structures that are fundamentally iterative in nature. As we are using Python in this book, this chapter focuses on Python data structures that can be used to implement the algorithms discussed in this book.

Chapter 3, *Sorting and Searching Algorithms*, presents core algorithms that are used for sorting and searching. These algorithms can later become the basis for more complex algorithms. The chapter starts by presenting different types of sorting algorithms. It also compares the performance of various approaches. Then, various algorithms for searching are presented. They are compared and their performance and complexity are quantified. Finally, this chapter presents the actual applications of these algorithms.

Chapter 4, *Designing Algorithms*, presents the core design concepts of various algorithms. It also explains different types of algorithms and discusses their strengths and weaknesses. Understanding these concepts is important when it comes to designing optimal complex algorithms. The chapter starts by discussing different types of algorithmic designs. Then, it presents the solution for the famous traveling salesman problem. It then discusses linear programming and its limitations. Finally, it presents a practical example that shows how linear programming can be used for capacity planning.

Chapter 5, *Graph Algorithms*, focuses on the algorithms for graph problems that are common in computer science. There are many computational problems that can best be represented in terms of graphs. This chapter presents methods for representing a graph and for searching a graph. Searching a graph means systematically following the edges of the graph so as to visit the vertices of the graph. A graph-searching algorithm can discover a lot about the structure of a graph. Many algorithms begin by searching their input graph to obtain this structural information. Several other graph algorithms elaborate on basic graph searching. Techniques for searching a graph lie at the heart of the field of graph algorithms. The first section discusses the two most common computational representations of graphs: as adjacency lists and as adjacency matrices. Next, a simple graph-searching algorithm called *breadth-first search* is presented and shows how to create a breadth-first tree. The following section presents the depth-first search and provides some standard results about the order in which a depth-first search visits vertices.

Chapter 6, *Unsupervised Machine Learning Algorithms*, introduces unsupervised machine learning algorithms. These algorithms are classified as unsupervised because the model or algorithm tries to learn inherent structures, patterns, and relationships from given data without any supervision. First, clustering methods are discussed. These are machine learning methods that try to find patterns of similarity and relationships among data samples in our dataset and then cluster these samples into various groups, such that each group or cluster of data samples has some similarity, based on the inherent attributes or features. The following section discusses dimensionality reduction algorithms, which are used when we end up having a number of features. Next, some algorithms that deal with anomaly detection are presented. Finally, this chapter presents association rule-mining, which is a data mining method used to examine and analyze large transactional datasets to identify patterns and rules of interest. These patterns represent interesting relationships and associations, among various items across transactions.

Chapter 7, *Traditional Supervised Learning Algorithms*, describes traditional supervised machine learning algorithms in relation to a set of machine learning problems in which there is a labeled dataset with input attributes and corresponding output labels or classes. These inputs and corresponding outputs are then used to learn a generalized system, which can be used to predict results for previously unseen data points. First, the concept of classification is introduced in the context of machine learning. Then, the simplest of the machine learning algorithms, linear regression, is presented. This is followed by one of the most important algorithms, the decision tree. The limitations and strengths of decision tree algorithms are discussed, followed by two important algorithms, SVM and XGBoost.

Chapter 8, *Neural Network Algorithms*, first introduces the main concepts and components of a typical neural network, which is becoming the most important type of machine learning technique. Then, it presents the various types of neural networks and also explains the various kinds of activation functions that are used to realize these neural networks. The backpropagation algorithm is then discussed in detail. This is the most widely used algorithm to converge the neural network problem. Next, the transfer learning technique is explained, which can be used to greatly simplify and partially automate the training of models. Finally, how to use deep learning to detect objects in multimedia data is presented as a real-world example.

Chapter 9, *Algorithms for Natural Language Processing*, presents algorithms for **natural language processing** (**NLP**). This chapter proceeds from the theoretical to the practical in a progressive manner. First, it presents the fundamentals, followed by the underlying mathematics. Then, it discusses one of the most widely used neural networks to design and implement a couple of important use cases for textual data. The limitations of NLP are also discussed. Finally, a case study is presented where a model is trained to detect the author of a paper based on the writing style.

Chapter 10, *Recommendation Engines,* focuses on recommendation engines, which are a way of modeling information available in relation to user preferences and then using this information to provide informed recommendations on the basis of that information. The basis of the recommendation engine is always the recorded interaction between the users and products. This chapter begins by presenting the basic idea behind recommendation engines. Then, it discusses various types of recommendation engines. Finally, this chapter discusses how recommendation engines are used to suggest items and products to different users.

Chapter 11, *Data Algorithms,* focuses on the issues related to data-centric algorithms. The chapter starts with a brief overview of the issues related to data. Then, the criteria for classifying data are presented. Next, a description of how to apply algorithms to streaming data applications is provided and then the topic of cryptography is presented. Finally, a practical example of extracting patterns from Twitter data is presented.

Chapter 12, *Cryptography,* introduces the algorithms related to cryptography. The chapter starts by presenting the background. Then, symmetrical encryption algorithms are discussed. MD5 and SHA hashing algorithms are explained and the limitations and weaknesses associated with implementing symmetric algorithms are presented. Next, asymmetric encryption algorithms are discussed and how they are used to create digital certificates. Finally, a practical example that summarizes all these techniques is discussed.

Chapter 13, *Large-Scale Algorithms,* explains how large-scale algorithms handle data that cannot fit into the memory of a single node and involve processing that requires multiple CPUs. This chapter starts by discussing what types of algorithms are best suited to be run in parallel. Then, it discusses the issues related to parallelizing the algorithms. It also presents the CUDA architecture and discusses how a single GPU or an array of GPUs can be used to accelerate the algorithms and what changes need to be made to the algorithm in order to effectively utilize the power of the GPU. Finally, this chapter discusses cluster computing and discusses how Apache Spark creates **resilient distributed datasets (RDDs)** to create an extremely fast parallel implementation of standard algorithms.

Chapter 14, *Practical Considerations,* starts with the important topic of explainability, which is becoming more and more important now that the logic behind automated decision making has been explained. Then, this chapter presents the ethics of using an algorithm and the possibilities of creating biases when implementing them. Next, the techniques for handling NP-hard problems are discussed in detail. Finally, ways to implement algorithms, and the real-world challenges associated with this, are summarized.

# To get the most out of this book

| Chapter number | Software required (with version) | Free/Proprietary | Hardware specifications | OS required |
|---|---|---|---|---|
| 1-14 | Python version 3.7.2 or later | Free | Min 4GB of RAM, 8GB +Recommended. | Windows/Linux/Mac |

If you are using the digital version of this book, we advise you to type the code yourself or access the code via the GitHub repository (link available in the next section). Doing so will help you avoid any potential errors related to the copying and pasting of code.

# Download the example code files

You can download the example code files for this book from your account at www.packt.com. If you purchased this book elsewhere, you can visit www.packtpub.com/support and register to have the files emailed directly to you.

You can download the code files by following these steps:

1. Log in or register at www.packt.com.
2. Select the **Support** tab.
3. Click on **Code Downloads**.
4. Enter the name of the book in the **Search** box and follow the onscreen instructions.

Once the file is downloaded, please make sure that you unzip or extract the folder using the latest version of:

- WinRAR/7-Zip for Windows
- Zipeg/iZip/UnRarX for Mac
- 7-Zip/PeaZip for Linux

The code bundle for the book is also hosted on GitHub at https://github.com/PacktPublishing/40-Algorithms-Every-Programmer-Should-Know. In case there's an update to the code, it will be updated on the existing GitHub repository.

We also have other code bundles from our rich catalog of books and videos available at https://github.com/PacktPublishing/. Check them out!

# Download the color images

We also provide a PDF file that has color images of the screenshots/diagrams used in this book. You can download it here: https://static.packt-cdn.com/downloads/ 9781789801217_ColorImages.pdf.

# Conventions used

There are a number of text conventions used throughout this book.

CodeInText: Indicates code words in text, database table names, folder names, filenames, file extensions, pathnames, dummy URLs, user input, and Twitter handles. Here is an example: "Let's see how to add a new element to a stack by using push or removing an element from a stack by using pop."

A block of code is set as follows:

```
define swap(x, y)
    buffer = x
    x = y
    y = buffer
```

When we wish to draw your attention to a particular part of a code block, the relevant lines or items are set in bold:

```
define swap(x, y)
    buffer = x
    x = y
    y = buffer
```

Any command-line input or output is written as follows:

```
pip install a_package
```

**Bold**: Indicates a new term, an important word, or words that you see on screen. For example, words in menus or dialog boxes appear in the text like this. Here is an example: "One way to reduce the complexity of an algorithm is to compromise on its accuracy, producing a type of algorithm called an **approximate algorithm**."

Warnings or important notes appear like this.

 Tips and tricks appear like this.

# Get in touch

Feedback from our readers is always welcome.

**General feedback**: If you have questions about any aspect of this book, mention the book title in the subject of your message and email us at customercare@packtpub.com.

**Errata**: Although we have taken every care to ensure the accuracy of our content, mistakes do happen. If you have found a mistake in this book, we would be grateful if you would report this to us. Please visit www.packtpub.com/support/errata, selecting your book, clicking on the Errata Submission Form link, and entering the details.

**Piracy**: If you come across any illegal copies of our works in any form on the internet, we would be grateful if you would provide us with the location address or website name. Please contact us at copyright@packt.com with a link to the material.

**If you are interested in becoming an author**: If there is a topic that you have expertise in, and you are interested in either writing or contributing to a book, please visit authors.packtpub.com.

# Reviews

Please leave a review. Once you have read and used this book, why not leave a review on the site that you purchased it from? Potential readers can then see and use your unbiased opinion to make purchase decisions, we at Packt can understand what you think about our products, and our authors can see your feedback on their book. Thank you!

For more information about Packt, please visit packt.com.

# Section 1: Fundamentals and Core Algorithms

# 1

This section introduces us to the core aspects of algorithms. We will explore what an algorithm is and how to design it, and also learn about the data structures used in algorithms. This section also gives a deep idea on sorting and searching algorithms along with the algorithms to solve graphical problems. The chapters included in this section are:

- Chapter 1, *Overview of Algorithms*
- Chapter 2, *Data Structures used in Algorithms*
- Chapter 3, *Sorting and Searching Algorithms*
- Chapter 4, *Designing Algorithms*
- Chapter 5, *Graph Algorithms*

# Section 1 Fundamentals and Core Algorithms

# Overview of Algorithms

1

This book covers the information needed to understand, classify, select, and implement important algorithms. In addition to explaining their logic, this book also discusses data structures, development environments, and production environments that are suitable for different classes of algorithms. We focus on modern machine learning algorithms that are becoming more and more important. Along with the logic, practical examples of the use of algorithms to solve actual everyday problems are also presented.

This chapter provides an insight into the fundamentals of algorithms. It starts with a section on the basic concepts needed to understand the workings of different algorithms. This section summarizes how people started using algorithms to mathematically formulate a certain class of problems. It also mentions the limitations of different algorithms. The next section explains the various ways to specify the logic of an algorithm. As Python is used in this book to write the algorithms, how to set up the environment to run the examples is explained. Then, the various ways that an algorithm's performance can be quantified and compared against other algorithms are discussed. Finally, this chapter discusses various ways a particular implementation of an algorithm can be validated.

To sum up, this chapter covers the following main points:

- What is an algorithm?
- Specifying the logic of an algorithm
- Introducing Python packages
- Algorithm design techniques
- Performance analysis
- Validating an algorithm

# What is an algorithm?

In the simplest terms, an algorithm is a set of rules for carrying out some calculations to solve a problem. It is designed to yield results for any valid input according to precisely defined instructions. If you look up the word algorithm in an English language dictionary (such as American Heritage), it defines the concept as follows:

> *"An algorithm is a finite set of unambiguous instructions that, given some set of initial conditions, can be performed in a prescribed sequence to achieve a certain goal and that has a recognizable set of end conditions."*

Designing an algorithm is an effort to create a mathematical recipe in the most efficient way that can effectively be used to solve a real-world problem. This recipe may be used as the basis for developing a more reusable and generic mathematical solution that can be applied to a wider set of similar problems.

# The phases of an algorithm

The different phases of developing, deploying, and finally using an algorithm are illustrated in the following diagram:

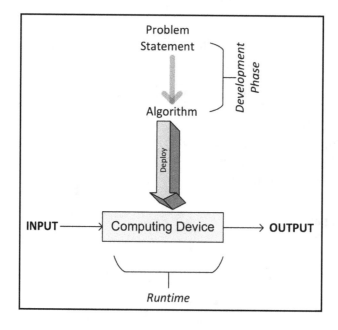

As we can see, the process starts with understanding the requirements from the problem statement that detail what needs to be done. Once the problem is clearly stated, it leads us to the development phase.

The development phase consists of two phases:

- **The design phase**: In the design phase, the architecture, logic, and implementation details of the algorithm are envisioned and documented. While designing an algorithm, we keep both accuracy and performance in mind. While searching for the solution to a given problem, in many cases we will end up having more than one alternative algorithm. The design phase of an algorithm is an iterative process that involves comparing different candidate algorithms. Some algorithms may provide simple and fast solutions but may compromise on accuracy. Other algorithms may be very accurate but may take considerable time to run due to their complexity. Some of these complex algorithms may be more efficient than others. Before making a choice, all the inherent tradeoffs of the candidate algorithms should be carefully studied. Particularly for a complex problem, designing an efficient algorithm is really important. A correctly designed algorithm will result in an efficient solution that will be capable of providing both satisfactory performance and reasonable accuracy at the same time.
- **The coding phase**: In the coding phase, the designed algorithm is converted into a computer program. It is important that the actual program implements all the logic and architecture suggested in the design phase.

The designing and coding phases of an algorithm are iterative in nature. Coming up with a design that meets both functional and non-functional requirements may take lots of time and effort. Functional requirements are those requirements that dictate what the right output for a given set of input data is. Non-functional requirements of an algorithm are mostly about the performance for a given size of data. Validation and performance analysis of an algorithm are discussed later in this chapter. Validating an algorithm is about verifying that an algorithm meets its functional requirements. Performance analysis of an algorithm is about verifying that it meets its main non-functional requirement: performance.

Once designed and implemented in a programming language of your choice, the code of the algorithm is ready to be deployed. Deploying an algorithm involves the design of the actual production environment where the code will run. The production environment needs to be designed according to the data and processing needs of the algorithm. For example, for parallelizable algorithms, a cluster with an appropriate number of computer nodes will be needed for the efficient execution of the algorithm. For data-intensive algorithms, a data ingress pipeline and the strategy to cache and store data may need to be designed. Designing a production environment is discussed in more detail in Chapter 13, *Large Scale Algorithms*, and Chapter 14, *Practical Considerations*. Once the production environment is designed and implemented, the algorithm is deployed, which takes the input data, processes it, and generates the output as per the requirements.

# Specifying the logic of an algorithm

When designing an algorithm, it is important to find different ways to specify its details. The ability to capture both its logic and architecture is required. Generally, just like building a home, it is important to specify the structure of an algorithm before actually implementing it. For more complex distributed algorithms, pre-planning the way their logic will be distributed across the cluster at running time is important for the iterative efficient design process. Through pseudocode and execution plans, both these needs are fulfilled and are discussed in the next section.

## Understanding pseudocode

The simplest way to specify the logic for an algorithm is to write the higher-level description of an algorithm in a semi-structured way, called **pseudocode**. Before writing the logic in pseudocode, it is helpful to first describe its main flow by writing the main steps in plain English. Then, this English description is converted into pseudocode, which is a structured way of writing this English description that closely represents the logic and flow for the algorithm. Well-written algorithm pseudocode should describe the high-level steps of the algorithm in reasonable detail, even if the detailed code is not relevant to the main flow and structure of the algorithm. The following figure shows the flow of steps:

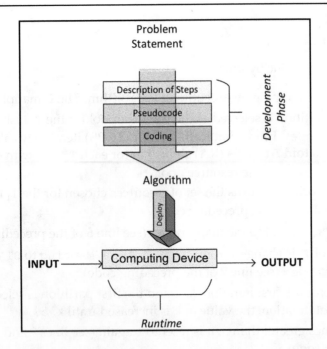

Note that once the pseudocode is written (as we will see in the next section), we are ready to code the algorithm using the programming language of our choice.

## A practical example of pseudocode

Figure 1.3 shows the pseudocode of a resource allocation algorithm called **SRPMP**. In cluster computing, there are many situations where there are parallel tasks that need to be run on a set of available resources, collectively called a **resource pool**. This algorithm assigns tasks to a resource and creates a mapping set, called $\Omega$. Note that the presented pseudocode captures the logic and flow of the algorithm, which is further explained in the following section:

```
 1: BEGIN Mapping_Phase
 2: Ω = { }
 3: k = 1
 4: FOREACH Tᵢ∈T
 5:     ωᵢ = RA (Δₖ, Tᵢ)
 6:     add {ωᵢ, Tᵢ} to Ω
 7:     state_change_Tᵢ [STATE 0: Idle/Unmapped] → [STATE 1: Idle/Mapped]
 8:     k=k+1
 9:     IF (k>q)
10:         k=1
11:     ENDIF
```

```
12: END FOREACH
13: END Mapping_Phase
```

Let's parse this algorithm line by line:

1. We start the mapping by executing the algorithm. The $\Omega$ mapping set is empty.

2. The first partition is selected as the resource pool for the $T_1$ task (see line 3 of the preceding code). **Television Rating Point (TRPS)** iteratively calls the **Rheumatoid Arthritis (RA)** algorithm for each $T_i$ task with one of the partitions chosen as the resource pool.

3. The RA algorithm returns the set of resources chosen for the $T_i$ task, represented by $\omega_i$ (see line 5 of the preceding code).

4. $T_i$ and $\omega_i$ are added to the mapping set (see line 6 of the preceding code).

5. The state of $T_i$ is changed from STATE 0:Idle/Mapping to STATE 1:Idle/Mapped (see line 7 of the preceding code).

6. Note that for the first iteration, k=1 and the first partition is selected. For each subsequent iteration, the value of k is increased until k>q.

7. If k becomes greater than q, it is reset to 1 again (see lines 9 and 10 of the preceding code).

8. This process is repeated until a mapping between all tasks and the set of resources they will use is determined and stored in a mapping set called $\Omega$.

9. Once each of the tasks is mapped to a set of the resources in the mapping phase, it is executed.

# Using snippets

With the popularity of simple but powerful coding language such as Python, an alternative approach is becoming popular, which is to represent the logic of the algorithm directly in the programming language in a somewhat simplified version. Like pseudocode, this selected code captures the important logic and structure of the proposed algorithm, avoiding detailed code. This selected code is sometimes called a **snippet**. In this book, snippets are used instead of pseudocode wherever possible as they save one additional step. For example, let's look at a simple snippet that is about a Python function that can be used to swap two variables:

```
define swap(x, y)
    buffer = x
    x = y
    y = buffer
```

Note that snippets cannot always replace pseudocode. In pseudocode, sometimes we abstract many lines of code as one line of pseudocode, expressing the logic of the algorithm without becoming distracted by unnecessary coding details.

# Creating an execution plan

Pseudocode and snippets are not always enough to specify all the logic related to more complex distributed algorithms. For example, distributed algorithms usually need to be divided into different coding phases at runtime that have a precedence order. The right strategy to divide the larger problem into an optimal number of phases with the right precedence constraints is crucial for the efficient execution of an algorithm.

We need to find a way to represent this strategy as well to completely represent the logic and structure of an algorithm. An execution plan is one of the ways of detailing how the algorithm will be subdivided into a bunch of tasks. A task can be mappers or reducers that can be grouped together in blocks called **stages**. The following diagram shows an execution plan that is generated by an Apache Spark runtime before executing an algorithm. It details the runtime tasks that the job created for executing our algorithm will be divided into:

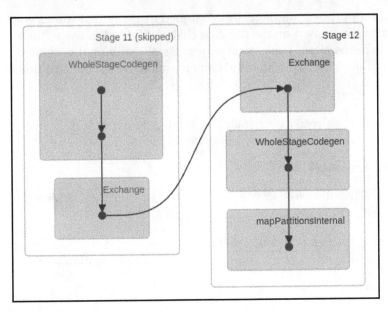

Note that the preceding diagram has five tasks that have been divided into two different stages: **Stage 11** and **Stage 12**.

# Introducing Python packages

Once designed, algorithms need to be implemented in a programming language as per the design. For this book, I chose the programming language Python. I chose it because Python is a flexible and open source programming language. Python is also the language of choice for increasingly important cloud computing infrastructures, such as **Amazon Web Services** (**AWS**), Microsoft Azure, and **Google Cloud Platform** (**GCP**).

The official Python home page is available at https://www.python.org/, which also has instructions for installation and a useful beginner's guide.

If you have not used Python before, it is a good idea to browse through this beginner's guide to self-study. A basic understanding of Python will help you to better understand the concepts presented in this book.

For this book, I expect you to use the recent version of Python 3. At the time of writing, the most recent version is 3.7.3, which is what we will use to run the exercises in this book.

# Python packages

Python is a general-purpose language. It is designed in a way that comes with bare minimum functionality. Based on the use case that you intend to use Python for, additional packages need to be installed. The easiest way to install additional packages is through the pip installer program. This pip command can be used to install the additional packages:

```
pip install a_package
```

The packages that have already been installed need to be periodically updated to get the latest functionality. This is achieved by using the upgrade flag:

```
pip install a_package --upgrade
```

Another Python distribution for scientific computing is Anaconda, which can be downloaded from http://continuum.io/downloads.

In addition to using the pip command to install new packages, for Anaconda distribution, we also have the option of using the following command to install new packages:

```
conda install a_package
```

To update the existing packages, the Anaconda distribution gives us the option to use the following command:

```
conda update a_package
```

There are all sorts of Python packages that are available. Some of the important packages that are relevant for algorithms are described in the following section.

# The SciPy ecosystem

Scientific Python (SciPy)—pronounced *sigh pie*—is a group of Python packages created for the scientific community. It contains many functions, including a wide range of random number generators, linear algebra routines, and optimizers. SciPy is a comprehensive package and, over time, people have developed many extensions to customize and extend the package according to their needs.

The following are the main packages that are part of this ecosystem:

- **NumPy**: For algorithms, the ability to create multi-dimensional data structures, such as arrays and matrices, is really important. NumPy offers a set of array and matrix data types that are important for statistics and data analysis. Details about NumPy can be found at `http://www.numpy.org/`.
- **scikit-learn**: This machine learning extension is one of the most popular extensions of SciPy. Scikit-learn provides a wide range of important machine learning algorithms, including classification, regression, clustering, and model validation. You can find more details about scikit-learn at `http://scikit-learn.org/`.
- **pandas**: pandas is an open source software library. It contains the tabular complex data structure that is used widely to input, output, and process tabular data in various algorithms. The pandas library contains many useful functions and it also offers highly optimized performance. More details about pandas can be found at `http://pandas.pydata.org/`.
- **Matplotlib**: Matplotlib provides tools to create powerful visualizations. Data can be presented as line plots, scatter plots, bar charts, histograms, pie charts, and so on. More information can be found at `https://matplotlib.org/`.
- **Seaborn**: Seaborn can be thought of as similar to the popular ggplot2 library in R. It is based on Matplotlib and offers an advanced interface for drawing brilliant statistical graphics. Further details can be found at `https://seaborn.pydata.org/`.
- **iPython**: iPython is an enhanced interactive console that is designed to facilitate the writing, testing, and debugging of Python code.
- **Running Python programs**: An interactive mode of programming is useful for learning and experimenting with code. Python programs can be saved in a text file with the `.py` extension and that file can be run from the console.

# Implementing Python via the Jupyter Notebook

Another way to run Python programs is through the Jupyter Notebook. The Jupyter Notebook provides a browser-based user interface to develop code. The Jupyter Notebook is used to present the code examples in this book. The ability to annotate and describe the code with texts and graphics makes it the perfect tool for presenting and explaining an algorithm and a great tool for learning.

To start the notebook, you need to start the `Juypter-notebook` process and then open your favorite browser and navigate to `http://localhost:8888`:

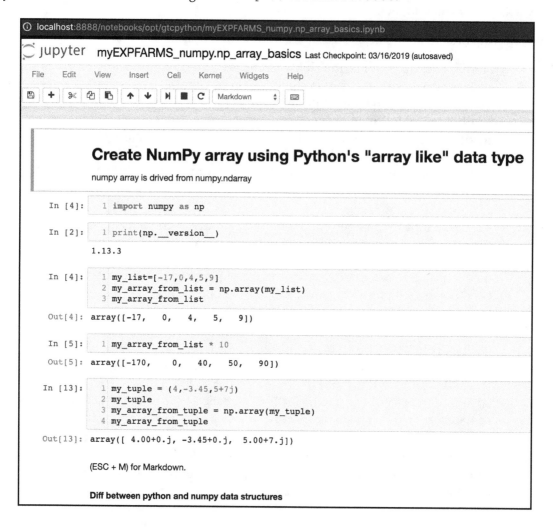

Note that a Jupyter Notebook consists of different blocks called **cells**.

# Algorithm design techniques

An algorithm is a mathematical solution to a real-world problem. When designing an algorithm, we keep the following three design concerns in mind as we work on designing and fine-tuning the algorithms:

- **Concern 1**: Is this algorithm producing the result we expected?
- **Concern 2**: Is this the most optimal way to get these results?
- **Concern 3**: How is the algorithm going to perform on larger datasets?

It is important to better understand the complexity of the problem itself before designing a solution for it. For example, it helps us to design an appropriate solution if we characterize the problem in terms of its needs and complexity. Generally, the algorithms can be divided into the following types based on the characteristics of the problem:

- **Data-intensive algorithms:** Data-intensive algorithms are designed to deal with a large amount of data. They are expected to have relatively simplistic processing requirements. A compression algorithm applied to a huge file is a good example of data-intensive algorithms. For such algorithms, the size of the data is expected to be much larger than the memory of the processing engine (a single node or cluster) and an iterative processing design may need to be developed to efficiently process the data according to the requirements.
- **Compute-intensive algorithms**: Compute-intensive algorithms have considerable processing requirements but do not involve large amounts of data. A simple example is the algorithm to find a very large prime number. Finding a strategy to divide the algorithm into different phases so that at least some of the phases are parallelized is key to maximizing the performance of the algorithm.
- **Both data and compute-intensive algorithms**: There are certain algorithms that deal with a large amount of data and also have considerable computing requirements. Algorithms used to perform sentiment analysis on live video feeds are a good example of where both the data and the processing requirements are huge in accomplishing the task. Such algorithms are the most resource-intensive algorithms and require careful design of the algorithm and intelligent allocation of available resources.

To characterize the problem in terms of its complexity and needs, it helps if we study its data and compute dimensions in more depth, which we will do in the following section.

# The data dimension

To categorize the data dimension of the problem, we look at its **volume**, **velocity**, and **variety** (the **3Vs**), which are defined as follows:

- **Volume**: The volume is the expected size of the data that the algorithm will process.
- **Velocity**: The velocity is the expected rate of new data generation when the algorithm is used. It can be zero.
- **Variety**: The variety quantifies how many different types of data the designed algorithm is expected to deal with.

The following figure shows the 3Vs of the data in more detail. The center of this diagram shows the simplest possible data, with a small volume and low variety and velocity. As we move away from the center, the complexity of the data increases. It can increase in one or more of the three dimensions. For example, in the dimension of velocity, we have the **Batch** process as the simplest, followed by the **Periodic** process, and then the **Near Real-Time** process. Finally, we have the **Real-Time** process, which is the most complex to handle in the context of data velocity. For example, a collection of live video feeds gathered by a group of monitoring cameras will have a high volume, high velocity, and high variety and may need an appropriate design to have the ability to store and process data effectively. On the other hand, a simple .csv file created in Excel will have a low volume, low velocity, and low variety:

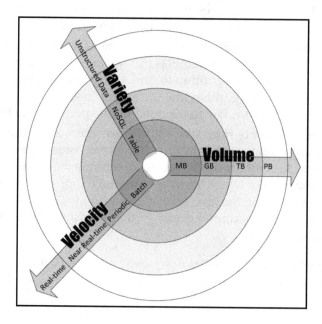

For example, if the input data is a simple `csv` file, then the volume, velocity, and variety of the data will be low. On the other hand, if the input data is the live stream of a security video camera, then the volume, velocity, and variety of the data will be quite high and this problem should be kept in mind while designing an algorithm for it.

# Compute dimension

The compute dimension is about the processing and computing needs of the problem at hand. The processing requirements of an algorithm will determine what sort of design is most efficient for it. For example, deep learning algorithms, in general, require lots of processing power. It means that for deep learning algorithms, it is important to have multi-node parallel architecture wherever possible.

# A practical example

Let's assume that we want to conduct sentiment analysis on a video. Sentiment analysis is where we try to flag different portions of a video with human emotions of sadness, happiness, fear, joy, frustration, and ecstasy. It is a compute-intensive job where lots of computing power is needed. As you will see in the following figure, to design the compute dimension, we have divided the processing into five tasks, consisting of two stages. All the data transformation and preparation is implemented in three mappers. For that, we divide the video into three different partitions, called **splits**. After the mappers are executed, the resulting processed video is inputted to the two aggregators, called **reducers**. To conduct the required sentiment analysis, the reducers group the video according to the emotions. Finally, the results are combined in the output:

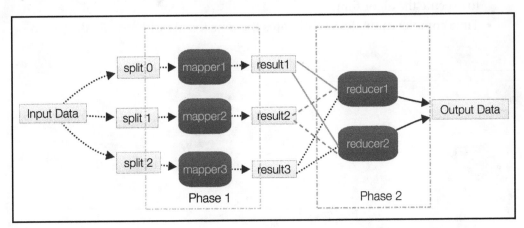

Note that the number of mappers directly translates to the runtime parallelism of the algorithm. The optimal number of mappers and reducers is dependent on the characteristics of the data, the type of algorithm that is needed to be used, and the number of resources available.

# Performance analysis

Analyzing the performance of an algorithm is an important part of its design. One of the ways to estimate the performance of an algorithm is to analyze its complexity.

Complexity theory is the study of how complicated algorithms are. To be useful, any algorithm should have three key features:

- It should be correct. An algorithm won't do you much good if it doesn't give you the right answers.
- A good algorithm should be understandable. The best algorithm in the world won't do you any good if it's too complicated for you to implement on a computer.
- A good algorithm should be efficient. Even if an algorithm produces a correct result, it won't help you much if it takes a thousand years or if it requires 1 billion terabytes of memory.

There are two possible types of analysis to quantify the complexity of an algorithm:

- Space complexity analysis: Estimates the runtime memory requirements needed to execute the algorithm.
- Time complexity analysis: Estimates the time the algorithm will take to run.

# Space complexity analysis

Space complexity analysis estimates the amount of memory required by the algorithm to process input data. While processing the input data, the algorithm needs to store the transient temporary data structures in memory. The way the algorithm is designed affects the number, type, and size of these data structures. In an age of distributed computing and with increasingly large amounts of data that needs to be processed, space complexity analysis is becoming more and more important. The size, type, and number of these data structures will dictate the memory requirements for the underlying hardware. Modern in-memory data structures used in distributed computing—such as **Resilient Distributed Datasets (RDDs)**—need to have efficient resource allocation mechanisms that are aware of the memory requirements at different execution phases of the algorithm.

Space complexity analysis is a must for the efficient design of algorithms. If proper space complexity analysis is not conducted while designing a particular algorithm, insufficient memory availability for the transient temporary data structures may trigger unnecessary disk spillovers, which could potentially considerably affect the performance and efficiency of the algorithm.

In this chapter, we will look deeper into time complexity. Space complexity will be discussed in Chapter 13, *Large-Scale Algorithms*, in more detail, where we will deal with large-scale distributed algorithms with complex runtime memory requirements.

# Time complexity analysis

Time complexity analysis estimates how long it will take for an algorithm to complete its assigned job based on its structure. In contrast to space complexity, time complexity is not dependent on any hardware that the algorithm will run on. Time complexity analysis solely depends on the structure of the algorithm itself. The overall goal of time complexity analysis is to try to answer these important questions—will this algorithm scale? How well will this algorithm handle larger datasets?

To answer these questions, we need to determine the effect on the performance of an algorithm as the size of the data is increased and make sure that the algorithm is designed in a way that not only makes it accurate but also scales well. The performance of an algorithm is becoming more and more important for larger datasets in today's world of "big data."

In many cases, we may have more than one approach available to design the algorithm. The goal of conducting time complexity analysis, in this case, will be as follows:

> *"Given a certain problem and more than one algorithm, which one is the most efficient to use in terms of time efficiency?"*

There can be two basic approaches to calculating the time complexity of an algorithm:

- **A post-implementation profiling approach**: In this approach, different candidate algorithms are implemented and their performance is compared.
- **A pre-implementation theoretical approach**: In this approach, the performance of each algorithm is approximated mathematically before running an algorithm.

The advantage of the theoretical approach is that it only depends on the structure of the algorithm itself. It does not depend on the actual hardware that will be used to run the algorithm, the choice of the software stack chosen at runtime, or the programming language used to implement the algorithm.

# Estimating the performance

The performance of a typical algorithm will depend on the type of the data given to it as an input. For example, if the data is already sorted according to the context of the problem we are trying to solve, the algorithm may perform blazingly fast. If the sorted input is used to benchmark this particular algorithm, then it will give an unrealistically good performance number, which will not be a true reflection of its real performance in most scenarios. To handle this dependency of algorithms on the input data, we have different types of cases to consider when conducting a performance analysis.

# The best case

In the best case, the data given as input is organized in a way that the algorithm will give its best performance. Best-case analysis gives the upper bound of the performance.

# The worst case

The second way to estimate the performance of an algorithm is to try to find the maximum possible time it will take to get the job done under a given set of conditions. This worst-case analysis of an algorithm is quite useful as we are guaranteeing that regardless of the conditions, the performance of the algorithm will always be better than the numbers that come out of our analysis. Worst-case analysis is especially useful for estimating the performance when dealing with complex problems with larger datasets. Worst-case analysis gives the lower bound of the performance of the algorithm.

# The average case

This starts by dividing the various possible inputs into various groups. Then, it conducts the performance analysis from one of the representative inputs from each group. Finally, it calculates the average of the performance of each of the groups.

Average-case analysis is not always accurate as it needs to consider all the different combinations and possibilities of input to the algorithm, which is not always easy to do.

# Selecting an algorithm

How do you know which one is a better solution? How do you know which algorithm runs faster? Time complexity and Big O notation (discussed later in this chapter) are really good tools for answering these types of questions.

To see where it can be useful, let's take a simple example where the objective is to sort a list of numbers. There are a couple of algorithms available that can do the job. The issue is how to choose the right one.

First, an observation that can be made is that if there are not too many numbers in the list, then it does not matter which algorithm do we choose to sort the list of numbers. So, if there are only 10 numbers in the list (n=10), then it does not matter which algorithm we choose as it would probably not take more than a few microseconds, even with a very badly designed algorithm. But as soon as the size of the list becomes 1 million, now the choice of the right algorithm will make a difference. A very badly written algorithm might even take a couple of hours to run, while a well-designed algorithm may finish sorting the list in a couple of seconds. So, for larger input datasets, it makes a lot of sense to invest time and effort, perform a performance analysis, and choose the correctly designed algorithm that will do the job required in an efficient manner.

# Big O notation

Big O notation is used to quantify the performance of various algorithms as the input size grows. Big O notation is one of the most popular methodologies used to conduct worst-case analysis. The different kinds of Big O notation types are discussed in this section.

## Constant time (O(1)) complexity

If an algorithm takes the same amount of time to run, independent of the size of the input data, it is said to run in constant time. It is represented by O(1). Let's take the example of accessing the $n^{th}$ element of an array. Regardless of the size of the array, it will take constant time to get the results. For example, the following function will return the first element of the array and has a complexity of O(1):

```
def getFirst(myList):
    return myList[0]
```

The output is shown as:

```
In [2]:     1  getFirst([1,2,3])

Out[2]:  1

In [3]:     1  getFirst( 1,2,3,4,5,6,7,8,9,10 )

Out[3]:  1
```

- Addition of a new element to a stack by using push or removing an element from a stack by using pop. Regardless of the size of the stack, it will take the same time to add or remove an element.
- Accessing the element of the hashtable (as discussed in Chapter 2, *Data Structures Used in Algorithms*).
- Bucket sort (as discussed in Chapter 2, *Data Structures Used in Algorithms*).

# Linear time (O(n)) complexity

An algorithm is said to have a complexity of linear time, represented by O(n), if the execution time is directly proportional to the size of the input. A simple example is to add the elements in a single-dimensional data structure:

```
def getSum(myList):
    sum = 0
    for item in myList:
        sum = sum + item
    return sum
```

Note the main loop of the algorithm. The number of iterations in the main loop increases linearly with an increasing value of *n*, producing an O(n) complexity in the following figure:

```
In [5]:     1 getSum([1,2,3])

Out[5]: 6

In [6]:     1 getSum([1,2,3,4])

Out[6]: 10
```

Some other examples of array operations are as follows:

- Searching an element
- Finding the minimum value among all the elements of an array

# Quadratic time (O(n²)) complexity

An algorithm is said to run in quadratic time if the execution time of an algorithm is proportional to the square of the input size; for example, a simple function that sums up a two-dimensional array, as follows:

```
def getSum(myList):
    sum = 0
    for row in myList:
        for item in row:
            sum += item
    return sum
```

Note the nested inner loop within the other main loop. This nested loop gives the preceding code the complexity of $O(n^2)$:

```
In [8]:     1  getSum([[1,2],[3,4]])

Out[8]:  10

In [9]:     1  getSum([[1,2,3],[4,5,6]])

Out[9]:  21
```

Another example is the **bubble sort algorithm** (as discussed in Chapter 2, *Data Structures Used in Algorithms*).

# Logarithmic time (O(logn)) complexity

An algorithm is said to run in logarithmic time if the execution time of the algorithm is proportional to the logarithm of the input size. With each iteration, the input size decreases by a constant multiple factor. An example of logarithmic is binary search. The binary search algorithm is used to find a particular element in a one-dimensional data structure, such as a Python list. The elements within the data structure need to be sorted in descending order. The binary search algorithm is implemented in a function named searchBinary, as follows:

```python
def searchBinary(myList,item):
    first = 0
    last = len(myList)-1
    foundFlag = False
    while( first<=last and not foundFlag):
        mid = (first + last)//2
        if myList[mid] == item :
            foundFlag = True
        else:
            if item < myList[mid]:
                last = mid - 1
            else:
                first = mid + 1
    return foundFlag
```

The main loop takes advantage of the fact that the list is ordered. It divides the list in half with each iteration until it gets to the result:

```
In [11]:   1  searchBinary([8,9,10,100,1000,2000,3000], 10)
           2

Out[11]:  True

In [12]:   1  searchBinary([8,9,10,100,1000,2000,3000], 5)

Out[12]:  False
```

After defining the function, it is tested to search a particular element in lines 11 and 12. The binary search algorithm is further discussed in `Chapter 3`, *Sorting and Searching Algorithms*.

Note that among the four types of Big O notation types presented, $O(n^2)$ has the worst performance and $O(\log n)$ has the best performance. In fact, $O(\log n)$'s performance can be thought of as the gold standard for the performance of any algorithm (which is not always achieved, though). On the other hand, $O(n^2)$ is not as bad as $O(n^3)$ but still, algorithms that fall in this class cannot be used on big data as the time complexity puts limitations on how much data they can realistically process.

One way to reduce the complexity of an algorithm is to compromise on its accuracy, producing a type of algorithm called an **approximate algorithm**.

The whole process of the performance evaluation of algorithms is iterative in nature, as shown in the following figure:

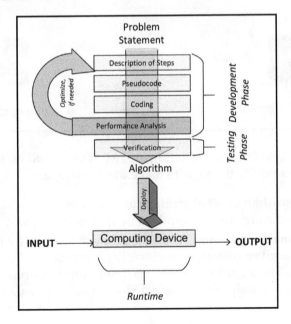

# Validating an algorithm

Validating an algorithm confirms that it is actually providing a mathematical solution to the problem we are trying to solve. A validation process should check the results for as many possible values and types of input values as possible.

# Exact, approximate, and randomized algorithms

Validating an algorithm also depends on the type of the algorithm as the testing techniques are different. Let's first differentiate between deterministic and randomized algorithms.

For deterministic algorithms, a particular input always generates exactly the same output. But for certain classes of algorithms, a sequence of random numbers is also taken as input, which makes the output different each time the algorithm is run. The k-means clustering algorithm, which is detailed in Chapter 6, *Unsupervised Machine Learning Algorithms*, is an example of such an algorithm:

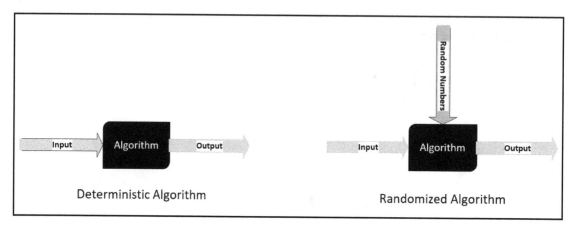

Algorithms can also be divided into the following two types based on assumptions or approximation used to simplify the logic to make them run faster:

- **An exact algorithm:** Exact algorithms are expected to produce a precise solution without introducing any assumptions or approximations.
- **An approximate algorithm:** When the problem complexity is too much to handle for the given resources, we simplify our problem by making some assumptions. The algorithms based on these simplifications or assumptions are called approximate algorithms, which doesn't quite give us the precise solution.

Let's look at an example to understand the difference between the exact and approximate algorithms—the famous traveling salesman problem, which was presented in 1930. A traveling salesman challenges you to find the shortest route for a particular salesman that visits each city (from a list of cities) and then returns to the origin, which is why he is named the traveling salesman. The first attempt to provide the solution will include generating all the permutations of cities and choosing the combination of cities that is cheapest. The complexity of this approach to provide the solution is O(n!), where $n$ is the number of cities. It is obvious that time complexity starts to become unmanageable beyond 30 cities.

If the number of cities is more than 30, one way of reducing the complexity is to introduce some approximations and assumptions.

For approximate algorithms, it is important to set the expectations for accuracy when gathering the requirements. Validating an approximation algorithm is about verifying that the error of the results is within an acceptable range.

# Explainability

When algorithms are used for critical cases, it becomes important to have the ability to explain the reason behind each and every result whenever needed. This is necessary to make sure that decisions based on the results of the algorithms do not introduce bias.

The ability to exactly identify the features that are used directly or indirectly to come up with a particular decision is called the **explainability** of an algorithm. Algorithms, when used for critical use cases, need to be evaluated for bias and prejudice. The ethical analysis of algorithms has become a standard part of the validation process for those algorithms that can affect decision-making that relates to the life of people.

For algorithms that deal with deep learning, explainability is difficult to achieve. For example, if an algorithm is used to refuse the mortgage application of a person, it is important to have the transparency and ability to explain the reason.

Algorithmic explainability is an active area of research. One of the effective techniques that has been recently developed is **Local Interpretable Model-Agnostic Explanations (LIME)**, as proposed in the proceedings of the 22nd **Association for Computing Machinery (ACM)** at the **Special Interest Group on Knowledge Discovery (SIGKDD)** international conference on knowledge discovery and data mining in 2016. LIME is based on a concept where small changes are induced to the input for each instance and then an effort to map the local decision boundary for that instance is made. It can then quantify the influence of each variable for that instance.

# Summary

This chapter was about learning the basics of algorithms. First, we learned about the different phases of developing an algorithm. We discussed the different ways of specifying the logic of an algorithm that are necessary for designing it. Then, we looked at how to design an algorithm. We learned two different ways of analyzing the performance of an algorithm. Finally, we studied different aspects of validating an algorithm.

After going through this chapter, we should be able to understand the pseudocode of an algorithm. We should understand the different phases in developing and deploying an algorithm. We also learned how to use Big O notation to evaluate the performance of an algorithm.

The next chapter is about the data structures used in algorithms. We will start by looking at the data structures available in Python. We will then look at how we can use these data structures to create more sophisticated data structures, such as stacks, queues, and trees, which are needed to develop complex algorithms.

# 2
# Data Structures Used in Algorithms

Algorithms need necessary in-memory data structures that can hold temporary data while executing. Choosing the right data structures is essential for their efficient implementation. Certain classes of algorithms are recursive or iterative in logic and need data structures that are specially designed for them. For example, a recursive algorithm may be more easily implemented, exhibiting better performance, if nested data structures are used. In this chapter, data structures are discussed in the context of algorithms. As we are using Python in this book, this chapter focuses on Python data structures, but the concepts presented in this chapter can be used in other languages such as Java and C++.

By the end of this chapter, you should be able to understand how Python handles complex data structures and which one should be used for a certain type of data.

Hence, here are the main points discussed in this chapter:

- Exploring data structures in Python
- Exploring abstract data type
- Stacks and queues
- Trees

# Exploring data structures in Python

In any language, data structures are used to store and manipulate complex data. In Python, data structures are storage containers to manage, organize, and search data in an efficient way. They are used to store a group of data elements called *collections* that need to be stored and processed together. In Python, there are five various data structures that can be used to store collections:

- **Lists**: Ordered mutable sequences of elements
- **Tuples**: Ordered immutable sequences of elements
- **Sets**: Unordered bags of elements
- **Dictionary**: Unordered bags of key-value pairs
- **Data frames**: Two-dimensional structures to store two-dimensional data

Let's look into them in more detail in the upcoming subsections.

# List

In Python, a list is the main data structure used to store a mutable sequence of elements. The sequence of data elements stored in the list need not be of the same type.

To create a list, the data elements need to be enclosed in [ ] and they need to be separated by a comma. For example, the following code creates four data elements together that are of different types:

```
>>> aList = ["John", 33,"Toronto", True]
>>> print(aList)
['John', 33, 'Toronto', True]Ex
```

In Python, a list is a handy way of creating one-dimensional writable data structures that are needed especially at different internal stages of algorithms.

# Using lists

Utility functions in data structures make them very useful as they can be used to manage data in lists.

Let's look into how we can use them:

- **List indexing**: As the position of an element is deterministic in a list, the index can be used to get an element at a particular position. The following code demonstrates the concept:

```
>>> bin_colors=['Red','Green','Blue','Yellow']
>>> bin_colors[1]
'Green'
```

The four-element list created by this code is shown in the following screenshot:

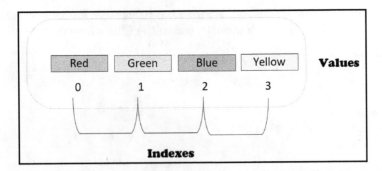

Note that the index starts from 0 and therefore **Green**, which is the second element, is retrieved by index **1**, that is, `bin_color[1]`.

- **List slicing**: Retrieving a subset of the elements of a list by specifying a range of indexes is called **slicing**. The following code can be used to create a slice of the list:

```
>>> bin_colors=['Red','Green','Blue','Yellow']
>>> bin_colors[0:2]
['Red', 'Green']
```

Note that lists are one of the most popular single-dimensional data structures in Python.

While slicing a list, the range is indicated as follows: the first number (inclusive) and the second number (exclusive). For example, `bin_colors[0:2]` will include `bin_color[0]` and `bin_color[1]` but not `bin_color[2]`. While using lists, this should be kept in mind as some users of the Python language complain that this is not very intuitive.

Let's have a look at the following code snippet:

```
>>> bin_colors=['Red','Green','Blue','Yellow']
>>> bin_colors[2:]
['Blue', 'Yellow']
>>> bin_colors[:2]
['Red', 'Green']
```

If the starting index is not specified, it means the beginning of the list, and if the ending index is not specified, it means the end of the list. The preceding code actually demonstrates this concept.

- **Negative indexing**: In Python, we also have negative indices, which count from the end of the list. This is demonstrated in the following code:

```
>>> bin_colors=['Red','Green','Blue','Yellow']
>>> bin_colors[:-1]
['Red', 'Green', 'Blue']
>>> bin_colors[:-2]
['Red', 'Green']
>>> bin_colors[-2:-1]
['Blue']
```

Note that negative indices are especially useful when we want to use the last element as a reference point instead of the first one.

- **Nesting**: An element of a list can be of a simple data type or a complex data type. This allows nesting in lists. For iterative and recursive algorithms, this provides important capabilities.

Let's have a look at the following code, which is an example of a list within a list (nesting):

```
>>> a = [1,2,[100,200,300],6]
>>> max(a[2])
300
>>> a[2][1]
200
```

- **Iteration**: Python allows iterating over each element on a list by using a `for` loop. This is demonstrated in the following example:

```
>>> bin_colors=['Red','Green','Blue','Yellow']
>>> for aColor in bin_colors:
        print(aColor + " Square")
Red Square
Green Square
```

```
Blue Square
Yellow Square
```

Note that the preceding code iterates through the list and prints each element.

# Lambda functions

There are a bunch of lambda functions that can be used on lists. They are specifically important in the context of algorithms and provide the ability to create a function on the fly. Sometimes, in the literature, they are also called *anonymous functions*. This section demonstrates their uses:

- **Filtering data**: To filter the data, first, we define a predicate, which is a function that inputs a single argument and returns a Boolean value. The following code demonstrates its use:

  ```
  >>> list(filter(lambda x: x > 100, [-5, 200, 300, -10, 10, 1000]))
  [200, 300, 1000]
  ```

  Note that, in this code, we filter a list using the lambda function, which specifies the filtering criteria. The filter function is designed to filter elements out of a sequence based on a defined criterion. The filter function in Python is usually used with lambda. In addition to lists, it can be used to filter elements from tuples or sets. For the preceding code, the defined criterion is x > 100. The code will iterate through all the elements of the list and will filter out the elements that do not pass this criterion.

- **Data transformation**: The map() function can be used for data transformation using a lambda function. An example is as follows:

  ```
  >>> list(map(lambda x: x ** 2, [11, 22, 33, 44,55]))
  [121, 484, 1089, 1936, 3025]
  ```

  Using the map function with a lambda function provides quite powerful functionality. When used with the map function, the lambda function can be used to specify a transformer that transforms each element of the given sequence. In the preceding code, the transformer is multiplication by two. So, we are using the map function to multiply each element in the list by two.

- **Data aggregation**: For data aggregation, the `reduce()` function can be used, which recursively runs a function to pairs of values on each element of the list:

```
from functools import reduce
def doSum(x1,x2):
    return x1+x2
x = reduce(doSum, [100, 122, 33, 4, 5, 6])
```

Note that the `reduce` function needs a data aggregation function to be defined. That data aggregation function in the preceding code is `functools`. It defines how it will aggregate the items of the given list. The aggregation will start from the first two elements and the result will replace the first two elements. This process of reduction is repeated until we reach the end, resulting in one aggregated number. x1 and x2 in the `doSum` function represent two numbers in each of these iterations and `doSum` represents the aggregation criterion for them.

The preceding code block results in a single value (which is 270).

# The range function

The `range` function can be used to easily generate a large list of numbers. It is used to auto-populate sequences of numbers in a list.

The `range` function is simple to use. We can use it by just specifying the number of elements we want in the list. By default, it starts from zero and increments by one:

```
>>> x = range(6)
>>> x
[0,1,2,3,4,5]
```

We can also specify the end number and the step:

```
>>> oddNum = range(3,29,2)
>>> oddNum
[3, 5, 7, 9, 11, 13, 15, 17, 19, 21, 23, 25, 27]
```

The preceding range function will give us odd numbers starting from 3 to 29.

# The time complexity of lists

The time complexity of various functions of a list can be summarized as follows using the Big O notation:

| Different methods | Time complexity |
|---|---|
| Insert an element | O(1) |
| Delete an element | O(n) (as in the worst case may have to iterate the whole list) |
| Slicing a list | O(n) |
| Element retrieval | O(n) |
| Copy | O(n) |

Please note that the time taken to add an individual element is independent of the size of the list. Other operations mentioned in the table are dependent on the size of the list. As the size of the list gets bigger, the impact on performance becomes more pronounced.

# Tuples

The second data structure that can be used to store a collection is a tuple. In contrast to lists, tuples are immutable (read-only) data structures. Tuples consist of several elements surrounded by ( ).

Like lists, elements within a tuple can be of different types. They also allow complex data types for their elements. So, there can be a tuple within a tuple providing a way to create a nested data structure. The capability to create nested data structures is especially useful in iterative and recursive algorithms.

The following code demonstrates how to create tuples:

```
>>> bin_colors=('Red','Green','Blue','Yellow')
>>> bin_colors[1]
'Green'
>>> bin_colors[2:]
('Blue', 'Yellow')
>>> bin_colors[:-1]
('Red', 'Green', 'Blue')
# Nested Tuple Data structure
>>> a = (1,2,(100,200,300),6)
>>> max(a[2])
300
>>> a[2][1]
200
```

Wherever possible, immutable data structures (such as tuples) should be preferred over mutable data structures (such as lists) due to performance. Especially when dealing with big data, immutable data structures are considerably faster than mutable ones. There is a price we pay for the ability to change data elements in lists, for example, and we should carefully analyze that it is really needed so we can implement the code as read-only tuples, which will be much faster.

Note that, in the preceding code, `a[2]` refers to the third element, which is a tuple, `(100,200,300)`. `a[2][1]` refers to the second element within this tuple, which is `200`.

## The time complexity of tuples

The time complexity of various functions of tuples can be summarized as follows (using Big O notation):

| Function | Time Complexity |
|----------|-----------------|
| Append | O(1) |

Note that `Append` is a function that adds an element toward the end of the already existing tuple. Its complexity is O(1).

## Dictionary

Holding data as key-value pairs is important especially in distributed algorithms. In Python, a collection of these key-value pairs is stored as a data structure called a *dictionary*. To create a dictionary, a key should be chosen as an attribute that is best suited to identify data throughout data processing. The value can be an element of any type, for example, a number or string. Python also always uses complex data types such as lists as values. Nested dictionaries can be created by using a dictionary as the data type of a value.

To create a simple dictionary that assigns colors to various variables, the key-value pairs need to be enclosed in { }. For example, the following code creates a simple dictionary consisting of three key-value pairs:

```
>>> bin_colors ={
      "manual_color": "Yellow",
      "approved_color": "Green",
      "refused_color": "Red"
    }
```

```
>>> print(bin_colors)
{'manual_color': 'Yellow', 'approved_color': 'Green', 'refused_color':
'Red'}
```

The three key-value pairs created by the preceding piece of code are also illustrated in the following screenshot:

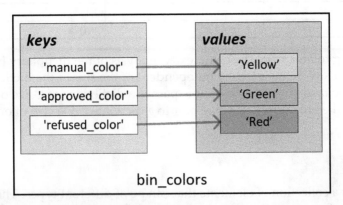

Now, let's see how to retrieve and update a value associated with a key:

1. To retrieve a value associated with a key, either the get function can be used or the key can be used as the index:

```
>>> bin_colors.get('approved_color')
'Green'
>>> bin_colors['approved_color']
'Green'
```

2. To update a value associated with a key, use the following code:

```
>>> bin_colors['approved_color']="Purple"
>>> print(bin_colors)
{'manual_color': 'Yellow', 'approved_color': 'Purple',
'refused_color': 'Red'}
```

Note that the preceding code shows how we can update a value related to a particular key in a dictionary.

# The time complexity of a dictionary

The following table gives the time complexity of a dictionary using Big O notation:

| Dictionary | Time complexity |
|---|---|
| Get a value or a key | O(1) |
| Set a value or a key | O(1) |
| Copy a dictionary | O(n) |

An important thing to note from the complexity analysis of the dictionary is that the time taken to get or set a key-value is totally independent of the size of the dictionary. This means that the time taken to add a key-value pair to a dictionary of a size of three is the same as the time taken to add a key-value pair to a dictionary of a size of one million.

# Sets

A set is defined as a collection of elements that can be of different types. The elements are enclosed within { }. For example, have a look at the following code block:

```
>>> green = {'grass', 'leaves'}
>>> print(green)
{'grass', 'leaves'}
```

The defining characteristic of a set is that it only stores the distinct value of each element. If we try to add another redundant element, it will ignore that, as illustrated in the following:

```
>>> green = {'grass', 'leaves','leaves'}
>>> print(green)
{'grass', 'leaves'}
```

To demonstrate what sort of operations can be done on sets, let's define two sets:

- A set named yellow, which has things that are yellow
- Another set named red, which has things that are red

Note that some things are common between these two sets. The two sets and their relationship can be represented with the help of the following Venn diagram:

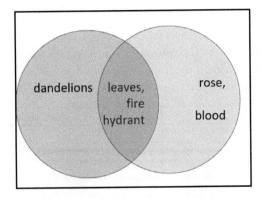

If we want to implement these two sets in Python, the code will look like this:

```
>>> yellow = {'dandelions', 'fire hydrant', 'leaves'}
>>> red = {'fire hydrant', 'blood', 'rose', 'leaves'}
```

Now, let's consider the following code, which demonstrates set operations using Python:

```
>>> yellow|red
{'dandelions', 'fire hydrant', 'blood', 'rose', 'leaves'}
>>> yellow&red
{'fire hydrant'}
```

As shown in the preceding code snippet, sets in Python can have operations such as unions and intersections. As we know, a union operation combines all of the elements of both sets, and the intersection operation will give a set of common elements between the two sets. Note the following:

- `yellow|red` is used to get the union of the preceding two defined sets.
- `yellow&red` is used to get the overlap between yellow and red.

# Time complexity analysis for sets

Following is the time complexity analysis for sets:

| Sets | Complexity |
|------|-----------|
| Add an element | O(1) |
| Remove an element | O(1) |
| Copy | O(n) |

An important thing to note from the complexity analysis of the sets is that the time taken to add an element is totally independent of the size of a particular set.

# DataFrames

A DataFrame is a data structure used to store tabular data available in Python's `pandas` package. It is one of the most important data structures for algorithms and is used to process traditional structured data. Let's consider the following table:

| id | name | age | decision |
|----|------|-----|----------|
| 1 | Fares | 32 | True |
| 2 | Elena | 23 | False |
| 3 | Steven | 40 | True |

Now, let's represent this using a DataFrame.

A simple DataFrame can be created by using the following code:

```
>>> import pandas as pd
>>> df = pd.DataFrame([
...              ['1', 'Fares', 32, True],
...              ['2', 'Elena', 23, False],
...              ['3', 'Steven', 40, True]])
>>> df.columns = ['id', 'name', 'age', 'decision']
>>> df
    id    name   age   decision
0   1    Fares    32      True
1   2    Elena    23     False
2   3   Steven    40      True
```

Note that, in the preceding code, `df.column` is a list that specifies the names of the columns.

 The DataFrame is also used in other popular languages and frameworks to implement a tabular data structure. Examples are R and the Apache Spark framework.

# Terminologies of DataFrames

Let's look into some of the terminologies that are used in the context of a DataFrame:

- **Axis**: In the pandas documentation, a single column or row of a DataFrame is called an axis.

- **Axes**: If there is more than one axis, they are called axes as a group.
- **Label**: A DataFrame allows the naming of both columns and rows with what's called a label.

# Creating a subset of a DataFrame

Fundamentally, there are two main ways of creating the subset of a DataFrame (say the name of the subset is myDF):

- Column selection
- Row selection

Let's see them one by one.

## Column selection

In machine learning algorithms, selecting the right set of features is an important task. Out of all of the features that we may have, not all of them may be needed at a particular stage of the algorithm. In Python, feature selection is achieved by column selection, which is explained in this section.

A column may be retrieved by *name*, as in the following:

```
>>> df[['name','age']]
      name   age
0    Fares    32
1    Elena    23
2   Steven    40
```

The positioning of a column is deterministic in a DataFrame. A column can be retrieved by its position as follows:

```
>>> df.iloc[:,3]
0 True
1 False
2 True
```

Note that, in this code, we are retrieving the first three rows of the DataFrame.

## Row selection

Each row in a DataFrame corresponds to a data point in our problem space. We need to perform row selection if we want to create a subset of the data elements we have in our problem space. This subset can be created by using one of the two following methods:

- By specifying their position
- By specifying a filter

A subset of rows can be retrieved by its position as follows:

```
>>> df.iloc[1:3,:]
   id name age decision
1  2  Elena 23 False
2  3  Steven 40 True
```

Note that the preceding code will return the first two rows and all columns.

To create a subset by specifying the filter, we need to use one or more columns to define the selection criterion. For example, a subset of data elements can be selected by this method, as follows:

```
>>> df[df.age>30]
   id    name  age  decision
0  1    Fares   32      True
2  3   Steven   40      True

>>> df[(df.age<35)&(df.decision==True)]
   id   name  age  decision
0  1   Fares   32      True
```

Note that this code creates a subset of rows that satisfies the condition stipulated in the filter.

# Matrix

A matrix is a two-dimensional data structure with a fixed number of columns and rows. Each element of a matrix can be referred to by its column and the row.

In Python, a matrix can be created by using the numpy array, as shown in the following code:

```
>>> myMatrix = np.array([[11, 12, 13], [21, 22, 23], [31, 32, 33]])
>>> print(myMatrix)
[[11 12 13]
[21 22 23]
[31 32 33]]
>>> print(type(myMatrix))
<class 'numpy.ndarray'>
```

Note that the preceding code will create a matrix that has three rows and three columns.

## Matrix operations

There are many operations available for matrix data manipulation. For example, let's try to transpose the preceding matrix. We will use the `transpose()` function, which will convert columns into rows and rows into columns:

```
>>> myMatrix.transpose()
array([[11, 21, 31],
       [12, 22, 32],
       [13, 23, 33]])
```

Note that matrix operations are used a lot in multimedia data manipulation.

Now that we have learned about data structures in Python, let's move onto the abstract data types in the next section.

# Exploring abstract data types

Abstraction, in general, is a concept used to define complex systems in terms of their common core functions. The use of this concept to create generic data structures gives birth to **Abstract Data Types** (**ADT**). By hiding the implementation level details and giving the user a generic, implementation-independent data structure, the use of ADTs creates algorithms that result in simpler and cleaner code. ADTs can be implemented in any programming language such as C++, Java, and Scala. In this section, we shall implement ADTs using Python. Let's start with vectors first.

# Vector

A vector is a single dimension structure to store data. They are one of the most popular data structures in Python. There are two ways of creating vectors in Python as follows:

- Using a Python list: The simplest way of creating a vector is by using a Python list, as follows:

```
>>> myVector = [22,33,44,55]
>>> print(myVector)
[22 33 44 55]
>>> print(type(myVector))
<class 'list'>
```

Note that this code will create a list with four elements.

- Using a `numpy` array: Another popular way of creating a vector is by using NumPy arrays, as follows:

```
>>> myVector = np.array([22,33,44,55])
>>> print(myVector)
[22 33 44 55]
>>> print(type(myVector))
<class 'numpy.ndarray'>
```

Note that we created `myVector` using `np.array` in this code.

In Python, we can represent integers using underscores to separate parts. It makes them more readable and less error-prone. This is especially useful when dealing with large numbers. So, one billion can be represented as a=1

# Stacks

A stack is a linear data structure to store a one-dimensional list. It can store items either in **Last-In, First-Out** (**LIFO**) or **First-In, Last-Out** (**FILO**) manner. The defining characteristic of a stack is the way elements are added and removed from it. A new element is added at one end and an element is removed from that end only.

Following are the operations related to stacks:

- **isEmpty:** Returns true if the stack is empty
- **push:** Adds a new element
- **pop**: Returns the element added most recently and removes it

The following diagram shows how push and pop operations can be used to add and remove data from a stack:

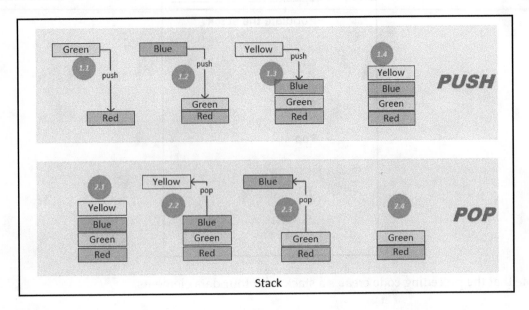

The top portion of the preceding diagram shows the use of push operations to add items to the stack. In steps **1.1**, **1.2**, and **1.3**, push operations are used three times to add three elements to the stack. The bottom portion of the preceding diagram is used to retrieve the stored values from the stack. In steps **2.2** and **2.3**, pop operations are used to retrieve two elements from the stack in LIFO format.

Let's create a class named Stack in Python, where we will define all of the operations related to the stack class. The code of this class will be as follows:

```
class Stack:
    def __init__(self):
        self.items = []
    def isEmpty(self):
        return self.items == []
    def push(self, item):
        self.items.append(item)
```

```
def pop(self):
    return self.items.pop()
def peek(self):
    return self.items[len(self.items)-1]
def size(self):
    return len(self.items)
```

To push four elements to the stack, the following code can be used:

---

**Populate the stack**

```
In [2]:  stack=Stack()
         stack.push('Red')
         stack.push('Green')
         stack.push("Blue")
         stack.push("Yellow")
```

**Pop**

```
In [3]:  stack.pop()
```
```
Out[3]:  'Yellow'
```

```
In [7]:  stack.isEmpty()
```
```
Out[7]:  False
```

---

Note that the preceding code creates a stack with four data elements.

# The time complexity of stacks

Let's look into the time complexity of stacks (using Big O notation):

| Operations | Time Complexity |
|---|---|
| push | O(1) |
| pop | O(1) |
| size | O(1) |
| peek | O(1) |

An important thing to note is that the performance of none of the four operations mentioned in the preceding table depends on the size of the stack.

# Practical example

A stack is used as the data structure in many use cases. For example, when a user wants to browse the history in a web browser, it is a LIFO data access pattern and a stack can be used to store the history. Another example is when a user wants to perform an Undo operation in word processing software.

# Queues

Like stacks, a queue stores *n* elements in a single-dimensional structure. The elements are added and removed in **FIFO** format. One end of the queue is called the *rear* and the other is called the *front*. When elements are removed from the front, the operation is called *dequeue*. When elements are added at the rear, the operation is called *enqueue*.

In the following diagram, the top portion shows the enqueue operation. Steps **1.1**, **1.2**, and **1.3** add three elements to the queue and the resultant queue is shown in **1.4**. Note that **Yellow** is the *rear* and **Red** is the *front*.

The bottom portion of the following diagram shows a dequeue operation. Steps **2.2**, **2.3**, and **2.4** remove elements from the queue one by one from the front of the queue:

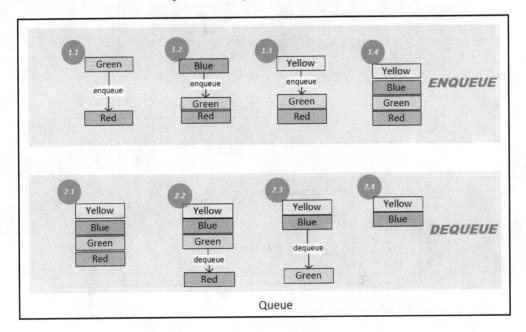

The queue shown in the preceding diagram can be implemented by using the following code:

```
class Queue(object):
    def __init__(self):
        self.items = []
    def isEmpty(self):
        return self.items == []
    def enqueue(self, item):
        self.items.insert(0,item)
    def dequeue(self):
        return self.items.pop()
    def size(self):
        return len(self.items)
```

Let's enqueue and dequeue elements as shown in the preceding diagram with the help of the following screenshot:

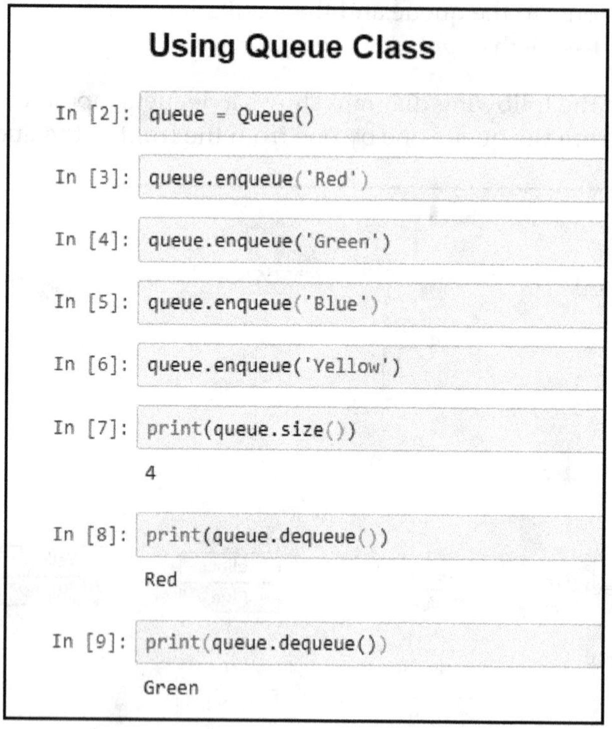

**Using Queue Class**

```
In [2]:  queue = Queue()

In [3]:  queue.enqueue('Red')

In [4]:  queue.enqueue('Green')

In [5]:  queue.enqueue('Blue')

In [6]:  queue.enqueue('Yellow')

In [7]:  print(queue.size())

         4

In [8]:  print(queue.dequeue())

         Red

In [9]:  print(queue.dequeue())

         Green
```

Note that the preceding code creates a queue first and then enqueues four items into it.

# The basic idea behind the use of stacks and queues

Let's look into the basic idea behind the use of stacks and queues using an analogy. Let's assume that we have a table where we put our incoming mail from our postal service, for example, Canada Mail. We stack it until we get some time to open and look at the mail, one by one. There are two possible ways of doing this:

- We put the letter in a stack and whenever we get a new letter, we put it on the top of the stack. When we want to read a letter, we start with the one that is on top. This is what we call a *stack*. Note that the latest letter to arrive will be on the top and will be processed first. Picking up a letter from the top of the list is called a *pop* operation. Whenever a new letter arrives, putting it on the top is called *push* operation. If we end up having a sizable stack and lots of letters are continuously arriving, there is a chance that we never get a chance to reach a very important letter waiting for us at the lower end of the stack.
- We put the letter in pile, but we want to handle the oldest letter first: each time we want to look at one or more letters, we take care to handle the oldest one first. This is what we call a *queue*. Adding a letter to the pile is called an *enqueue* operation. Removing the letter from the pile is called *dequeue* operation.

# Tree

In the context of algorithms, a tree is one of the most useful data structures due to its hierarchical data storage capabilities. While designing algorithms, we use trees wherever we need to represent hierarchical relationships among the data elements that we need to store or process.

Let's look deeper into this interesting and quite important data structure.

Each tree has a finite set of nodes so that it has a starting data element called a *root* and a set of nodes joined together by links called *branches*.

# Terminology

Let's look into some of the terminology related to the tree data structure:

| | |
|---|---|
| Root node | A node with no parent is called the *root* node. For example, in the following diagram, the root node is **A**. In algorithms, usually, the root node holds the most important value in the tree structure. |
| Level of a node | The distance from the root node is the level of a node. For example, in the following diagram, the level of nodes **D**, **E**, and **F** is two. |
| Siblings nodes | Two nodes in a tree are called *siblings* if they are at the same level. For example, if we check the following diagram, nodes **B** and **C** are siblings. |
| Child and parent node | A node, **F**, is a child of node **C**, if both are directly connected and the level of node **C** is less than node **F**. Conversely, node **C** is a parent of node **F**. Nodes **C** and **F** in the following diagram show this parent-child relationship. |
| Degree of a node | The degree of a node is the number of children it has. For example, in the following diagram, node **B** has a degree of two. |
| Degree of a tree | The degree of a tree is equal to the maximum degree that can be found among the constituent nodes of a tree. For example, the tree presented in the following diagram has a degree of two. |
| Subtree | A subtree of a tree is a portion of the tree with the chosen node as the root node of the subtree and all of the children as the nodes of the tree. For example, a subtree at node **E** of the tree presented in the following diagram consists of node **E** as the root node and node **G** and **H** as the two children. |
| Leaf node | A node in a tree with no children is called a *leaf* node. For example, in the following figure, **D, G, H,** and **F** are the four leaf nodes. |
| Internal node | Any node that is neither a root nor a leaf node is an internal node. An internal node will have at least one parent and at least one child node. |

Note that trees are a kind of network or graph that we will study in Chapter 6, *Unsupervised Machine Learning Algorithms*. For graphs and network analysis, we use the terms link or edge instead of branches. Most of the other terminology remains unchanged.

# Types of trees

There are different types of trees, which are explained as follows:

- **Binary tree:** If the degree of a tree is two, that tree is called a *binary tree*. For example, the tree shown in the following diagram is a binary tree as it has a degree of two:

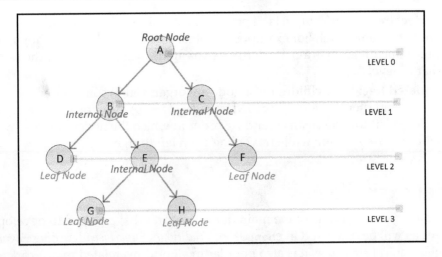

Note that the preceding diagram shows a tree that has four levels with eight nodes.

- **Full tree:** A full tree is the one in which all of the nodes are of the same degree, which will be equal to the degree of the tree. The following diagram shows the kinds of trees discussed earlier:

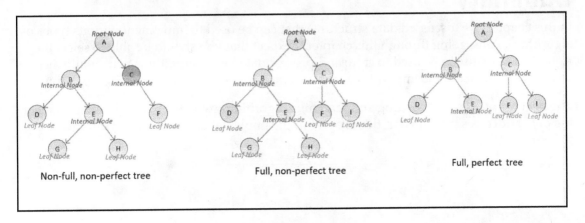

Note that the binary tree on the left is not a full tree, as node **C** has a degree of one and all other nodes have a degree of two. The tree in the middle and the one on the left are both full trees.

- **Perfect tree:** A perfect tree is a special type of full tree in which all the leaf nodes are at the same level. For example, the binary tree on the right as shown in the preceding diagram is a perfect, full tree as all the leaf nodes are at the same level, that is, **level 2**.
- **Ordered tree**: If the children of a node are organized in some order according to particular criteria, the tree is called an *ordered tree*. A tree, for example, can be ordered left to right in an ascending order in which the nodes at the same level will increase in value while traversing from left to right.

## Practical examples

An abstract data type tree is one of the main data structures that are used in developing decision trees as will be discussed in Chapter 7, *Traditional Supervised Learning Algorithms*. Due to its hierarchical structure, it is also popular in algorithms related to network analysis as will be discussed in detail in Chapter 6, *Unsupervised Machine Learning Algorithms*. Trees are also used in various search and sort algorithms where divide and conquer strategies need to be implemented.

# Summary

In this chapter, we discussed data structures that can be used to implement various types of algorithms. After going through this chapter, I expect that you should be able to select the right data structure to be used to store and process data by an algorithm. You should also be able to understand the implications of our choice on the performance of the algorithm.

The next chapter is about sorting and searching algorithms, where we will be using some of the data structures presented in this chapter in the implementation of the algorithms.

# 3
# Sorting and Searching Algorithms

In this chapter, we will look at the algorithms that are used for sorting and searching. This is an important class of algorithms that can be used on their own or can become the foundation for more complex algorithms (presented in the later chapters of this book). This chapter starts by presenting different types of sorting algorithms. It compares the performance of various approaches to designing a sorting algorithm. Then, some searching algorithms are presented in detail. Finally, a practical example of the sorting and searching algorithms presented in this chapter is explored.

By the end of this chapter, you will be able to understand the various algorithms that are used for sorting and searching, and you will be able to apprehend their strengths and weaknesses. As searching and sorting algorithms are the building blocks for most of the more complex algorithms, understanding them in detail will help you understand modern complex algorithms as well.

The following are the main concepts discussed in this chapter:

- Introducing sorting algorithms
- Introducing searching algorithms
- A practical example

Let's first look at some sorting algorithms.

# Introducing Sorting Algorithms

In the era of big data, the ability to efficiently sort and search items in a complex data structure is quite important as it is needed by many modern algorithms. The right strategy to sort and search data will depend on the size and type of the data, as discussed in this chapter. While the end result is exactly the same, the right sorting and searching algorithm will be needed for an efficient solution to a real-world problem.

The following sorting algorithms are presented in this chapter:

- Bubble sort
- Merge sort
- Insertion sort
- Shell sort
- Selection sort

# Swapping Variables in Python

When implementing sorting and searching algorithms, we need to swap the values of two variables. In Python, there is a simple way to swap two variables, which is as follows:

```
var1 = 1
var2 = 2
var1,var2 = var2,var1
>>> print (var1,var2)
>>> 2 1
```

Let's see how it works:

This simple way of swapping values is used throughout the sorting and searching algorithms in this chapter.

Let's start by looking at the bubble sort algorithm in the next section.

# Bubble Sort

Bubble sort is the simplest and slowest algorithm used for sorting. It is designed in a way that the highest value in its list bubbles its way to the top as the algorithm loops through iterations. As its worst-case performance is $O(N^2)$, as discussed previously, it should be used for smaller datasets.

## Understanding the Logic Behind Bubble Sort

Bubble sort is based on various iterations, called **passes**. For a list of size $N$, bubble sort will have $N-1$ passes. Let's focus on the first iteration: pass one.

The goal of pass one is pushing the highest value to the top of the list. We will see the highest value of the list bubbling its way to the top as pass one progresses.

Bubble sort compares adjacent neighbor values. If the value at a higher position is higher in value than the value at a lower index, we exchange the values. This iteration continues until we reach the end of the list. This is shown in the following diagram:

| | | | | | | | |
|--|--|--|--|--|--|--|--|
| 25 | 21 | 22 | 24 | 23 | 27 | 26 | Exchange |
| 21 | 25 | 22 | 24 | 23 | 27 | 26 | Exchange |
| 21 | 22 | 25 | 24 | 23 | 27 | 26 | Exchange |
| 21 | 22 | 24 | 25 | 23 | 27 | 26 | Exchange |
| 21 | 22 | 24 | 23 | 25 | 27 | 26 | No Exchange |
| 21 | 22 | 24 | 23 | 25 | 27 | 26 | Exchange |
| 21 | 22 | 24 | 23 | 25 | 26 | 27 | |

—1st Pass→

**Bubble Sort**

Let's now see how bubble sort can be implemented using Python:

```
#Pass 1 of Bubble Sort
lastElementIndex = len(list)-1
print(0,list)
for idx in range(lastElementIndex):
            if list[idx]>list[idx+1]:
list[idx],list[idx+1]=list[idx+1],list[idx]
print(idx+1,list)
```

If we implement pass one of bubble sort in Python, it will look as follows:

```
In [91]:  1  lastElementIndex = len(list)-1
          2  print(0,list)
          3  for idx in range(lastElementIndex):
          4              if list[idx]>list[idx+1]:
          5                      list[idx],list[idx+1]=list[idx+1],list[idx]
          6              print(idx+1,list)

0 [25, 21, 22, 24, 23, 27, 26]
1 [21, 25, 22, 24, 23, 27, 26]
2 [21, 22, 25, 24, 23, 27, 26]
3 [21, 22, 24, 25, 23, 27, 26]
4 [21, 22, 24, 23, 25, 27, 26]
5 [21, 22, 24, 23, 25, 27, 26]
6 [21, 22, 24, 23, 25, 26, 27]
```

Once the first pass is complete, the highest value is at the top of the list. The algorithm next moves on to the second pass. The goal of the second pass is to move the second highest value to the second highest position in the list. To do that, the algorithm will again compare adjacent neighbor values, exchanging them if they are not in order. The second pass will exclude the top element, which was put in the right place by pass one and need not be touched again.

After completing pass two, the algorithm keeps on performing pass three and so on until all the data points of the list are in ascending order. The algorithm will need *N-1* passes for a list of size *N* to completely sort it. The complete implementation of bubble sort in Python is as follows:

```
In [5]:  def BubbleSort(list):
         # Excahnge the elements to arrange in order
             lastElementIndex = len(list)-1
             for passNo in range(lastElementIndex,0,-1):
                 for idx in range(passNo):
                     if list[idx]>list[idx+1]:
                         list[idx],list[idx+1]=list[idx+1],list[idx]
             return list
```

Now let's look into the performance of the BubbleSort algorithm.

# A Performance Analysis of Bubble Sort

It is easier to see that bubble sort involves two levels of loops:

- **An outer loop**: This is also called **passes**. For example, pass one is the first iteration of the outer loop.
- **An inner loop**: This is when the remaining unsorted elements in the list are sorted, until the highest value is bubbled to the right. The first pass will have *N-1* comparisons, the second pass will have *N-2* comparisons, and each subsequent pass will reduce the number of comparisons by one.

Due to two levels of looping, the worst-case runtime complexity would be $O(n^2)$.

# Insertion Sort

The basic idea of insertion sort is that in each iteration, we remove a data point from the data structure we have and then insert it into its right position. That is why we call this **the insertion sort algorithm**. In the first iteration, we select the two data points and sort them. Then, we expand our selection and select the third data point and find its correct position, based on its value. The algorithm progresses until all the data points are moved to their correct positions. This process is shown in the following diagram:

| 25 | 26 | 22 | 24 | 27 | 23 | 21 | Insert 25 |
|----|----|----|----|----|----|----|-----------|
| 25 | 26 | 22 | 24 | 27 | 23 | 21 | Insert 26 |
| 22 | 25 | 26 | 24 | 27 | 23 | 21 | Insert 22 |
| 22 | 24 | 25 | 26 | 27 | 23 | 21 | Insert 24 |
| 22 | 24 | 25 | 26 | 27 | 23 | 21 | Insert 27 |
| 22 | 23 | 24 | 25 | 26 | 27 | 21 | Insert 23 |
| 21 | 22 | 23 | 24 | 25 | 26 | 27 | Insert 21 |

**Insertion Sort**

The insertion sort algorithm can be coded in Python as follows:

```python
def InsertionSort(list):
    for i in range(1, len(list)):
        j = i-1
        element_next = list[i]
        while (list[j] > element_next) and (j >= 0):
            list[j+1] = list[j]
            j=j-1
        list[j+1] = element_next
    return list
```

Note that in the main loop, we iterate throughout all of the list. In each iteration, the two adjacent elements are `list[j]` (the current element) and `list[i]` (the next element).

In `list[j] > element_next` and `j >= 0`, we compare the current element with the next element.

Let's use this code to sort an array:

```
In [134]:   1  list = [25,26,22,24,27,23,21]

In [135]:   1  InsertionSort(list)
            2  print(list)

            [21, 22, 23, 24, 25, 26, 27]
```

Let's look at the performance of the insertion sort algorithm.

It's obvious from the description of the algorithm that if the data structure is already sorted, insertion sort will perform very fast. In fact, if the data structure is sorted, then the insertion sort will have a linear running time; that is, O(n). The worst case is when each of the inner loops has to move all the elements in the list. If the inner loop is defined by *i*, the worst-case performance of the insertion sort algorithm is given by the following:

$$w(N) = \sum_{i=1}^{N-1} i = \frac{(N-1)N}{2} = \frac{N^2 - N}{2}$$

$$w(N) \approx \frac{1}{2}N^2 = O(N^2)$$

The total number of passes is shown in the following diagram:

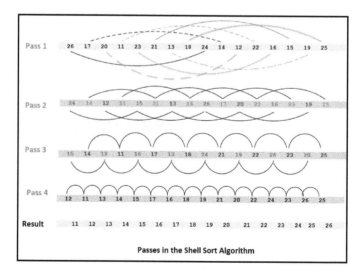

**Passes in the Shell Sort Algorithm**

In general, insertion can be used on small data structures. For larger data structures, insertion sort is not recommended due to quadratic average performance.

# Merge Sort

We have presented, so far, two sorting algorithms: bubble sort and insertion sort. The performance of both of them will be better if the data is partially sorted. The third algorithm presented in this chapter is **the merge sort algorithm**, which was developed in 1940 by John von Neumann. The defining feature of this algorithm is that its performance is not dependent on whether the input data is sorted. Like MapReduce and other big data algorithms, it is based on a divide and conquer strategy. In the first phase, called splitting, the algorithm keeps on dividing the data into two parts recursively, until the size of the data is less than the defined threshold. In the second phase, called **merging**, the algorithm keeps on merging and processing until we get the final result. The logic of this algorithm is explained in the following diagram:

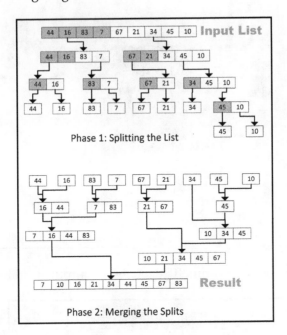

Let's first look into the pseudocode of the merge sort algorithm:

```
mergeSort(list, start, end)
    if(start < end)
        midPoint = (end - start) / 2 + start
        mergeSort(list, start, midPoint)
```

```
mergeSort(list, midPoint + 1, start)
merge(list, start, midPoint, end)
```

As we can see the algorithm has the following three steps:

1. It divides the input list into two equal parts
2. It uses recursion to split until the length of each list is 1
3. Then, it merges the sorted parts into a sorted list and returns it

The code for implementing `MergeSort` is shown here:

```
In [6]: def MergeSort(list):
            if len(list)>1:
                mid = len(list)//2 #splits list in half
                left = list[:mid]
                right = list[mid:]

                MergeSort(left) #repeats until length of each list is 1
                MergeSort(right)

                a = 0
                b = 0
                c = 0
                while a < len(left) and b < len(right):
                    if left[a] < right[b]:
                        list[c]=left[a]
                        a = a + 1
                    else:
                        list[c]=right[b]
                        b = b + 1
                    c = c + 1
                while a < len(left):
                    list[c]=left[a]
                    a = a + 1
                    c = c + 1

                while b < len(right):
                    list[c]=right[b]
                    b = b + 1
                    c = c + 1
            return list
```

When the preceding Python code is run, it generates an output, as follows:

```
In [180]:   1  list = [44,16,83,7,67,21,34,45,10]
            2  MergeSort(list)
            3  print(list)
            4
            5

            [7, 10, 16, 21, 34, 44, 45, 67, 83]
```

Note that the code results are in a sorted list.

# Shell Sort

The bubble sort algorithm compares immediate neighbors and exchanges them if they are out of order. If we have a partially sorted list, bubble sort should give reasonable performance as it will exit as soon as no more swapping of elements occurs in a loop.

But for a totally unsorted list, sized $N$, you can argue that bubble sort will have to fully iterate through $N$-1 passes in order to get it fully sorted.

Donald Shell proposed Shell sort (named after him), which questions the importance of selecting immediate neighbors for comparison and swapping.

Now, let's understand this concept.

In pass one, instead of selecting immediate neighbors, we use elements that are at a fixed gap, eventually sorting a sublist consisting of a pair of data points. This is shown in the following diagram. In pass two, it sorts sublists containing four data points (see the following diagram). In subsequent passes, the number of data points per sublist keeps on increasing and the number of sublists keeps on decreasing until we reach a situation where there is just one sublist that consists of all the data points. At this point, we can assume that the list is sorted:

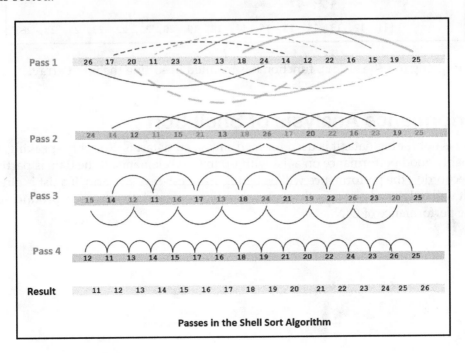

**Passes in the Shell Sort Algorithm**

In Python, the code for implementing the Shell sort algorithm is as follows:

```
def ShellSort(list):
    distance = len(list) // 2
    while distance > 0:
        for i in range(distance, len(list)):
            temp = input_list[i]
            j = i
# Sort the sub list for this distance
            while j >= distance and list[j - distance] > temp:
                list[j] = list[j - distance]
                j = j-distance
            list[j] = temp
# Reduce the distance for the next element
        distance = distance//2
    return list
```

The preceding code can be used to sort the list, as follows:

```
In [119]:    1  list = [26,17,20,11,23,21,13,18,24,14,12,22,16,15,19,25]

In [120]:    1  shellSort(list)
             2  print(list)

             [11, 12, 13, 14, 15, 16, 17, 18, 19, 20, 21, 22, 23, 24, 25, 26]
```

Note that calling the ShellSort function has resulted in sorting the input array.

# A Performance Analysis of Shell Sort

Shell sort is not for big data. It is used for medium-sized datasets. Roughly speaking, it has a reasonably good performance on a list with up to 6,000 elements. If the data is partially in the correct order, the performance will be better. In a best-case scenario, if a list is already sorted, it will only need one pass through $N$ elements to validate the order, producing a best-case performance of $O(N)$.

# Selection Sort

As we saw earlier in this chapter, bubble sort is one of the simplest sorting algorithms. Selection sort is an improvement on bubble sort, where we try to minimize the total number of swaps required with the algorithm. It is designed to make one swap for each pass, compared to *N*-1 passes with the bubble sort algorithm. Instead of bubbling the largest value toward the top in baby steps (as done in bubble sort, resulting in *N*-1 swaps), we look for the largest value in each pass and move it toward the top. So, after the first pass, the largest value will be at the top. After the second pass, the second largest value will be next to the top value. As the algorithm progresses, the subsequent values will move to their correct place based on their values. The last value will be moved after the (*N*-1)[th] pass. So, selection sort takes *N*-1 passes to sort *N* items:

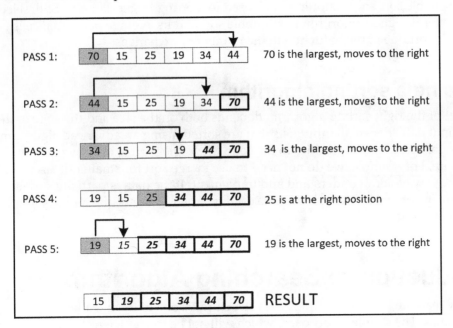

The implementation of selection sort in Python is shown here:

```
def SelectionSort(list):
    for fill_slot in range(len(list) - 1, 0, -1):
        max_index = 0
        for location in range(1, fill_slot + 1):
            if list[location] > list[max_index]:
                max_index = location
        list[fill_slot],list[max_index] = list[max_index],list[fill_slot]
```

When the selection sort algorithm is executed, it will result in the following output:

```
In [202]:   1  list = [70,15,25,19,34,44]
            2  SelectionSort(list)
            3  print(list)

            [15, 19, 25, 34, 44, 70]
```

Note that the final output is the sorted list.

## The performance of the selection sort algorithm

Selection sort's worst-case performance is $O(N^2)$. Note that its worst performance is similar to bubble sort and it should not be used for sorting larger datasets. Still, selection sort is a better designed algorithm than bubble sort and its average performance is better than bubble sort due to the reduction in the number of exchanges.

## Choosing a sorting algorithm

The choice of the right sorting algorithm depends both on the size and the state of the current input data. For small input lists that are sorted, using an advanced algorithm will introduce unnecessary complexities to the code, with a negligible improvement in performance. For example, we do not need to use merge sort for smaller datasets. Bubble sort will be way easier to understand and implement. If the data is partially sorted, we can take advantage of that by using insertion sort. For larger datasets, the merge sort algorithm is the best one to use.

# Introduction to Searching Algorithms

Efficiently searching data in complex data structures is one of the most important functionalities. The simplest approach, which will not be that efficient, is to search for the required data in each data point. But, as the data becomes bigger in size, we need more sophisticated algorithms designed for searching data.

The following searching algorithms are presented in this section:

- Linear search
- Binary search
- Interpolation search

Let's look at each of them in more detail.

# Linear Search

One of the simplest strategies for searching data is to simply loop through each element looking for the target. Each data point is searched for a match and when a match is found, the results are returned and the algorithm exits the loop. Otherwise, the algorithm keeps on searching until it reaches the end of the data. The obvious disadvantage of linear search is that it is very slow due to the inherent exhaustive search. The advantage is that the data does not need to be sorted, as required by the other algorithms presented in this chapter.

Let's look at the code for linear search:

```
def LinearSearch(list, item):
    index = 0
    found = False
# Match the value with each data element
    while index < len(list) and found is False:
        if list[index] == item:
            found = True
        else:
            index = index + 1
    return found
```

Let's now look at the output of the preceding code:

```
1  list = [12, 33, 11, 99, 22, 55, 90]
2  print(LinearSearch(list, 12))
3  print(LinearSearch(list, 91))

True
False
```

Note that running the LinearSearch function returns a True value if it can successfully find the data.

## The Performance of Linear Search

As discussed, linear search is a simple algorithm that performs an exhaustive search. Its worst-case behavior is *O(N)*.

# Binary Search

The pre-requisite of the binary search algorithm is sorted data. The algorithm iteratively divides a list into two parts and keeps a track of the lowest and highest indices until it finds the value it is looking for:

```
def BinarySearch(list, item):
    first = 0
    last = len(list)-1
    found = False

while first<=last and not found:
    midpoint = (first + last)//2
    if list[midpoint] == item:
        found = True
    else:
        if item < list[midpoint]:
            last = midpoint-1
        else:
            first = midpoint+1
return found
```

The output is as follows:

```
In [14]:   1  list = [12, 33, 11, 99, 22, 55, 90]
           2  sorted_list = BubbleSort(list)
           3  print(BinarySearch(list, 12))
           4  print(BinarySearch(list, 91))

           True
           False
```

Note that calling the `BinarySearch` function will return `True` if the value is found in the input list.

# The Performance of Binary Search

Binary search is so named because at each iteration, the algorithm bifurcates the data into two parts. If the data has *N* items, it will take a maximum of O(logN) steps to iterate. This means that the algorithm has an *O(logN)* runtime.

# Interpolation Search

Binary search is based on the logic that it focuses on the middle section of the data. Interpolation search is more sophisticated. It uses the target value to estimate the position of the element in the sorted array. Let's try to understand it by using an example. Let's assume we want to search for a word in an English dictionary, such as the word *river*. We will use this information to interpolate and start searching for words starting with *r*. A more generalized interpolation search can be programmed as follows:

```
def IntPolsearch(list,x ):
    idx0 = 0
    idxn = (len(list) - 1)
    found = False
    while idx0 <= idxn and x >= list[idx0] and x <= list[idxn]:
    # Find the mid point
        mid = idx0 +int(((float(idxn - idx0)/( list[idxn] - list[idx0])) *
( x - list[idx0])))
 # Compare the value at mid point with search value
        if list[mid] == x:
            found = True
            return found
    if list[mid] < x:
            idx0 = mid + 1
 return found
```

The output is as follows:

```
In [16]:  1  list = [12, 33, 11, 99, 22, 55, 90]
          2  sorted_list = BubbleSort(list)
          3  print(IntPolsearch(list, 12))
          4  print(IntPolsearch(list,91))

          True
          False
```

Note that before using `IntPolsearch`, the array first needs to be sorted using a sorting algorithm.

# The Performance of Interpolation Search

If the data is unevenly distributed, the performance of the interpolation search algorithm will be poor. The worst-case performance of this algorithm is $O(N)$ and if the data is somewhat reasonably uniform, the best performance is $O(\log(\log N))$.

# Practical Applications

The ability to efficiently and accurately search data in a given data repository is critical to many real-life applications. Depending on your choice of searching algorithm, you may need to sort the data first as well. The choice of the right sorting and searching algorithms will depend on the type and the size of the data, as well as the nature of the problem you are trying to solve.

Let's try to use the algorithms presented in this chapter to solve the problem of matching a new applicant at the immigration department of a certain country with historical records. When someone applies for a visa to enter the country, the system tries to match the applicant with the existing historical records. If at least one match is found, then the system further calculates the number of times that the individual has been approved or refused in the past. On the other hand, if no match is found, the system classes the applicant as a new applicant and issues them a new identifier. The ability to search, locate, and identify a person in the historical data is critical for the system. This information is important because if someone has applied in the past and the application is known to have been refused, then this may affect that individual's current application in a negative way. Similarly, if someone's application is known to have been approved in the past, this approval may increase the chances of that individual getting approval for their current application. Typically, the historical database will have millions of rows, and we will need a well-designed solution to match new applicants in the historical database.

Let's assume that the historical table in the database looks like the following:

| Personal ID | Application ID | First name | Surname | DOB | Decision | Decision date |
|---|---|---|---|---|---|---|
| 45583 | 677862 | John | Doe | 2000-09-19 | Approved | 2018-08-07 |
| 54543 | 877653 | Xman | Xsir | 1970-03-10 | Rejected | 2018-06-07 |
| 34332 | 344565 | Agro | Waka | 1973-02-15 | Rejected | 2018-05-05 |
| 45583 | 677864 | John | Doe | 2000-09-19 | Approved | 2018-03-02 |
| 22331 | 344553 | Kal | Sorts | 1975-01-02 | Approved | 2018-04-15 |

In this table, the first column, `Personal ID`, is associated with each of the unique applicants in the historical database. If there are 30 million unique applicants in the historical database, then there will be 30 million unique personal IDs. Each personal ID identifies an applicant in the historical database system.

The second column we have is `Application ID`. Each application ID identifies a unique application in the system. A person may have applied more than once in the past. So, this means that in the historical database, we will have more unique application IDs than personal IDs. John Doe will only have one personal ID but has two application IDs, as shown in the preceding table.

The preceding table only shows a sample of the historical dataset. Let's assume that we have close to 1 million rows in our historical dataset, which contains the records of the last 10 years of applicants. New applicants are continuously arriving at the average rate of around 2 applicants per minute. For each applicant, we need to do the following:

- Issue a new application ID for the applicant.
- See if there is a match with an applicant in the historical database.
- If a match is found, use the personal ID for that applicant, as found in the historical database. We also need to determine that how many times the application has been approved or refused in the historical database.
- If no match is found, then we need to issue a new personal ID for that individual.

Suppose a new person arrives with the following credentials:

- First Name: John
- Surname: Doe
- DOB: 2000-09-19

Now, how can we design an application that can perform an efficient and cost-effective search?

One strategy for searching the new application in the database can be devised as follows:

- Sort the historical database by DOB.
- Each time a new person arrives, issue a new application ID to the applicant.
- Fetch all the records that match that date of birth. This will be the primary search.
- Out of the records that have come up as matches, perform a secondary search using the first and last name.
- If a match is found, use Personal ID to refer to the applicants. Calculate the number of approvals and refusals.
- If no match is found, issue a new personal ID to the applicant.

Let's try choosing the right algorithm to sort the historical database. We can safely rule out bubble sort as the size of the data is huge. Shell sort will perform better, but only if we have partially sorted lists. So, merge sort may be the best option for sorting the historical database.

When a new person arrives, we need to locate and search that person in the historical database. As the data is already sorted, either interpolation search or binary search can be used. Because applicants are likely to be equally spread out, as per DOB, we can safely use binary search.

Initially, we search based on DOB, which returns a set of applicants sharing the same date of birth. Now, we need to find the required person within the small subset of people who share the same date of birth. As we have successfully reduced the data to a small subset, any of the search algorithms, including bubble sort, can be used to search for the applicant. Note that we have simplified the secondary search problem here a bit. We also need to calculate the total number of approvals and refusals by aggregating the search results, if more than one match is found.

In a real-world scenario, each individual needs to be identified in the secondary search using some fuzzy search algorithm, as the first and last names may be spelled slightly differently. The search may need to use some kind of distance algorithm to implement the fuzzy search, where the data points whose similarity is above a defined threshold are considered the same.

# Summary

In this chapter, we presented a set of sorting and searching algorithms. We also discussed the strengths and weaknesses of different sorting and searching algorithms. We quantified the performance of these algorithms and learned when to use each algorithm.

In the next chapter, we will study dynamic algorithms. We will also look at a practical example of designing an algorithm and the details of the page ranking algorithm. Finally, we will study the linear programming algorithm.

# 4
# Designing Algorithms

This chapter presents the core design concepts of various algorithms. It discusses the strengths and weaknesses of various techniques for designing algorithms. By understanding these concepts, you will learn how to design efficient algorithms.

This chapter starts by discussing the different choices available to you when designing algorithms. Then, it discusses the importance of characterizing the particular problem that we are trying to solve. Next, it uses the famous **Traveling Salesman Problem (TSP)** as a use case and applies the different design techniques that we will be presenting. Then, it introduces linear programming and discusses its applications. Finally, it presents how linear programming can be used to solve a real-world problem.

By the end of this chapter, you should be able to understand the basic concepts of designing an efficient algorithm.

The following concepts are discussed in this chapter:

- The various approaches to designing an algorithm
- Understanding the trade-offs involved in choosing the correct design for an algorithm
- Best practices of formulating a real-world problem
- Solving a real-world optimization problem

Let's first look at the basic concepts of designing an algorithm.

# Introducing the basic concepts of designing an algorithm

An algorithm, according to the American Heritage Dictionary, is defined as follows:

> *"A finite set of unambiguous instructions that given some set of initial conditions can be performed in a prescribed sequence to achieve a certain goal and that has a recognizable set of end conditions."*

Designing an algorithm is about coming up with this *"finite set of unambiguous instructions"* in the most efficient way to *"achieve a certain goal."* For a complex real-world problem, designing an algorithm is a tedious task. To come up with a good design, we first need to fully understand the problem we are trying to solve. We start by figuring out *what* needs to be done (that is, understanding the requirements) before looking into *how* it will be done (that is, designing the algorithm). Understanding the problem includes addressing both the functional and non-functional requirements of the problem. Let's look at what these are:

- Functional requirements formally specify the input and output interfaces of the problem that we want to solve and the functions associated with them. Functional requirements help us understand data processing, data manipulation, and the calculations that need to be implemented to generate the result.
- Non-functional requirements set the expectations about the performance and security aspects of the algorithm.

Note that designing an algorithm is about addressing both the functional and non-functional requirements in the best possible way under the given set of circumstances and keeping in mind the set of resources available to run the designed algorithm.

To come up with a good response that can meet the functional and non-functional requirements, our design should respect the following three concerns, as discussed in Chapter 1, *Overview of Algorithms*:

- Concern 1: Will the designed algorithm produce the result we expect?
- Concern 2: Is this the optimal way to get these results?
- Concern 3: How is the algorithm going to perform on larger datasets?

In this section, let's look at these concerns one by one.

# Concern 1 – Will the designed algorithm produce the result we expect?

An algorithm is a mathematical solution to a real-world problem. To be useful, it should produce accurate results. How to verify the correctness of an algorithm should not be an afterthought; instead, it should be baked into the design of the algorithm. Before strategizing how to verify an algorithm, we need to think about the following two aspects:

- **Defining the truth**: To verify the algorithm, we need some known correct results for a given set of inputs. These known correct results are called the **truths**, in the context of the problem we are trying to solve. The **truth** is important as it is used as a reference when we iteratively work on evolving our algorithm toward a better solution.
- **Choosing metrics**: We also need to think about how are we going to quantify the deviation from the defined truth. Choosing the correct metrics will help us to accurately quantify the quality of our algorithm.

For example, for machine learning algorithms, we can use existing labeled data as the truth. We can choose one or more metrics, such as accuracy, recall, or precision, to quantify deviation from the truth. It is important to note that, in some use cases, the correct output is not a single value. Instead, the correct output is defined as the range for a given set of inputs. As we work on the design and development of our algorithm, the objective will be to iteratively improve the algorithm until it is within the range specified in the requirements.

# Concern 2 – Is this the optimal way to get these results?

The second concern is about finding the answer to the following question:

*Is this the optimal solution and can we verify that no other solution exists for this problem that is better than our solution?*

At first glance, this question looks quite simple to answer. However, for a certain class of algorithms, researchers have unsuccessfully spent decades verifying whether a particular solution generated by an algorithm is also the best and that no other solution exists that can give better results. So, it becomes important that we first understand the problem, its requirements, and the resources available to run the algorithm. We need to acknowledge the following statement:

*Should we aim to find the optimal solution for this problem? Finding and verifying the optimal solution is so time-consuming and complex that a workable solution based on heuristics is our best bet.*

So, understanding the problem and its complexities is important and helps us estimate the resource requirements.

Before we start looking deeper into this, first, let's define a couple of terms here:

- **Polynomial algorithm:** If an algorithm has a time complexity of $O(n^k)$, we call it a polynomial algorithm, where $k$ is a constant.
- **Certificate:** A proposed candidate solution produced at the end of an iteration is called a **certificate**. As we progress iteratively in solving a particular problem, we typically generate a series of certificates. If the solution is moving toward convergence, each generated certificate will be better than the previous one. At some point, when our certificate meets the requirements, we will choose that certificate as the final solution.

In Chapter 1, *Overview of Algorithms*, we introduced Big O notation, which can be used to analyze the time complexity of an algorithm. In the context of analyzing time complexity, we are looking at the following different time intervals:

- The time it takes for an algorithm to produce a proposed solution, called a certificate $(t_r)$
- The time it takes to verify the proposed solution (certificate), $t_s$

# Characterizing the complexity of the problem

Over the years, the research community has divided problems into various categories according to their complexity. Before we attempt to design the solution to a problem, it makes sense to first try to characterize it. Generally, there are three types of problems:

- Type 1: Problems for which we can guarantee that a polynomial algorithm exists that can be used to solve them

- Type 2: Problems for which we can prove that they cannot be solved by a polynomial algorithm
- Type 3: Problems for which we are unable to find a polynomial algorithm to solve them, but we are also unable to prove that a polynomial solution for those problems is impossible to find

Let's look at the various classes of problems:

- **Non-Deterministic Polynomial (NP)**: For a problem to be an NP problem, it has to meet the following condition:
    - It is guaranteed that there is a polynomial algorithm that can be used to verify that the candidate solution (certificate) is optimal.
- **Polynominal (P)**: These are types of problems that can be thought of as a subset of NP. In addition to meeting the condition of an NP problem, P problems need to meet another condition:
    - It is guaranteed that there is at least one polynomial algorithm that can be used to solve them.

The relationship between **P** and **NP** problems is shown in the following diagram:

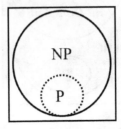

If a problem is NP, is it P as well? This is one of the greatest problems in computer science that remains unresolved. Millennium Prize Problems, selected by the Clay Mathematics Institute, has announced a 1 million dollar prize for the solution to this problem as it will have a major impact on fields such as AI, cryptography, and theoretical computer sciences:

Let's continue the list of various classes of problems:

- **NP-complete**: The NP-complete category contains the hardest problems of all NP problems. An NP-complete problem meets the following two conditions:
    - There are no known polynomial algorithms to generate a certificate.
    - There are known polynomial algorithms to verify that the proposed certificate is optimal.
- **NP-hard**: The NP-hard category contains problems that are at least as hard as any problem in the NP category, but that do not themselves need to be in the NP category.

Now, let's try to draw a diagram to illustrate these different classes of problems:

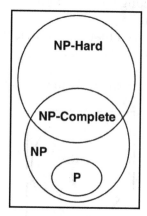

Note that it is still to be proven by the research community whether P = NP. Although this has not yet been proven, it is extremely likely that P ≠ NP. In that case, no polynomial solution exists for NP-complete problems. Note that the preceding diagram is based on this assumption.

# Concern 3 – How is the algorithm going to perform on larger datasets?

An algorithm processes data in a defined way to produce a result. Generally, as the size of the data increases, it takes more and more time to process the data and calculate the required results. The term *big data* is sometimes used to roughly identify datasets that are expected to be challenging for the infrastructure and algorithms to work with due to their volume, variety, and velocity. A well-designed algorithm should be scalable, which means that it should be designed in a way that means, wherever possible, it should be able to run efficiently, making use of the available resources and generating the correct results in a reasonable timeframe. The design of the algorithm becomes even more important when dealing with big data. To quantify the scalability of an algorithm, we need to keep the following two aspects in mind:

- **The increase in resource requirements as the input data is increased**: Estimating a requirement such as this is called space complexity analysis.
- **The increase in the time taken to run as the input data is increased**: Estimating this is called time complexity analysis.

Note that we are living in an era that is defined by data explosion. The term *big data* has become mainstream as it captures the size and complexity of the data that is typically required to be processed by modern algorithms.

While in the development-and-testing phase, many algorithms use only a small sample of data. When designing an algorithm, it is important to look into the scalability aspect of the algorithms. In particular, it is important to carefully analyze (that is, test or predict) the effect of an algorithm's performance as datasets increase in size.

# Understanding algorithmic strategies

A well-designed algorithm tries to optimize the use of the available resources most efficiently by dividing the problem into smaller subproblems wherever possible. There are different algorithmic strategies for designing algorithms. An algorithmic strategy deals with the following three aspects of an algorithm list containing aspects of the missing algorithm.

We will present the following three strategies in this section:

- The divide-and-conquer strategy
- The dynamic programming strategy
- The greedy algorithm strategy

# Understanding the divide-and-conquer strategy

One of the strategies is to find a way to divide a larger problem into smaller problems that can be solved independently of each other. The subsolutions produced by these subproblems are then combined to generate the overall solution of the problem. This is called the **divide-and-conquer** strategy.

Mathematically, if we are designing a solution for a problem ($P$) with $n$ inputs that needs to process dataset $d$, we split the problem into $k$ subproblems, $P_1$ to $P_k$. Each of the subproblems will process a partition of the dataset, $d$. Typically, we will have $P_1$ to $P_k$ processing $d_1$ to $d_k$.

Let's look at a practical example.

## Practical example – divide-and-conquer applied to Apache Spark

Apache Spark is an open source framework that is used to solve complex distributed problems. It implements a divide-and-conquer strategy to solve problems. To process a problem, it divides the problem into various subproblems and processes them independently of each other. We will demonstrate this by using a simple example of counting words from a list.

Let's assume that we have the following list of words:

```
wordsList = [python, java, ottawa, news, java, ottawa]
```

We want to calculate the frequency of each word in this list. For that, we will apply the divide-and-conquer strategy to solve this problem in an efficient way.

The implementation of divide-and-conquer is shown in the following diagram:

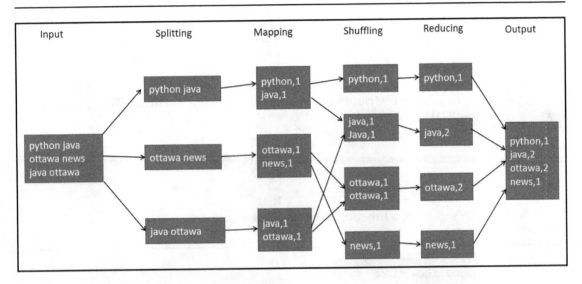

The preceding diagram shows the following phases into which a problem is divided:

1. **Splitting**: The input data is divided into partitions that can be processed independently of each other. This is called splitting. We have three *splits* in the preceding figure.
2. **Mapping**: Any operation that can run independently on a split is called a map. In the preceding diagram, the map operation coverts each of the words in the partition to key-value pairs. Corresponding to the three splits, there are three mappers that are run in parallel.
3. **Shuffling**: Shuffling is the process of bringing similar keys together. Once the similar keys are brought together, aggregation functions can be run on their values. Note that *shuffling* is a performance-intensive operation as similar keys need to be brought together that can be originally distributed across the network.
4. **Reducing**: Running an aggregation function on the values of similar keys is called reducing. In the preceding diagram, we have to count the number of words.

Let's see how we can write the code to implement this. To demonstrate the divide-and-conquer strategy, we need a distributed computing framework. We will run Python running on Apache Spark for this:

1. First, in order to use Apache Spark, we will create a runtime context of Apache Spark:

```
import findspark
findspark.init()
```

```
from pyspark.sql import SparkSession
spark = SparkSession.builder.master("local[*]").getOrCreate()
sc = spark.sparkContext
```

2. Now, let's create a sample list containing some words. We will convert this list into Spark's native distributed data structure, called a **Resilient Distributed Dataset (RDD)**:

```
wordsList = ['python', 'java', 'ottawa', 'ottawa', 'java','news']
wordsRDD = sc.parallelize(wordsList, 4)
# Print out the type of wordsRDD
print (wordsRDD.collect())
```

3. Now, let's use a `map` function to convert the words into a key-value pair:

```
In [19]:  wordPairs = wordsRDD.map(lambda w: (w, 1))
          print (wordPairs.collect())

          [('python', 1), ('java', 1), ('ottawa', 1), ('ottawa', 1), ('java', 1), ('news', 1)]
```

4. Let's use the `reduce` function to aggregate and get the final result:

```
In [20]:  wordCountsCollected = wordPairs.reduceByKey(lambda x,y: x+y)
          print(wordCountsCollected.collect())

          [('python', 1), ('java', 2), ('ottawa', 2), ('news', 1)]
```

This shows how we can use the divide-and-conquer strategy to count the number of words.

 Modern cloud computing infrastructures, such as Microsoft Azure, Amazon Web Services, and Google Cloud, achieve scalability by implementing a divide-and-conquer strategy either directly or indirectly behind the scenes.

# Understanding the dynamic programming strategy

Dynamic programming was a strategy proposed in the 1950s by Richard Bellman to optimize certain classes of algorithms. It is based on an intelligent caching mechanism that tries to reuse heavy computations. This intelligent caching mechanism is called **memorization**.

Dynamic programming gives good performance benefits when the problem we are trying to solve can be divided into subproblems. The subproblems partly involve a calculation that is repeated in those subproblems. The idea is to perform that calculation once (which is the time-consuming step) and then reuse it on the other subproblems. This is achieved using memorization, which is especially useful in solving recursive problems that may evaluate the same inputs multiple times.

# Understanding greedy algorithms

Before we dive deep into this section, let's first define two terms:

- **Algorithmic overheads**: Whenever we try to find the optimal solution to a certain problem, it takes some time. As the problems that we are trying to optimize become more and more complex, the time it takes to find the optimal solution also increases. We represent algorithmic overheads with $\Omega_i$.
- **Delta from optimal**: For a given optimization problem, there exists an optimal solution. Typically, we iteratively optimize the solution using our chosen algorithm. For a given problem, there always exists a perfect solution, called the **optimal solution**, to the current problem. As discussed, based on the classification of the problem we are trying to solve, it's possible for the optimal solution to be unknown or that it would take an unreasonable amount of time to calculate and verify it. Assuming that the optimal solution is known, the difference from optimal for the current solution in the $i^{th}$ iteration is called **delta from optimal** and is represented by $\Delta_i$.

For complex problems, we have two possible strategies:

- **Strategy 1:** Spend more time finding a solution nearest to optimal so that $\Delta_i$ is as small as possible.
- **Strategy 2:** Minimize the algorithmic overhead, $\Omega_i$. Use the quick-and-dirty approach and just use a workable solution.

Greedy algorithms are based on strategy 2, where we do not make an effort to find a global optimal and choose to minimize the algorithm overheads instead.

Using a greedy algorithm is a quick and simple strategy of finding the global optimal value for multistage problems. It is based on selecting the local optimal values without making an effort to verify whether local optimal values are globally optimal as well. Generally, unless we are lucky, a greedy algorithm will not result in a value that can be considered globally optimal. However, finding a global optimal value is a time-consuming task. Hence, the greedy algorithm is fast compared to the divide-and-conquer and dynamic programming algorithms.

Generally, a greedy algorithm is defined as follows:

1. Let's assume that we have a dataset, $D$. In this dataset, choose an element, $k$.
2. Let's assume the candidate solution or certificate is $S$. Consider including $k$ in the solution, $S$. If it can be included, then the solution is *Union(S, e)*.
3. Repeat the process until $S$ is filled up or $D$ is exhausted.

# Practical application – solving the TSP

Let's first look at the problem statement for the TSP, which is a well-known problem that was coined as a challenge in the 1930s. The TSP is an NP-hard problem. To start with, we can randomly generate a tour that meets the condition of visiting all of the cities without caring about the optimal solution. Then, we can work to improve the solution with each iteration. Each tour generated in an iteration is called a candidate solution (also called a certificate). Proving that a certificate is optimal requires an exponentially increasing amount of time. Instead, different heuristics-based solutions are used that generate tours that are near to optimal but are not optimal.

A traveling salesman needs to visit a given list of cities to get their job done:

| INPUT | A list of $n$ cities (denoted as $V$) and the distances between each pair of cities, $d_{ij}$ $(1 \le i, j \le n)$ |
|---|---|
| OUTPUT | The shortest tour that visits each city exactly once and returns to the initial city |

Note the following:

- The distances between the cities on the list are known,
- Each city in the given list needs to be visited *exactly* once.

Can we generate the travel plan for the salesman? What will be the optimal solution that can minimize the total distance traveled by the traveling salesman?

The following are the distances between five Canadian cities that we can use for the TSP:

|  | Ottawa | Montreal | Kingston | Toronto | Sudbury |
|---|---|---|---|---|---|
| Ottawa | - | 199 | 196 | 450 | 484 |
| Montreal | 199 | - | 287 | 542 | 680 |
| Kingston | 196 | 287 | - | 263 | 634 |
| Toronto | 450 | 542 | 263 | - | 400 |
| Sudbury | 484 | 680 | 634 | 400 | - |

Note that the objective is to get a tour that starts and ends in the initial city. For example, a typical tour can be Ottawa–Sudbury–Montreal–Kingston–Toronto–Ottawa with a cost of 484 + 680 + 287 + 263 + 450 = 2,164. Is this the tour in which the salesman has to travel the minimum distance? What will be the optimal solution that can minimize the total distance traveled by the traveling salesman? I will leave this up to you to think about and calculate.

# Using a brute-force strategy

The first solution that comes to mind to solve the TSP is using brute force to come up with the shortest path in which the salesperson visits every city exactly once and returns to the initial city. So, the brute-force strategy works as follows:

1. Evaluate all possible tours.
2. Choose the one for which we get the shortest distance.

The problem is that for $n$ number of cities there are $(n-1)!$ possible tours. It means that five cities will produce $4! = 24$ tours and we will select the one that corresponds to the lowest distance. It is obvious that this method will only work since we do not have too many cities. As the number of cities increases, the brute-force strategy becomes unstable due to a large number of permutations generated by using this approach.

Let's see how we can implement the brute-force strategy in Python.

First, note that a tour, {1,2,3}, represents a tour of the city from city 1 to city 2 and city 3. The total distance in a tour is the total distance covered in a tour. We will assume that the distance between the cities is the shortest distance between them (which is the Euclidean distance).

Let's first define three utility functions:

- distance_points: Calculates the absolute distance between two points
- distance_tour: Calculates the total distance the salesperson has to cover in a given tour
- generate_cities: Randomly generates a set of *n* cities located in a rectangle of width 500 and height 300

Let's look at the following code:

```python
import random
from itertools import permutations
alltours = permutations

def distance_tour(aTour):
    return sum(distance_points(aTour[i - 1], aTour[i])
            for i in range(len(aTour)))

aCity = complex

def distance_points(first, second): return abs(first - second)

def generate_cities (number_of_cities):
    seed=111;width=500;height=300
    random.seed((number_of_cities, seed))
    return frozenset(aCity(random.randint(1, width), random.randint(1,
height))
        for c in range(number_of_cities))
```

In the preceding code, we implemented alltours from the permutations function of the itertools package. We have also represented the distance with a complex number. This means the following:

- Calculating the distance between two cities, *a* and *b*, is as simple as distance (a,b),
- We can create *n* number of cities just by calling generate_cities (n).

Now let's define a function, `brute_force`, that generates all the possible tours of the cities. Once it has generated all possible tours, it will choose the one with the shortest distance:

```
def brute_force(cities):
    "Generate all possible tours of the cities and choose the shortest
    tour."
    return shortest_tour(alltours(cities))

def shortest_tour(tours): return min(tours, key=distance_tour)
```

Now let's define the utility functions that can help us plot the cites. We will define the following functions:

- `visualize_tour`: Plots all the cities and links in a particular tour. It also highlights the city from where the tour started.
- `visualize_segment`: Used by `visualize_tour` to plot cites and links in a segment.

Look at the following code:

```
%matplotlib inline
import matplotlib.pyplot as plt
def visualize_tour(tour, style='bo-'):
    if len(tour) > 1000: plt.figure(figsize=(15, 10))
    start = tour[0:1]
    visualize_segment(tour + start, style)
    visualize_segment(start, 'rD')
def visualize_segment (segment, style='bo-'):
    plt.plot([X(c) for c in segment], [Y(c) for c in segment], style,
clip_on=False)
    plt.axis('scaled')
    plt.axis('off')
def X(city): "X axis"; return city.real
def Y(city): "Y axis"; return city.imag
```

Let's implement a function, `tsp()`, that does the following:

1. Generates the tour based on the algorithm and number of cities requested
2. Calculates the time it took for the algorithm to run
3. Generates a plot

Once `tsp()` is defined, we can use it to create a tour:

```
[ ]  from time import clock
     from collections import Counter
     def tsp(algorithm, cities):
         t0   = clock()
         tour = algorithm(cities)
         t1   = clock()
         assert Counter(tour) == Counter(cities) # Every city appears exactly once in tour
         visualize_tour(tour)
         print("{}: {} cities ⇒ tour length {:.0f} (in {:.3f} sec)".format(
             name(algorithm), len(tour), distance_tour(tour), t1 - t0))

     def name(algorithm): return algorithm.__name__.replace('_tsp', '')


[ ]  tsp(brute_force, generate_cities(10))

 ⤷   brute_force: 10 cities ⇒ tour length 1218 (in 10.962 sec)
```

Note that we have used it to generate the tour for 10 cities. As *n* = *10,* it will generate *(10-1)!* = *362,880* possible permutations. If *n* increases, the number of permutations sharply increases and the brute-force method cannot be used.

# Using a greedy algorithm

If we use a greedy algorithm to solve the TSP, then, at each step, we can choose a city that seems reasonable, instead of finding a city to visit that will result in the best overall path. So, whenever we need to select a city, we just select the nearest city without bothering to verify that this choice will result in the globally optimal path.

The approach of the greedy algorithm is simple:

1. Start from any city.
2. At each step, keep building the tour by moving to the next city where the nearest neighborhood has not been visited before.
3. Repeat *step 2*.

Let's define a function named `greedy_algorithm` that can implement this logic:

```
def greedy_algorithm(cities, start=None):
    C = start or first(cities)
    tour = [C]
    unvisited = set(cities - {C})
    while unvisited:
        C = nearest_neighbor(C, unvisited)
        tour.append(C)
        unvisited.remove(C)
    return tour

def first(collection): return next(iter(collection))

def nearest_neighbor(A, cities):
    return min(cities, key=lambda C: distance_points(C, A))
```

Now, let's use `greedy_algorithm` to create a tour for 2,000 cities:

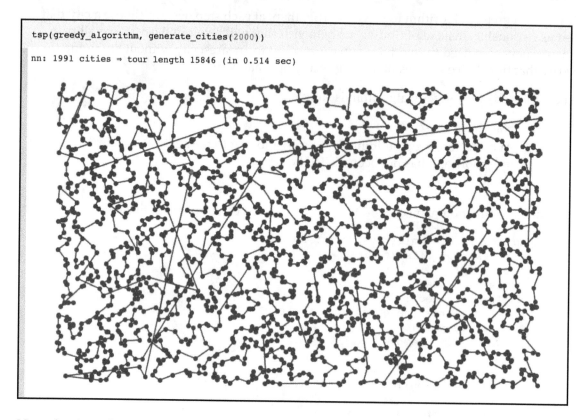

```
tsp(greedy_algorithm, generate_cities(2000))

nn: 1991 cities ⇒ tour length 15846 (in 0.514 sec)
```

Note that it took only 0.514 seconds to generate the tour for 2,000 cities. If we had used the brute-force method, it would have generated *(2000-1)!* permutations, which is almost infinity.

Note that the greedy algorithm is based on heuristics and there is no proof that the solution will be optimal.

Now, let's look at the design of the PageRank algorithm.

# Presenting the PageRank algorithm

As a practical example, let's look at the PageRank algorithm, which was initially used by Google to rank the search results of a user query. It generates a number that quantifies the importance of search results in the context of the query the user has executed. This was designed by two Ph.D. students, Larry Page and Sergey Brin, at Stanford in the late 1990s, who also went on to start Google.

> The PageRank algorithm was named after Larry Page, who created it with Sergey Brin while studying at Stanford University.

Let's first formally define the problem for which PageRank was initially designed.

# Problem definition

Whenever a user enters a query on a search engine on the web, it typically results in a large number of results. To make the results useful for the end user, it is important to rank the web pages using some criteria. The results that are displayed use this ranking to summarize the results for the user and are dependent on the criteria defined by the underlying algorithm being used.

# Implementing the PageRank algorithm

The most important part of the PageRank algorithm is to come up with the best way to calculate the importance of each page that is returned by the query results. To calculate a number from 0 to 1 that can quantify the importance of a particular page, the algorithm incorporates information from the following two components:

- **Information that was specific to the query entered by the user**: This component estimates, in the context of the query entered by the user, how relevant the content of the web page is. The content of the page is directly dependent on the author of the page.
- **Information that was not relevant to the query entered by the user**: This component tries to quantify the importance of each web page in the context of its links, views, and neighborhood. This component is difficult to calculate as web pages are heterogeneous and coming up with criteria that can be applied across the web is difficult to develop.

In order to implement the PageRank algorithm in Python, first, let's import the necessary libraries:

```
import numpy as np
import networkx as nx
import matplotlib.pyplot as plt
%matplotlib inline
```

For the purpose of demonstration, let's assume that we are analyzing only five webpages in the network. Let's call this set of pages `myPages` and together they are in a network named `myWeb`:

```
myWeb = nx.DiGraph()
myPages = range(1,5)
```

Now, let's connect them randomly to simulate an actual network:

```
connections = [(1,3),(2,1),(2,3),(3,1),(3,2),(3,4),(4,5),(5,1),(5,4)]
myWeb.add_nodes_from(myPages)
myWeb.add_edges_from(connections)
```

Now, let's plot this graph:

```
pos=nx.shell_layout(myWeb)
nx.draw(myWeb, pos, arrows=True, with_labels=True)
plt.show()
```

It creates the visual representation of our network, as follows:

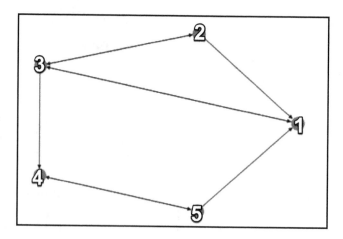

In the PageRank algorithm, the patterns of a web page are contained in a matrix called the transition matrix. There are algorithms that constantly update the transition matrix to capture the constantly changing state of the web. The size of the transition matrix is $n \times n$, where $n$ is the number of nodes. The numbers in the matrix are the probability that a visitor will next go to that link due to the outbound link.

In our case, the preceding graph shows the static web that we have. Let's define a function that can be used to create the transition matrix:

```
def createPageRank(aGraph):
    nodes_set = len(aGraph)
    M = nx.to_numpy_matrix(aGraph)
    outwards = np.squeeze(np.asarray(np.sum(M, axis=1)))
    prob_outwards = np.array(
    [1.0/count
        if count>0 else 0.0 for count in outwards])
    G = np.asarray(np.multiply(M.T, prob_outwards))
    p = np.ones(nodes_set) / float(nodes_set)
    if np.min(np.sum(G,axis=0)) < 1.0:
        print ('WARN: G is substochastic')
    return G, p
```

Note that this function will return G, which represents the transition matrix for our graph.

Let's generate the transition matrix for our graph:

```
[6]  G, p = createPageRank(myWeb)
     print (G)
```

```
[→]  [[0.   0.5   0.33333333  0.   0.5  ]
      [0.   0.    0.33333333  0.   0.   ]
      [1.   0.5   0.          0.   0.   ]
      [0.   0.    0.33333333  0.   0.5  ]
      [0.   0.    0.          1.   0.  ]]
```

Note that the transition matrix is *5 x 5* for our graph. Each column corresponds to each node in the graph. For example, column **2** is about the second node. There is a 0.5 probability that the visitor will navigate from node **2** to node **1** or node **3**. Note that the diagonal of the transition matrix is 0 as in our graph, there is no outbound link from a node to itself. In an actual network, it may be possible.

Note that the transition matrix is a sparse matrix. As the number of nodes increases, most of its values will be 0.

# Understanding linear programming

The basic algorithm behind linear programming was developed by George Dantzig at the University of California at Berkeley in the early 1940s. Dantzig used this concept to experiment with logistical supply-and-capacity planning for troops while working for the US Air Force. At the end of the Second World War, Dantzig started working for the Pentagon and matured his algorithm into a technique that he named linear programming. It was used for military combat planning.

Today, it is used to solve important real-world problems that relate to minimizing or maximizing a variable based on certain constraints. Some examples of these problems are as follows:

- Minimizing the time to repair a car at a mechanic shop based on the resources
- Allocating available distributed resources in a distributed computing environment to minimize response times
- Maximizing the profit of a company based on the optimal assignment of resources within the company

# Formulating a linear programming problem

The conditions to use linear programming are as follows:

- We should be able to formulate the problem through a set of equations.
- The variables used in the equation must be linear.

# Defining the objective function

Note that the objective of each of the preceding three examples is about minimizing or maximizing a variable. This objective is mathematically formulated as a linear function of other variables and is called the objective function. The aim of a linear programming problem is to minimize or maximize the objective function while remaining within the specified constraints.

## Specifying constraints

When trying to minimize or maximize something, there are certain constraints in real-world problems that need to be respected. For example, when trying to minimize the time it takes to repair a car, we also need to consider that there is a limited number of mechanics available. Specifying each constraint through a linear equation is an important part of formulating a linear programming problem.

# Practical application – capacity planning with linear programming

Let's look at a practical use case where linear programming can be used to solve a real-world problem. Let's assume that we want to maximize the profits of a state-of-the-art factory that manufactures two different types of robots:

- **Advanced model (A)**: This provides full functionality. Manufacturing each unit of the advanced model results in a profit of $4,200.
- **Basic model (B)**: This only provides basic functionality. Manufacturing each unit of the basic model results in a profit of $2,800.

There are three different types of people needed to manufacture a robot. The exact number of days needed to manufacture a robot of each type are as follows:

| Type of Robot | Technician | AI Specialist | Engineer |
|---|---|---|---|
| Robot A: advanced model | 3 days | 4 days | 4 days |
| Robot B: basic model | 2 days | 3 days | 3 days |

The factory runs on 30-day cycles. A single AI specialist is available for 30 days in a cycle. Each of the two engineers will take 8 days off in 30 days. So, an engineer is available only for 22 days in a cycle. There is a single technician available for 20 days in a 30-day cycle.

The following table shows the number of people we have in the factory:

| | Technician | AI Specialist | Engineer |
|---|---|---|---|
| Number of people | 1 | 1 | 2 |
| Total number of days in a cycle | 1 x 20 = 20 days | 1 x 30 = 30 days | 2 x 22 = 44 days |

This can be modeled as follows:

- Maximum profit = 4200A + 2800B
- This is subject to the following:
  - A ≥ 0: The number of advanced robots produced can be 0 or more.
  - B ≥ 0: The number of basic robots produced can be 0 or more.
  - 3A + 2B ≤ 20: These are the constraints of the technician's availability.
  - 4A+3B ≤ 30: These are the constraints of the AI specialist's availability.
  - 4A+ 3B ≤ 44: These are the constraints of the engineers' availability.

First, we import the Python package named `pulp`, which is used to implement ;linear programming:

```
import pulp
```

Then, we call the `LpProblem` function in this package to instantiate the problem class. We name the instance `Profit maximising problem`:

```
# Instantiate our problem class
model = pulp.LpProblem("Profit maximising problem", pulp.LpMaximize)
```

Then, we define two linear variables, `A` and `B`. Variable `A` represents the number of advanced robots that are produced and variable `B` represents the number of basic robots that are produced:

```
A = pulp.LpVariable('A', lowBound=0, cat='Integer')
B = pulp.LpVariable('B', lowBound=0, cat='Integer')
```

We define the objective function and constraints as follows:

```
# Objective function
model += 5000 * A + 2500 * B, "Profit"

# Constraints
model += 3 * A + 2 * B <= 20
model += 4 * A + 3 * B <= 30
model += 4 * A + 3 * B <= 44
```

We use the `solve` function to generate a solution:

```
# Solve our problem
model.solve()
pulp.LpStatus[model.status]
```

Then, we print the values of A and B and the value of the objective function:

```
In [147]:  # Print our decision variable values
           print (A.varValue)
           print (B.varValue)

           6.0
           1.0

In [148]:  # Print our objective function value
           print (pulp.value(model.objective))

           32500.0
```

Linear programming is extensively used in the manufacturing industry to find the optimal number of products that should be used to optimize the use of available resources.

And here we come to the end of this chapter! Let's summarize what we have learned.

# Summary

In this chapter, we looked at various approaches to designing an algorithm. We looked at the trade-offs involved in choosing the correct design of an algorithm. We looked at the best practices of formulating a real-world problem. We also looked at how to solve a real-world optimization problem. The lessons learned from this chapter can be used to implement well-designed algorithms.

In the next chapter, we will focus on graph-based algorithms. We will start by looking at different ways of representing graphs. Then, we will study the techniques to establish a neighborhood around various data points to conduct a particular investigation. Finally, we will study the optimal ways to search for information from graphs.

# 5
# Graph Algorithms

There is a class of computational problems that can be best represented in terms of graphs. Such problems can be solved using a class of algorithms called **graph algorithms**. For example, graph algorithms can be used to efficiently search a value in a graphical representation of data. To work efficiently, these algorithms will first need to discover the structure of the graph. They also need to find the right strategy for following the edges of the graph to read the data stored in the vertices. As graph algorithms need to search values in order to work, efficient searching strategies lie at the center of designing efficient graph algorithms. Using graph algorithms is one of the most efficient ways of searching for information in complex, interconnected data structures that are linked through meaningful relationships. In today's era of big data, social media, and distributed data, such techniques are becoming increasingly important and useful.

In this chapter, we will start by presenting the basic concepts behind graph algorithms. Then, we will present the basics of network analysis theory. Next, we will look at the various techniques that can be used to traverse graphs. Finally, we will look at a case study showing how graph algorithms can be used for fraud detection.

In this chapter, we will go through the following concepts:

- Different ways of representing graphs
- Introducing network theory analysis
- Understanding graph traversals
- Case study: fraud analytics
- Techniques for establishing a neighborhood in our problem space

By the end of this chapter, you will have a good understanding of what graphs are and how to work with them to represent interconnected data structures and mine information from entities that are related by direct or indirect relationships, as well as use them to solve some complex real-world problems.

# Representations of graphs

A graph is a structure that represents data in terms of vertices and edges. A graph is represented as `aGraph` = $(\mathcal{V}, \mathcal{E})$, where $\mathcal{V}$ represents a set of vertices and $\mathcal{E}$ represents a set of edges. Note that `aGraph` has $|\mathcal{V}|$ vertices and $|\mathcal{E}|$ edges.

A vertex, $v \in \mathcal{V}$, represents a real-world object, such as a person, a computer, or an activity. An edge, $v \in \mathcal{E}$, connects two vertices in a network:

$e(v_1, v_2) \mid e \in \mathcal{E}\ \&\ v_i \in \mathcal{V}$

The preceding equation indicates that in a graph, all edges belong to a set, $\mathcal{E}$, and all vertices belong to a set, $\mathcal{V}$.

An edge connects two vertices and so represents a relationship between them. For example, it can represent the following relationships:

- Friendships between people
- A person connected to a friend on LinkedIn
- A physical connection of two nodes in a cluster
- A person attending a research conference

In this chapter, we will be using the `networkx` Python package to represent graphs. Let's try to create a simple graph using the `networtx` package in Python. To begin with, let's try to create an empty graph, `aGraph`, with no vertex or node:

```
import networkx as nx
G = nx.Graph()
```

Let's add a single vertex:

```
G.add_node("Mike")
```

We can also add a bunch of vertices using a list:

```
G.add_nodes_from(["Amine", "Wassim", "Nick"])
```

We can also add one edge between the existing vertices, as shown:

```
G.add_edge("Mike", "Amine")
```

Let's now print the edges and vertices:

```
In [5]:   1  list(G.nodes)
Out[5]:  ['Mike', 'Amine', 'Wassim', 'Nick']

In [6]:   1  list(G.edges)
Out[6]:  [('Mike', 'Amine')]
```

Please note that if we are adding an edge, this also leads to adding the associated vertices, if they do not already exist, as shown here:

```
G.add_edge("Amine","Imran")
```

If we print the list of nodes, the following is the output that we observe:

```
In [9]:   1  list(G.edges)
Out[9]:  [('Mike', 'Amine'), ('Amine', 'Imran')]
```

Note that the request to add a vertex that already exists is silently ignored. The request is ignored or entertained based on the type of graph we have created.

# Types of graphs

Graphs can be classified into four kinds, namely the following:

- Undirected graphs
- Directed graphs
- Undirected multigraphs
- Directed multigraphs

Let's now look through each one in detail.

# Undirected graphs

In most cases, the relationships that the constituent nodes of a graph represent can be thought of as undirectional. Such relationships do not impose any order on the relationship. Such edges are called **undirected edges** and the resultant graph is called an **undirected graph**. An undirected graph is shown here:

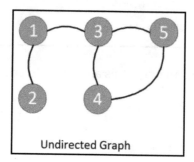

Undirected Graph

Some examples of undirectional relationships are as follows:

- Mike and Amine (Mike and Amine know each other).
- Node **A** and Node **B** are connected (this is a peer-to-peer connection).

# Directed graphs

A graph where the relationship between the nodes in the graph has some sense of direction is called a **directed graph**. A directed graph is shown here:

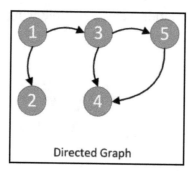

Directed Graph

Some examples of directed relationships are as follows:

- Mike and his house (Mike lives in a house, but his house does not live in Mike).
- John manages Paul (John is the manager of Paul).

# Undirected multigraphs

Sometimes, nodes have more than one type of relationship between them. In that case, there can be more than one edge connecting the same two nodes. These kinds of graphs, where multiples parallel edges are allowed on the same nodes, are called **multigraphs**. We have to explicitly indicate whether a particular graph is a multigraph or not. Parallel edges may represent different types of relationships between the nodes.

A multigraph is shown in the following figure:

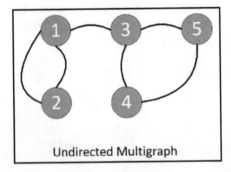

Undirected Multigraph

An example of a multidirectional relationship is if Mike and John are classmates are well as co-workers.

# Directed multigraphs

If there is a directional relationship between nodes in a multigraph, we call it a **directed multigraph**:

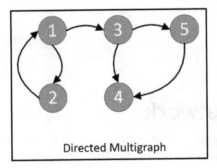

Directed Multigraph

An example of a directed multigraph is that Mike reports to John in the office, and John teaches Mike the Python programming language.

# Special types of edges

Edges connect various vertices of a graph together and represent the relationship between themselves. In addition to simple edges, they can be of the following special types:

- **Self-edge**: Sometimes, a particular vertex can have a relationship with itself. For example, John transfers money from his business account to his personal account. Such a special relationship can be represented by a self-directed edge.
- **Hyperedge**: Sometimes, more than one vertex is connected by the same edge. An edge that connects more than one vertex to represent such a relationship is called a hyperedge. For example, suppose all three of Mike, John, and Sarah are working on one specific project.

 A graph that has one or more hyperedges is called a **hypergraph**.

A diagram of a self-edge and hyperedge graph is shown here:

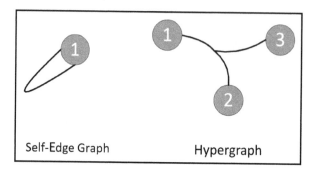

Self-Edge Graph                    Hypergraph

Note that one particular graph can have more than one special type of edge node. This means that one particular graph can have both self-edges and hyper edges at the same time.

# Ego-centered networks

The direct neighborhood of a particular vertex, *m*, may have enough important information to conduct a conclusive analysis for the node. The ego-center, or egonet, is based on this idea. An egonet of a particular vertex, *m*, consists of all the vertices directly connected to *m* plus node *m* itself. The node *m* is called the **ego** and the one-hop neighbors it is connected to are called **alters**.

The ego network of a particular node, 3, is shown in the following graph:

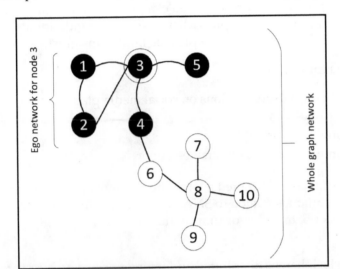

Note that the egonet represents one degree neighborhood. This concept can be extended to n-degree neighborhoods, which consist of all the vertices n-hop away from the vertex of interest.

# Social network analysis

**Social network analysis (SNA)** is one of the important applications of graph theory. A network graph analysis is considered social network analysis if the following apply:

- The vertices of the graph represent people.
- The edges between them represent social relationships between them, such as a friendship, a common hobby, kinship, a sexual relationship, dislikes, and so on.
- The business question that we are trying to answer through graph analysis has some strong social aspect to it.

Human behavior is reflected in SNA and should always be kept in mind while working on SNA. By mapping human relationships in a graph, SNA gives good insights into human interactions, which can help us understand their actions.

By creating a neighborhood around each individual and analyzing the actions of an individual based on its social relationship, you can produce interesting, and sometimes surprising, insights. The alternative approaches to analyzing individuals in isolation, based on their individual job functions, can only provide limited insights.

So, SNA can be used for the following:

- Understanding a users's actions on social media platforms, such as Facebook, Twitter, or LinkedIn
- Understanding fraud
- Understanding society's criminal behavior

 LinkedIn has contributed a lot to the research and development of new techniques related to SNA. In fact, LinkedIn can be thought of as a pioneer of many algorithms in this area.

Thus, SNA—due to its inherent distributed and interconnected architecture of social networks—is one of the most powerful use cases for graph theory. Another way to abstract a graph is by considering it as a network and applying an algorithm designed for networks. This whole area is called **network analysis theory**, which we will discuss next.

# Introducing network analysis theory

We know that interconnected data can be represented as a network. In network analysis theory, we study the details of the methodologies developed to explore and analyze data represented as a network . Let's look at some important aspects of network analysis theory in this section.

First, note that a vertex in a network acts as the basic unit. A network is an interconnected web of vertices where each connection represents the relationship between various entities under investigation. It is important to quantify the usefulness and importance of a vertex in a network in the context of the problem we are trying to solve. There are various techniques that can help us quantify the importance.

Let's look at some of the important concepts used in network analysis theory.

# Understanding the shortest path

A path is a sequence of nodes between a start node and an end node, where no node appears twice on the path. A path represents a route between the chosen start and end vertex. It will be set of vertices, *p*, connecting the start vertex with the end vertex. No vertex is repeated in *p*.

The length of a path is calculated by counting the constituent edges. Out of all the options, the path with the smallest length is called the **shortest path**. Calculation of the shortest path is used extensively in graph theory algorithms but is not always straightforward to calculate. There are different algorithms that can be used to find the shortest path between a start node and an end node. One of the most popular algorithms that can be used to find the shortest distance between the start node and the end node is **Dijkstra's algorithm**, published in the late 1950s. It calculates the shortest path in a graph. It can be used by **Global Positioning System (GPS)** devices to calculate the minimum distance between a source and destination. Dijkstra's algorithm is also used in network routing algorithms.

 There is a battle between Google and Apple to design the best shortest-distance algorithm for Google Maps and Apple Maps. The challenge they face is making the algorithm fast enough to calculate the shortest path within seconds.

Later in this chapter, we will discuss the **breadth-first search (BFS) algorithm**, which can be modified to be converted into Dijkstra's algorithm. BFS assumes the same cost of traversing each path in a given graph. For Dijkstra's algorithm, the cost of traversing a graph can be different and it needs to be incorporated to modify BFS into Dijkstra's algorithm.

As indicated, Dijkstra's algorithm is a single sourced algorithm that calculates the shortest path. If we want to solve all pairs of shortest paths, then the **Floyd-Warshall algorithm** can be used.

# Creating a neighborhood

Finding strategies to create a neighborhood around nodes of interest is pivotal for graph algorithms. Methodologies to create neighborhoods are based on selecting direct associates with the vertex of interest. One way of creating a neighborhood is by choosing a k-order strategy that selects the vertices that are *k* hops away from the vertex of interest.

Let's look at the various criteria for creating neighborhoods.

# Triangles

In graph theory, finding vertices that are well-connected to each other is important for the purpose of analysis. One technique is to try to identify triangles, which are a subgraph that consists of three nodes directly connected to each other, in the network.

Let's look at the use case of fraud detection, which we have also used as a case study towards the end of this chapter. If an egonet of a node, $m$, consists of three vertices, including vertex $m$, then this egonet is a triangle. Vertex $m$ will be the ego and the two connected vertices will be alters, say vertex $A$ and vertex $B$. If both alters are known fraudulent cases, we can safely declare vertex $m$ as fraudulent as well. If one of the alters is involved in fraud, we cannot come up with conclusive evidence, but we will need to conduct a further search into the evidence of fraud.

# Density

Let's first define a fully connected network. We call a graph where every vertex is directly connected to every other vertex a **fully connected network**.

If we have a fully connected network, $N$, then the number of edges in the network can be represented by the following:

$$Edges_{total} = \binom{N}{2} = \frac{N(N-1)}{2}$$

Now, this is where density comes into play. Density measures the number of observed edges to the maximum number of edges, if **Edges$_{Observed}$** is the number of edges we want to observe. It can be framed as follows:

$$density = \frac{Edges_{observed}}{Edges_{total}}$$

Note that for a triangle, the density of the network is 1 and this represents the highest possible connected network.

# Understanding centrality measures

There are different measures for understanding the centrality of a particular vertex in a graph or subgraph. For example, they can quantify the importance of a person in a social network or the importance of a building in a city.

The following centrality measures are widely used in graph analysis:

- Degree
- Betweenness
- Closeness
- Eigenvector

Let's discuss them in detail.

## Degree

The number of edges connected to a particular vertex is called its **degree**. It can indicate how well connected a particular vertex is and its ability to quickly spread a message across a network.

Let's consider aGraph = $(\mathcal{V}, \mathcal{E})$, where $\mathcal{V}$ represents a set of vertices and $\mathcal{E}$ represents a set of edges. Recall that aGraph has $|\mathcal{V}|$ vertices and $|\mathcal{E}|$ edges. If we divide the degree of a node by $(|\mathcal{V}| -1)$, it is called **degree centrality**:

$$C_{DC_a} = \frac{deg(a)}{|\mathcal{V}| - 1}$$

Now, let's look at a specific example. Consider the following graph:

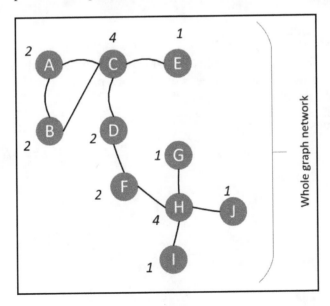

Now, in the preceding graph, vertex **C** has a degree of **4**. Its degree centrality can be calculated as follows:

$$C_{DC_c} = \frac{deg(c)}{|\mathcal{V}| - 1} = \frac{4}{10 - 1} = 0.44$$

# Betweenness

Betweenness is the measure of centrality in a graph. In the context of social media, it will quantify the probability that a person is part of the communication in a subgroup. For a computer network, betweenness will quantify the negative effect on communication between the graph nodes, in the event of vertex failure.

To calculate the betweenness of vertex *a* in a certain `aGraph` = $(V, \mathcal{E})$, follow these steps:

1. Compute the shortest paths between each pair of vertices in `aGraph`. Let's represent this with $n_{shortest_{Total}}$.

2. From $n_{shortest_{Total}}$, count the number of shortest paths that pass through vertex *a*. Let's represent this with $n_{shortest_a}$.

3. Calculate the betweenness with $$C_{betweenness_a} = \frac{n_{shortest_a}}{n_{shortest_{Total}}}.$$

# Fairness and closeness

Let's take a graph, *g*. The fairness of vertex *a* in graph *g* is defined as the sum of vertex *a*'s distance from other vertices. Note that the centrality of a particular vertex quantifies its total distance from all the other vertices.

The opposite of fairness is closeness.

# Eigenvector centrality

Eigenvector centrality gives scores to all vertices in a graph that measure their importance in the network. The score will be an indicator of the connectivity of a particular node to other important nodes in the whole network. When Google created the **PageRank algorithm**, which assigns a score to each web page on the internet (in order to express its importance), the idea was derived from the eigenvector centrality measure.

# Calculating centrality metrics using Python

Let's create a network and then try to calculate its centrality metrics. The following code block illustrates this:

```
import networkx as nx
import matplotlib.pyplot as plt
vertices = range(1,10)
edges = [(7,2), (2,3), (7,4), (4,5), (7,3), (7,5), (1,6),(1,7),(2,8),(2,9)]
G = nx.Graph()
G.add_nodes_from(vertices)
G.add_edges_from(edges)
nx.draw(G, with_labels=True,node_color='y',node_size=800)
```

The graph produced by this code is as follows:

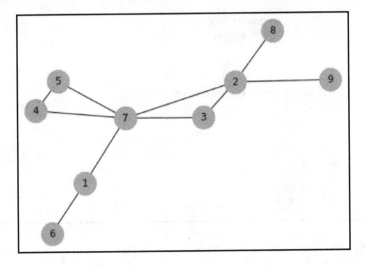

So far, we have studied different measures of centrality. Let's calculate them for the preceding example:

```
In [8]:    1  nx.degree_centrality(G)

Out[8]:  {1: 0.25,
          2: 0.5,
          3: 0.25,
          4: 0.25,
          5: 0.25,
          6: 0.125,
          7: 0.625,
          8: 0.125,
          9: 0.125}

In [9]:    1  nx.betweenness_centrality(G)

Out[9]:  {1: 0.25,
          2: 0.46428571428571425,
          3: 0.0,
          4: 0.0,
          5: 0.0,
          6: 0.0,
          7: 0.7142857142857142,
          8: 0.0,
          9: 0.0}

In [10]:   1  nx.closeness_centrality(G)

Out[10]: {1: 0.5,
          2: 0.6153846153846154,
          3: 0.5333333333333333,
          4: 0.47058823529411764,
          5: 0.47058823529411764,
          6: 0.34782608695652173,
          7: 0.7272727272727273,
          8: 0.4,
          9: 0.4}

In [11]:   1  centrality = nx.eigenvector_centrality(G)
           2  sorted((v, '{:0.2f}'.format(c)) for v, c in centrality.items())

Out[11]: [(1, '0.24'),
          (2, '0.45'),
          (3, '0.36'),
          (4, '0.32'),
          (5, '0.32'),
          (6, '0.08'),
          (7, '0.59'),
          (8, '0.16'),
          (9, '0.16')]
```

Note that the metrics of centrality are expected to give the centrality measure of a particular vertex in a graph or subgraph. Looking at the graph, the vertex labeled 7 seems to have the most central location. Vertex **7** has the highest values in all four metrics of centrality, thus reflecting its importance in this context.

Now let's look into how we can retrieve information from the graphs. Graphs are complex data structures with lots of information stored both in vertices and edges. Let's look at some strategies that can be used to navigate through graphs efficiently in order to gather information from them to answer queries.

# Understanding graph traversals

To make use of graphs, information needs to be mined from them. Graph traversal is defined as the strategy used to make sure that every vertex and edge is visited in an orderly manner. An effort is made to make sure that each vertex and edge is visited exactly once; no more and no less. Broadly, there can be two different ways of traveling a graph to search the data in it. Going by breadth is called **breadth-first search** (**BFS**) and going by depth is called **depth-first search** (**DFS**). Let's look at them one by one.

# Breadth-first search

BFS works best when there is a concept of layers or levels of neighborhoods in the aGraph we are dealing with. For example, when the connections of a person in LinkedIn are expressed as a graph, there are first-level connections and then there are second-level connections, which directly translate to the layers.

The BFS algorithm starts from a root vertex and explores the vertices in the neighborhood vertices. It then moves to the next neighborhood level and repeats the process.

Let's look at a BFS algorithm. For that, let's first consider the following undirected graph:

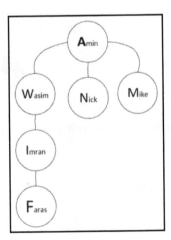

Let's start by calculating the immediate neighborhood of each vertex and store that in a list, called an **adjacency list**. In Python, we can use the dictionary data structure to store it:

```
graph={ 'Amin'   : {'Wasim', 'Nick', 'Mike'},
        'Wasim' : {'Imran', 'Amin'},
        'Imran' : {'Wasim','Faras'},
        'Faras' : {'Imran'},
        'Mike'  : {'Amin'},
        'Nick'  :  {'Amin'}}
```

To implement it in Python, we proceed as follows.

We will first explain the initialization and then the main loop.

# Initialization

We will use two data structures:

- visited: This contains all the vertices that have been visited. Initially, it will be empty.
- queue: This contains all the vertices that we have want to visit in next iterations.

# The main loop

Next, we will implement the main loop. It will keep on looping until there isn't even a single element in the queue. For each node in the queue, if it has already been visited, then it visits its neighbor.

We can implement this main loop in Python as follows:

1. First, we pop the first node from the queue and choose that as current node of this iteration.

   ```
   node = queue.pop(0)
   ```

2. Then, we check that the node is not in the visited list. If it is not, we add it to the list of visited nodes and use neighbors to represent its directly connected nodes

   ```
   visited.append(node)
   neighbours = graph[node]
   ```

3. Now we will add neighbours of nodes to the queue:

```
for neighbour in neighbours:
    queue.append(neighbour)
```

4. Once the main loop is complete, the `visited` data structure is returned, which contains all the nodes traversed.

5. The complete code, with both initialization and the main loop, will be as follows:

```
def bfs(graph, start):
    visited = []
    queue = [start]

    while queue:
        node = queue.pop(0)
        if node not in visited:
            visited.append(node)
            neighbours = graph[node]
            for neighbour in neighbours:
                queue.append(neighbour)
    return visited
```

Let's look at the exhaustive search traversal pattern for the graph that we defined using BFS. To visit all the nodes, the traversal pattern is shown in the following figure. It can be observed that while executing, it always maintains two data structures:

- **Visited**: Contains all the nodes that have been visited
- **Queue**: Contains nodes yet to be visited

Here's how the algorithm works:

1. It starts from the first node, which is the only node, **Amin**, on level one.
2. Then, it moves to level two and visits all three nodes **Wasim, Nick,** and **Mike** one by one.
3. After that, it moves to level three and level four, which have only one node each, **Imran** and **Faras**.

Once all the nodes have been visited, they are added to the **Visited** data structure and the iterations stop:

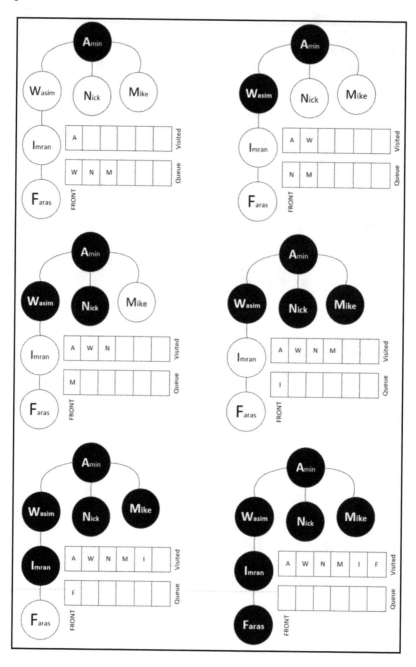

Now, let's try to find a specific person from this graph using BFS. Let's specify the data that we are searching for and observe the results:

```
In [97]: bfs(graph,'Amin')
Out[97]: ['Amin', 'Wasim', 'Nick', 'Mike', 'Imran', 'Faras']
```

Now let's look into the depth-first search algorithm.

# Depth-first search

DFS is the alternative to BFS, used to search data from a graph. The factor that differentiates DFS from BFS is that after starting from the root vertex, the algorithm goes down as far as possible in each of the unique single paths one by one. For each path, once it has successfully reached the ultimate depth, it flags all the vertices associated with that path as visited. After completing the path, the algorithm backtracks. If it can find another path from the root node that has yet to be visited, the algorithm repeats the previous process. The algorithm keeps on moving in the new branch until all the branches have been visited.

Note that a graph may have a cyclic method. As mentioned, we use a Boolean flag to keep track of the vertices that have been processed to avoid iterating in cycles.

To implement DFS, we will use a stack data structure, which was discussed in detail in Chapter 2, *Data Structures Used in Algorithms*. Remember that stack is based on the **Last In, First Out** (**LIFO**) principle. This contrasts with a queue, which was used for BFS, which works on the **First In, First Out** (**FIFO**) principal.

The following code is used for DFS:

```
def dfs(graph, start, visited=None):
    if visited is None:
        visited = set()
    visited.add(start)
    print(start)
    for next in graph[start] - visited:
        dfs(graph, next, visited)
    return visited
```

Let's again use the following code to test the `dfs` function defined previously:

```
graph={ 'Amin' : {'Wasim', 'Nick', 'Mike'},
        'Wasim' : {'Imran', 'Amin'},
        'Imran' : {'Wasim','Faras'},
        'Faras' : {'Imran'},
        'Mike'  :{'Amin'},
        'Nick'  :{'Amin'}}
```

If we run this algorithm, the output will look like the following:

```
Out[94]: {'Amin', 'Faras', 'Imran', 'Mike', 'Nick', 'Wasim'}
```

Let's look at the exhaustive traversal pattern of this graph using the DFS methodology:

1. The iteration starts from the top node, **Amin**.
2. Then, it moves to level two, **Wasim**. From there, it moves toward the lower levels until it reaches the end, which is the **Imran** and **Fares** nodes.
3. After completing the first full branch, it backtracks and then goes to level two to visit **Nick** and **Mike**.

The traversal pattern is shown in the following figure:

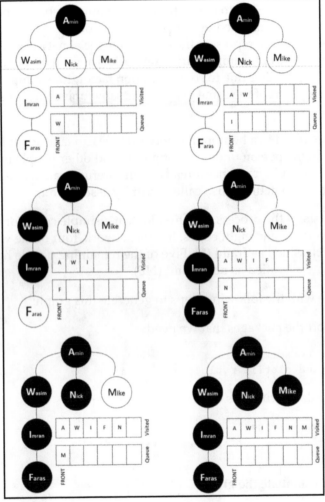

 Note that DFS can be used in trees as well.

Let's now look at a case study, which explains how the concepts we have discussed so far in this chapter can be used to solve a real-world problem.

# Case study – fraud analytics

Let's look at how we can use SNA to detect fraud. With humans being social animals, human behavior is said to be affected by the people that you are surrounded by. The word **homophily** has been coined to represent the effect their social network has on a person. Extending this concept, a **homophilic network** is a group of people who are likely to be associated with each other due to some common factor; for example, having the same origin or hobbies, being part of the same gang or the same university, or some combination of other factors.

If we want to analyze fraud in a homophilic network, we can take advantage of the relationships between the person under investigation and other people in the network, whose risk of involvement in fraud has already been carefully calculated. Flagging a person due to their company is sometimes also called **guilt by association**.

In an effort to understand the process, let's first look at a simple case. For that, let's use a network with nine vertices and eight edges. In this network, four of the vertices are known fraud cases and are classified as **fraud (F)**. Five of the remaining people have no fraud-related history and are classified as **non-fraud (NF)**.

We will write a code with the following steps to generate this graph:

1. Let's import the packages that we need:

   ```
   import networkx as nx
   import matplotlib.pyplot as plt
   ```

2. Define the data structures of `vertices` and `edges`:

   ```
   vertices = range(1,10)
   edges= [(7,2), (2,3), (7,4), (4,5), (7,3), (7,5),
   (1,6),(1,7),(2,8),(2,9)]
   ```

3. Let's first instantiate the graph:

   ```
   G = nx.Graph()
   ```

4. Now, let's draw the graph:

   ```
   G.add_nodes_from(vertices)
   G.add_edges_from(edges)
   pos=nx.spring_layout(G)
   ```

5. Let's define the NF nodes:

```
nx.draw_networkx_nodes( G,pos,
                        nodelist=[1,4,3,8,9],
                        with_labels=True,
                        node_color='g',
                        node_size=1300)
```

6. Now, let's create the nodes that are known to be involved in fraud:

```
nx.draw_networkx_nodes(G,pos,
                       nodelist=[2,5,6,7],
                       with_labels=True,
                       node_color='r',
                       node_size=1300)
```

7. Let's create labels for the nodes:

```
nx.draw_networkx_edges(G,pos,edges,width=3,alpha=0.5,edge_color='b'
) labels={} labels[1]=r'1 NF' labels[2]=r'2 F' labels[3]=r'3 NF'
labels[4]=r'4 NF' labels[5]=r'5 F' labels[6]=r'6 F' labels[7]=r'7
F' labels[8]=r'8 NF' labels[9]=r'9 NF'
nx.draw_networkx_labels(G,pos,labels,font_size=16)
```

Once the preceding code runs, it will show us a graph like this:

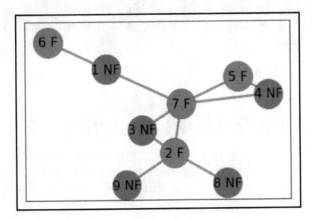

Note that we have already conducted detailed analysis to classify each node as a graph or non-graph. Let's assume that we add another vertex, named *q*, to the network, as shown in the following figure. We have no prior information about this person and whether this person is involved in fraud or not. We want to classify this person as **NF** or **F** based on their links to the existing members of the social network:

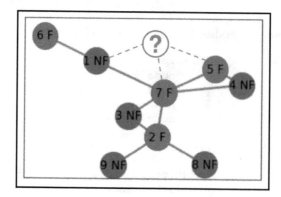

We have devised two ways to classify this new person, represented by node *q*, as **F** or **NF**:

- Using a simple method that does not use centrality metrics and additional information about the type of fraud
- Using a watchtower methodology, which is an advanced technique that uses the centrality metrics of the existing nodes, as well as additional information about the type of fraud

We will discuss each method in detail.

# Conducting simple fraud analytics

The simple technique of fraud analytics is based on the assumption that in a network, the behaviour of a person is affected by the people they are connected to. In a network, two vertices are more likely to have similar behaviour if they are associated with each other.

Based on this assumption, we devise a simple technique. If we want to find the probability that a certain node, $a$, belongs to $F$, the probability is represented by $P(F/q)$ and is calculated as follows:

$$P(F|q) = \frac{1}{degree_q} \sum_{n_j \in Neighborhood_n | class(n_j) = F} w(n, n_j) DOS_{normalized_j}$$

Let's apply this to the preceding figure, where $Neighborhood_n$ represents the neighborhood of vertex $n$ and $w(n, nj)$ represents the weight of the connection between $n$ and $nj$. Also, $degree_q$ is the degree of node $q$. Then, the probability is calculated as follows:

$$P(F|q) = \frac{1+1}{3} = \frac{2}{3} = .67$$

Based on this analysis, the likelihood of this person being involved in fraud is 67%. We need to set a threshold. If the threshold is 30%, then this person is above the threshold value and we can safely flag them as F.

Note that this process needs to be repeated for each of the new nodes in the network.

Now, let's look at an advanced way of conducting fraud analytics.

# Presenting the watchtower fraud analytics methodology

The previous, simple fraud analytics technique has the following two limitations:

- It does not evaluate the importance of each vertex in the social network. A connection to a hub that is involved in fraud may have different implications than a relationship with a remote, isolated person.
- When labeling someone as a known case of fraud in an existing network, we do not consider the severity of the crime.

The watchtower fraud analytics methodology addresses these two limitations. First, let's look at a couple of concepts.

# Scoring negative outcomes

If a person is known to be involved in fraud, we say that there is a negative outcome associated with this individual. Not every negative outcome is of the same severity or seriousness. A person known to be impersonating another person will have a more serious type of negative outcome associated with them, compared to someone who is just trying to use an expired $20 gift card, in an innovative way to make it valid.

From a score of 1 to 10, we rate various negative outcomes as follows:

| Negative outcome | Negative outcome score |
|---|---|
| Impersonation | 10 |
| Involvement in credit card theft | 8 |
| Fake check submission | 7 |
| Criminal record | 6 |
| No record | 0 |

Note that these scores will be based on our analysis of fraud cases and their impact from historical data.

# Degree of suspicion

The **degree of suspicion (DOS)** quantifies our level of suspicion that a person may be involved in fraud. A DOS value of 0 means that this is a low-risk person and a DOS value of 9 means that this is a high-risk person.

Analysis of historical data shows that professional fraudsters have important positions in their social networks. To incorporate this, first we calculate all of the four centrality metrics of each vertex in our network. We then take the average of these vertices. This translates to the importance of that particular person in the network.

If a person associated with a vertex is involved in fraud, we illustrate this negative outcome by scoring the person using the pre-determined values shown in the preceding table. This is done so that the severity of the crime is reflected in the value of each individual DOS.

Finally, we multiply the average of the centrality metrics and the negative outcome score to get the value of the DOS. We normalize the DOS by dividing it by the maximum value of the DOS in the network.

Let's calculate the DOS for each of the nine nodes in the previous network:

| | Node 1 | Node 2 | Node 3 | Node 4 | Node 5 | Node 6 | Node 7 | Node 8 | Node 9 |
|---|---|---|---|---|---|---|---|---|---|
| Degree of centrality | 0.25 | 0.5 | 0.25 | 0.25 | 0.25 | 0.13 | 0.63 | 0.13 | 0.13 |
| Betweenness | 0.25 | 0.47 | 0 | 0 | 0 | 0 | 0.71 | 0 | 0 |
| Closeness | 0.5 | 0.61 | 0.53 | 0.47 | 0.47 | 0.34 | 0.72 | 0.4 | 0.4 |
| Eigenvector | 0.24 | 0.45 | 0.36 | 0.32 | 0.32 | 0.08 | 0.59 | 0.16 | 0.16 |
| Average of centrality Metrics | 0.31 | 0.51 | 0.29 | 0.26 | 0.26 | 0.14 | 0.66 | 0.17 | 0.17 |
| Negative outcome score | 0 | 6 | 0 | 0 | 7 | 8 | 10 | 0 | 0 |
| DOS | 0 | 3 | 0 | 0 | 1.82 | 1.1 | 6.625 | 0 | 0 |
| Normalized DOS | 0 | 0.47 | 0 | 0 | 0.27 | 0.17 | 1 | 0 | 0 |

Each of the nodes and their normalized DOS is shown in the following figure:

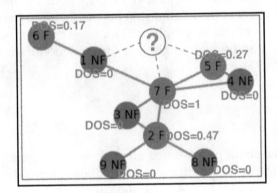

In order to calculate the DOS of the new node that has been added, we will use the following formula:

$$DOS_k = \frac{1}{degree_k} \sum_{n_j \in Neighborhood_n} w(n, n_j) DOS_{normalized_j}$$

Using the relevant values, we will calculate the DOS as follows:

$$DOS_k = \frac{(0 + 1 + 0.27)}{3} = 0.42$$

This will indicate the risk of fraud associated with this new node added to the system. It means that on a scale of 0 to 1, this person has a DOS value of 0.42. We can create different risk bins for the DOS, as follows:

| Value of the DOS | Risk classification |
|---|---|
| DOS = 0 | No risk |
| 0<DOS<=0.10 | Low risk |
| 0.10<DOS<=0.3 | Medium risk |
| DOS>0.3 | High risk |

Based on these criteria, it can be seen that the new individual is a high-risk person and should be flagged.

Usually, a time dimension is not involved when conducting such an analysis. But now, there are some advanced techniques that look at the growth of a graph as time progresses. This allows researchers to look at the relationship between vertices as the network evolves. Although such time-series analysis on graphs will increase the complexity of the problem by many times, it may give additional insight into the evidence of fraud that was not possible otherwise.

# Summary

In this chapter, we learned about graph-based algorithms. After going through this chapter, I expect that we should be able to use different techniques of representing, searching, and processing data represented as graphs. We also developed skills to be able to calculate the shortest distance between two vertices and we built neighborhoods in our problem space. This knowledge should help us use graph theory to address problems such as fraud detection.

In the next chapter, we will focus on different unsupervised machine learning algorithms. Many of the use-case techniques discussed in this chapter complement unsupervised learning algorithms, which will be discussed in detail in the next chapter. Finding evidence of fraud in a dataset is an example of such use cases.

# Section 2: Machine Learning Algorithms

**2**

This section explains the different kinds of machine learning algorithms, such as unsupervised machine learning algorithms and traditional supervised learning algorithms, in detail and also introduces us to algorithms for natural language processing. The section ends with introducing us to recommendation engines. The chapters included in this section are:

# 6
# Unsupervised Machine Learning Algorithms

This chapter is about unsupervised machine learning algorithms. The chapter starts with an introduction to unsupervised learning techniques. Then, we will learn about two clustering algorithms: k-means clustering and hierarchical clustering algorithms. The next section looks at a dimensionality reduction algorithm, which may be effective when we have a large number of input variables. The following section shows how unsupervised learning can be used for anomaly detection. Finally, we will look at one of the most powerful unsupervised learning techniques, association rules mining. This section also explains how patterns discovered from association rules mining represent interesting relationships between the various data elements across transactions that can help us in our data-driven decision making.

By the end of this chapter, the reader should be able to understand how unsupervised learning can be used to solve some real-world problems. The reader will understand the basic algorithms and methodologies that are currently being used for unsupervised learning.

In this chapter, we will cover the following topics:

- Unsupervised learning
- Clustering algorithms
- Dimensionality reduction
- Anomaly detection algorithms
- Association rules mining

# Introducing unsupervised learning

The simplest definition of unsupervised learning is that it is the process of providing some sort of structure to unstructured data by discovering and utilizing the inherent patterns of the data. If data is not produced by some random process, it will have some patterns between its data elements in its multidimensional problem space. Unsupervised learning algorithms work by discovering these patterns and using them to provide some structure to the dataset. This concept is shown in the following diagram:

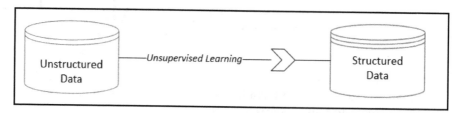

Note that unsupervised learning adds structure by discovering new features from the existing patterns.

# Unsupervised learning in the data-mining life cycle

To understand the role of unsupervised learning, it is important to first look at the overall life cycle of the data-mining process. There are different methodologies that divide the life cycle of the data-mining process into different independent stages, called **phases**. Currently, there are two popular ways to represent the data-mining life cycle:

- **CRISP-DM (Cross-Industry Standard Process for Data Mining)** life cycle
- **SEMMA (Sample, Explore, Modify, Model, Access)** data-mining process

CRISP-DM was developed by a consortium of data miners who belonged to various companies, including Chrysler and **SPSS (Statistical Package for Social Science)**. SEMMA was proposed by **SAS (Statistical Analysis System)**. Let's look at one of these two representations of the data-mining life cycle, CRISP-DM, and try to understand the place of unsupervised learning in the data-mining life cycle. Note that SEMMA has somewhat similar phases within its life cycle.

If we look at the CRISP-DM life cycle, we can see that it consists of six distinct phases, which are shown in the following figure:

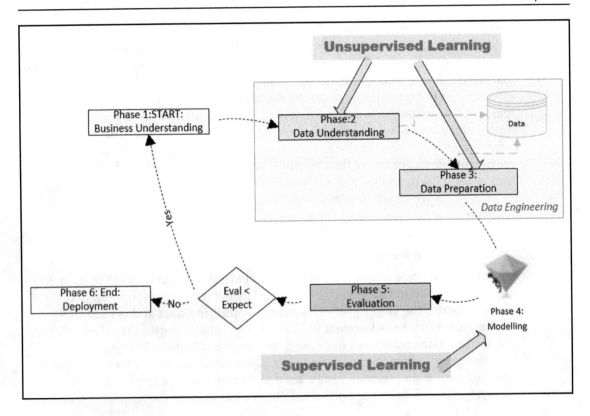

Let's understand each phase one by one:

- **Phase 1: Business Understanding**: This is about gathering the requirements and involves trying to fully understand the problem in depth from a business point of view. Defining the scope of the problem and properly rephrasing it according to **machine learning** (**ML**) is an important part of this phase—for example, for a binary classification problem, sometimes it is helpful to phrase the requirements in terms of a hypothesis that can be proved or rejected. This phase is also about documenting the expectations for the machine learning model that will be trained downstream in Phase 4—for example, for a classification problem, we need to document the minimum acceptable accuracy of the model that can be deployed in production.

 It is important to note that Phase 1 of the CRISP-DM life cycle is about business understanding. It focuses on what needs to be done, not on how it will be done.

- **Phase 2: Data Understanding**: This is about understanding the data that is available for data mining. In this phase, we will find out whether the right datasets are available for the problem we are trying to solve. After identifying the datasets, we need to understand the quality of the data and its structure. We need to find out what patterns can be extracted out of the data that can potentially lead us toward important insights. We will also try to find the right feature that can be used as the label (or the target variable) according to the requirements gathered in Phase 1. Unsupervised learning algorithms can play a powerful role in achieving the objectives of Phase 2. Unsupervised algorithms can be used for the following purposes:

  - To discover patterns in the dataset
  - To understand the structure of the dataset by analyzing the discovered patterns
  - To identify or derive the target variable

- **Phase 3: Data Preparation**: This is about preparing the data for the ML model that we will train in Phase 4. The available labeled data is divided into two unequal parts. The larger portion is called the **training data** and is used for training the model downstream in Phase 4. The smaller portion is called the **testing data** and is used in Phase 5 for model evaluation. In this phase, the unsupervised machine learning algorithms can be used as a tool to prepare the data—for example, they can be used to convert unstructured data into structured data, providing additional dimensions that can be helpful in training the model.

- **Phase 4: Modeling**: This is the phase where we use supervised learning to formulate the patterns that we have discovered. We are expected to successfully prepare the data according to the requirements of our chosen supervised learning algorithm. This is also the phase in which the particular feature that will be used as the label will be identified. In Phase 3, we divided the data into testing and training sets. In this phase, we form mathematical formulations to represent the relationships in our patterns of interest. This is done by training the model using the training data that was created in Phase 3. As mentioned before, the resulting mathematical formulation will depend on our choice of algorithm.

- **Phase 5: Evaluation**: This phase is about testing the newly trained model using the test data from Phase 3. If the evaluation matches the expectations set in Phase 1, then we need iterate through all the preceding phases again, starting with Phase 1. This is illustrated in the preceding image.

- **Phase 6: Deployment**: If the evaluation meets or exceeds the expectations described in Phase 5, then the trained model is deployed in production and starts generating a solution to the problem we defined in Phase 1.

Phase 2 (Data Understanding) and Phase 3 (Data Preparation) of the CRISP-DM life cycle are all about understanding the data and preparing it for training the model. These phases involve data processing. Some organizations employ specialists for this data engineering phase.

It is obvious that the process of suggesting a solution to a problem is fully data driven. A combination of supervised and unsupervised machine learning is used to formulate a workable solution. This chapter focuses on the unsupervised learning part of the solution.

 Data engineering comprises Phase 2 and Phase 3, and is the most time-consuming part of machine learning. It can take as much as 70% of the time and resources of a typical ML project. The unsupervised learning algorithms can play an important role in data engineering.

The following sections provide more details regarding unsupervised algorithms.

# Current research trends in unsupervised learning

For years, research into machine learning algorithms was more focused on supervised learning techniques. As supervised learning techniques can be directly used for inference, their benefits in terms of time, cost, and accuracy are relatively easily measurable. The power of unsupervised machine learning algorithms has been recognized more recently. As unsupervised learning is not guided, it is less dependent on assumptions and can potentially converge the solution in any dimension. Although it is more difficult to control the scope and processing requirements of unsupervised learning algorithms, they have more potential to unearth the hidden patterns. Researchers are also working to combine unsupervised machine learning techniques with supervised learning techniques in order to design new powerful algorithms.

# Practical examples

Currently, unsupervised learning is used to get a better sense of the data and provide it with more structure—for example, it is used in marketing segmentation, fraud detection, and market basket analysis (which is discussed later in this chapter). Let's look at a couple of examples.

# Voice categorization

Unsupervised learning can be used to classify individual voices in a voice file. It uses the fact that each individual's voice has distinct characteristics, creating potentially separable audio patterns. These patterns can then be used for voice recognition—for example, Google uses this technique in their Google Home devices to train them to differentiate between different people's voices. Once trained, Google Home can personalize the response for each user individually.

For example, let's assume that we have a recorded conversation of three people talking to each other for half an hour. Using unsupervised learning algorithms, we can identify the voices of distinct people in this dataset. Note that through unsupervised learning, we are adding structure to the given set of unstructured data. This structure gives us additional useful dimensions in our problem space that can be used to gain insights and to prepare data for our chosen machine learning algorithm. The following diagram shows how unsupervised learning is used for voice recognition:

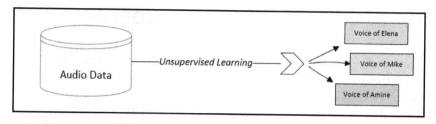

Note that, in this case, unsupervised learning suggests that we add a new feature with three distinct levels.

# Document categorization

Unsupervised machine learning algorithms can also be applied to a repository of unstructured textual data—for example, if we have a dataset of PDF documents, then unsupervised learning can be used to do the following:

- Discover various topics in the dataset
- Associate each PDF document to one of the discovered topics

This use of unsupervised learning for document classification is shown in the following figure. This is another example in which we are adding more structure to unstructured data:

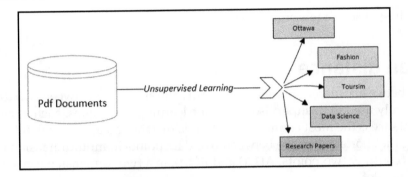

Figure 6.4: Using unsupervised learning for document classification

Note that, in this case, unsupervised learning suggests that we add a new feature with five distinct levels.

# Understanding clustering algorithms

One of the simplest and most powerful techniques used in unsupervised learning is based on grouping similar patterns together through clustering algorithms. It is used to understand a particular aspect of the data that is related to the problem we are trying to solve. Clustering algorithms look for natural grouping in data items. As the group is not based on any target or assumptions, it is classified as an unsupervised learning technique.

Groupings created by various clustering algorithms are based on finding the similarities between various data points in the problem space. The best way to determine the similarities between data points will vary from problem to problem and will depend on the nature of the problem we are dealing with. Let's look at the various methods that can be used to calculate the similarities between various data points.

# Quantifying similarities

The reliability of the grouping created by clustering algorithms is based on the assumption that we can accurately quantify the similarities or closeness between various data points in the problem space. This is done by using various distance measures. The following are three of the most popular methods that are used to quantify similarities:

- Euclidean distance measure
- Manhattan distance measure
- Cosine distance measure

Let's look at these distance measures in more detail.

# Euclidean distance

The distance between different points can quantify the similarity between two data points and is extensively used in unsupervised machine learning techniques, such as clustering. Euclidean distance is the most common and simple distance measure used. It is calculated by measuring the shortest distance between two data points in multidimensional space. For example, let's consider two points, **A(1,1)** and **B(4,4)**, in a two -dimensional space, as shown in the following plot:

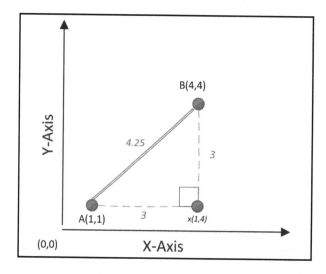

To calculate the distance between **A** and **B**—that is *d(A,B)*, we can use the following Pythagorean formula:

$$d(A, B) = \sqrt{(a_2 - b_2)^2 + (a_1 - b_1)^2} = \sqrt{(4 - 1)^2 + (4 - 1)^2} = \sqrt{9 + 9} = 4.25$$

Note that this calculation is for a two-dimensional problem space. For an *n*-dimensional problem space, we can calculate the distance between two points **A** and **B** as follows:

$$d(A, B) = \sqrt{\sum_{i=1}^{n} (a_i - b_i)^2}$$

# Manhattan distance

In many situations, measuring the shortest distance between two points using the Euclidean distance measure will not truly represent the similarity or closeness between two points—for example, if two data points represent locations on a map, then the actual distance from point A to point B using ground transportation, such as a car or taxi, will be more than the distance calculated by the Euclidean distance. For situations such as these, we use Manhattan distance, which marks the longest route between two points and is a better reflection of the closeness of two points in the context of source and destination points that can be traveled to in a busy city. The comparison between the Manhattan and Euclidean distance measures is shown in the following plot:

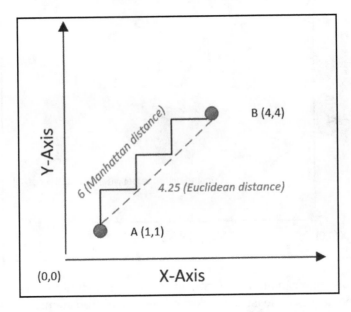

Note that the Manhattan distance will always be equal or larger than the corresponding Euclidean distance calculated.

# Cosine distance

Euclidean and Manhattan distance measures do not perform well in high-dimensional space. In a high-dimensional problem space, cosine distance more accurately reflects the closeness between two data points in a multidimensional problem space. The cosine distance measure is calculated by measuring the cosine angle created by two points connected to a reference point. If the data points are close, then the angle will be narrow, irrespective of the dimensions they have. On the other hand, if they are far away, then the angle will be large:

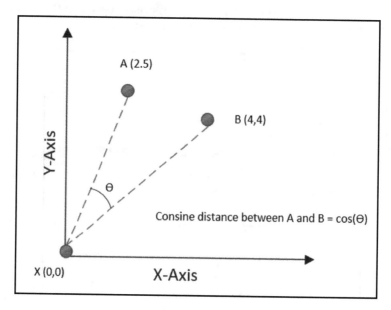

 Textual data can almost be considered a highly dimensional space. As the cosine distance measure works very well with h-dimensional spaces, it is a good choice when dealing with textual data.

Note that in the preceding figure, the cosine of the angle between **A(2,5)** and **B(4.4)** is the cosine distance. The reference between these points is the origin—that is, **X(0,0)**. But in reality, any point in the problem space can act as the reference data point, and it does not have to be the origin.

# K-means clustering algorithm

The name of the k-means clustering algorithm comes from the fact that it tries to create a number of clusters, *k*, calculating the means to find the closeness between the data points. It uses a relatively simple clustering approach, but is still popular because of its scalability and speed. Algorithmically, k-means clustering uses an iterative logic that moves the centers of the clusters until they reflect the most representative data point of the grouping they belong to.

It is important to note that k-means algorithms lack one of the very basic functionalities needed for clustering. That missing functionality is that for a given dataset, the k-means algorithm cannot determine the most appropriate number of clusters. The most appropriate number of clusters, *k*, is dependent on the number of natural groupings in a particular dataset. The philosophy behind this omission is to keep the algorithm as simple as possible, maximizing its performance. This lean-and-mean design makes k-means suitable for larger datasets. The assumption is that an external mechanism will be used to calculate *k*. The best way to determine *k* will depend on the problem we are trying to solve. In some cases, *k* is directly specified by the clustering problem's context—for example, if we want to divide a class of data-science students into two clusters, one consisting of the students with the data science skill and the other with programming skills, then *k* will be two. In some other problems, the value of *k* may not be obvious. In such cases, an iterative trial-and-error procedure or a heuristic-based algorithm will have to be used to estimate the most appropriate number of clusters for a given dataset.

# The logic of k-means clustering

This section describes the logic of the k-means clustering algorithm. Let's look at them one by one.

## Initialization

In order to group them, the k-means algorithm uses a distance measure to find the similarity or closeness between data points. Before using the k-means algorithm, the most appropriate distance measure needs to be selected. By default, the Euclidean distance measure will be used. Also, if the dataset has outliers, then a mechanism needs to be devised to determine the criteria that are to be identified and remove the outliers of the dataset.

# The steps of the k-means algorithm

The steps involved in the k-means clustering algorithm are as follows:

| Step 1 | We choose the number of clusters, $k$. |
|--------|---------------------------------------|
| Step 2 | Among the data points, we randomly choose $k$ points as cluster centers. |
| Step 3 | Based on the selected distance measure, we iteratively compute the distance from each point in the problem space to each of the $k$ cluster centers. Based on the size of the dataset, this may be a time-consuming step—for example, if there are 10,000 points in the cluster and $k = 3$, this means that 30,000 distances need to be calculated. |
| Step 4 | We assign each data point in the problem space to the nearest cluster center. |
| Step 5 | Now each data point in our problem space has an assigned cluster center. But we are not done, as the selection of the initial cluster centers was based on random selection. We need to verify that the current randomly selected cluster centers are actually the center of gravity of each cluster. We recalculate the cluster centers by computing the mean of the constituent data points of each of the $k$ clusters. This step explains why this algorithm is called k-means. |
| Step 6 | If the cluster centers have shifted in step 5, this means that we need to recompute the cluster assignment for each data point. For this, we will go back to step 3 to repeat that compute-intensive step. If the cluster centers have not shifted or if our predetermined stop condition (for example, the number of maximum iterations) has been satisfied, then we are done. |

The following figure shows the result of running the k-means algorithm in a two-dimensional problem space:

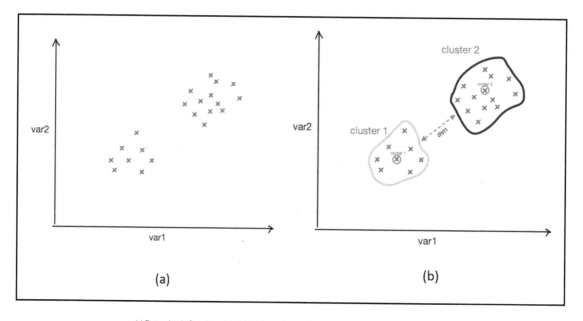

(a) Data points before clustering; (b) Resultant clusters after running the k-means clustering algorithm

Note that the two resulting clusters created after running k-means are well differentiated in this case.

## Stop condition

For the k-means algorithm, the default stop condition is when there is no more shifting of cluster centers in step 5. But as with many other algorithms, k-means algorithms may take lot of time to converge, especially while processing large datasets in a high-dimensional problem space. Instead of waiting for the algorithm to converge, we can also explicitly define the stop condition as follows:

- By specifying the maximum execution time:
    - **Stop condition**: $t > t_{max}$, where $t$ is the current execution time and $t_{max}$ is the maximum execution time we have set for the algorithm.

- By specifying the maximum iterations:
    - **Stop condition**: if $m > m_{max}$, where $m$ is the current iteration and $m_{max}$ is the maximum number of iterations we have set for the algorithm.

# Coding the k-means algorithm

Let's look at how we can code the k-means algorithm in Python:

1. First, let's import the packages that we will need to code for the k-means algorithm. Note that we are importing the `sklearn` package for k-means clustering:

```
from sklearn import cluster
import pandas as pd
import numpy as np
```

2. To use k-means clustering, let's create 20 data points in a two-dimensional problem space that we will be using for k-means clustering:

```
dataset = pd.DataFrame({
    'x': [11, 21, 28, 17, 29, 33, 24, 45, 45, 52, 51, 52, 55, 53,
55, 61, 62, 70, 72, 10],
    'y': [39, 36, 30, 52, 53, 46, 55, 59, 63, 70, 66, 63, 58, 23,
14, 8, 18, 7, 24, 10]
})
```

3. Let's have two clusters ($k = 2$) and then create the cluster by calling the `fit` functions:

```
myKmeans = cluster.KMeans (n_clusters=2)
myKmeans.fit(dataset)
```

4. Let's create a variable named `centroid` that is an array that holds the location of the center of the clusters formed. In our case, as $k = 2$, the array will have a size of 2. Let's also create another variable named `label` that represents the assignment of each data point to one of the two clusters. As there are 20 data points, this array will have a size of 20:

```
centroids = myKmeans.cluster_centers_
labels = myKmeans.labels_
```

5. Now let's print these two arrays, `centroids` and `labels`:

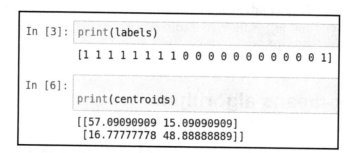

```
In [3]: print(labels)

        [1 1 1 1 1 1 1 0 0 0 0 0 0 0 0 0 0 0 0 1]

In [6]:
        print(centroids)

        [[57.09090909 15.09090909]
         [16.77777778 48.88888889]]
```

Note that the first array shows the assignment of the cluster with each data point and the second one shows the two cluster centers.

6. Let's plot and look at the clusters using `matplotlib`:

```
In [16]:  import matplotlib.pyplot as plt
          plt.scatter(dataset['x'],dataset['y'], s=10)
          plt.scatter(centers[0],centers[1],s=100)
          plt.show()
```

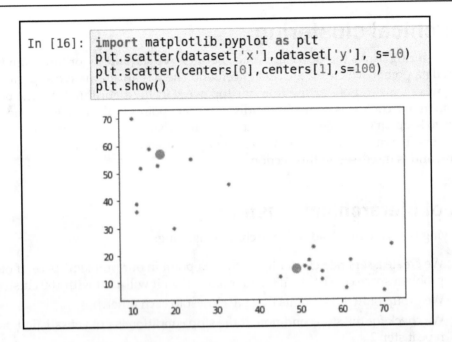

Note that the bigger dots in the plot are the centroids as determined by the k-means algorithm.

# Limitation of k-means clustering

The k-means algorithm is designed to be a simple and fast algorithm. Because of the intentional simplicity in its design, it comes with the following limitations:

- The biggest limitation of k-means clustering is that the initial number of clusters has to be predetermined.
- The initial assignment of cluster centers is random. This means that each time the algorithm is run, it may give slightly different clusters.
- Each data point is assigned to only one cluster.
- k-means clustering is sensitive to outliers.

# Hierarchical clustering

k-means clustering uses a top-down approach because we start the algorithm from the most important data points, which are the cluster centers. There is an alternative approach of clustering where, instead of starting from the top, we start the algorithm from the bottom. The bottom in this context is each of the individual data points in the problem space. The solution is to keep on grouping similar data points together as it progresses up toward the cluster centers. This alternative bottom-up approach is used by hierarchical clustering algorithms, and is discussed in this section.

## Steps of hierarchical clustering

The following steps are involved in hierarchical clustering:

1. We create a separate cluster for each data point in our problem space. If our problem space consists of 100 data points, then it will start with 100 clusters.
2. We group only those points that are closest to each other.
3. We check for the stop condition; if the stop condition is not yet satisfied, then we repeat step 2.

The resulting clustered structure is called a **dendrogram**.

In a dendrogram, the height of the vertical lines determines how close the items are, as shown in the following diagram:

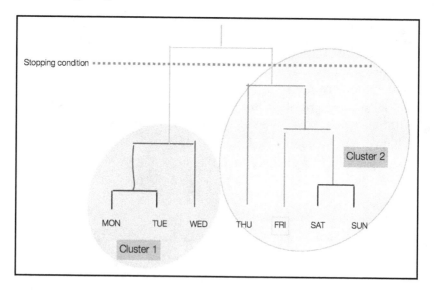

Note that the stopping condition is shown as a dotted line in the preceding figure.

# Coding a hierarchical clustering algorithm

Let's learn how we can code a hierarchical algorithm in Python:

1.  We will first import `AgglomerativeClustering` from
    the `sklearn.cluster` library, along with the `pandas` and `numpy` packages:

    ```
    from sklearn.cluster import AgglomerativeClustering
    import pandas as pd
    import numpy as np
    ```

2.  Then we will create 20 data points in a two-dimensional problem space:

    ```
    dataset = pd.DataFrame({
        'x': [11, 21, 28, 17, 29, 33, 24, 45, 45, 52, 51, 52, 55, 53,
    55, 61, 62, 70, 72, 10],
        'y': [39, 36, 30, 52, 53, 46, 55, 59, 63, 70, 66, 63, 58, 23,
    14, 8, 18, 7, 24, 10]
    })
    ```

3.  Then we create the hierarchical cluster by specifying the hyperparameters. We
    use the `fit_predict` function to actually process the algorithm:

    ```
    cluster = AgglomerativeClustering(n_clusters=2,
    affinity='euclidean', linkage='ward')
    cluster.fit_predict(dataset)
    ```

4.  Now let's look at the association of each data point to the two clusters that were
    created:

    ```
    In [3]:    1 print(cluster.labels_)

    [0 0 0 0 0 0 0 1 1 1 1 1 1 1 1 1 1 1 1 0]
    ```

You can see that the cluster assignment for both hierarchical and k-means
algorithms are very similar.

# Evaluating the clusters

The objective of good quality clustering is that the data points that belong to the separate clusters should be differentiable. This implies the following:

- The data points that belong to the same cluster should be as similar as possible.
- Data points that belong to separate clusters should be as different as possible.

Human intuition can be used to evaluate the clustering results by visualizing the clusters, but there are mathematical methods that can quantify the quality of the clusters. Silhouette analysis is one such technique that compares the tightness and separation in the clusters created by the k-means algorithm. The silhouette draws a plot that displays the closeness each point in a particular cluster has with respect to the other points in the neighboring clusters. It associates a number in the range of [-0, 1] with each cluster. The following table shows what the figures in this range signify:

| Range | Meaning | Description |
|---|---|---|
| 0.71–1.0 | Excellent | This means that the k-means clustering resulted in groups that are quite differentiable from each other. |
| 0.51–0.70 | Reasonable | This means that the k-means clustering resulted in groups that are somewhat differentiable from each other. |
| 0.26–0.50 | Weak | This means that the k-means clustering resulted in grouping, but the quality of the grouping should not be relied upon. |
| <0.25 | No clustering has been found | Using the parameters selected and the data used, it was not possible to create grouping using k-means clustering. |

Note that each cluster in the problem space will get a separate score.

# Application of clustering

Clustering is used wherever we needed to discover the underlying patterns in datasets.

In government use cases, clustering can be used for the following:

- Crime-hotspot analysis
- Demographic social analysis

In market research, clustering can be used for the following:

- Market segmentation
- Targeted advertisements
- Customer categorization

**Principal component analysis (PCA)** is also used for generally exploring the data and removing noise from real-time data, such as stock-market trading.

# Dimensionality reduction

Each feature in our data corresponds to a dimension in our problem space. Minimizing the number of features to make our problem space simpler is called **dimensionality reduction**. It can be done in one of the following two ways:

- **Feature selection**: Selecting a set of features that are important in the context of the problem we are trying to solve
- **Feature aggregation**: Combining two or more features to reduce dimensions using one of the following algorithms:
    - **PCA**: A linear unsupervised ML algorithm
    - **Linear discriminant analysis (LDA)**: A linear supervised ML algorithm
    - **Kernel principal component analysis**: A nonlinear algorithm

Let's look deeper at one of the popular dimensionality reduction algorithms, namely PCA, in more detail.

# Principal component analysis

PCA is an unsupervised machine learning technique that can be used to reduce dimensions using linear transformation. In the following figure, we can see two principle components, **PC1** and **PC2**, which show the shape of the spread of the data points. PC1 and PC2 can be used to summarize the data points with appropriate coefficients:

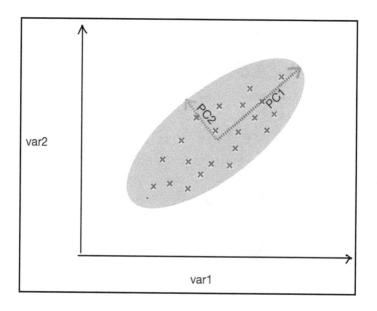

Let's consider the following code:

```
from sklearn.decomposition import PCA
iris = pd.read_csv('iris.csv')
X = iris.drop('Species', axis=1)
pca = PCA(n_components=4)
pca.fit(X)
```

Now let's print the coefficients of our PCA model:

```
In [36]:  print(pd.DataFrame(pca.components_,columns=X.columns))

          Sepal.Length  Sepal.Width  Petal.Length  Petal.Width          Coefficients for PC1
       0      0.361387    -0.084523      0.856671      0.358289          Coefficients for PC2
       1      0.656589     0.730161     -0.173373     -0.075481          Coefficients for PC3
       2     -0.582030     0.597911      0.076236      0.545831          Coefficients for PC4
       3     -0.315487     0.319723      0.479839     -0.753657
```

Note that the original DataFrame has four features, Sepal.Length, Sepal.Width, Petal.Length, and Petal.Width. The preceding DataFrame specifies the coefficients of the four principal components, PC1, PC2, PC3, and PC4—for example, the first row specifies the coefficients of PC1 that can be used to replace the original four variables.

Based on these coefficients, we can calculate the PCA components for our input DataFrame X:

```
pca_df=(pd.DataFrame(pca.components_,columns=X.columns))

# Let us calculate PC1 using coefficients that are generated
X['PC1'] = X['Sepal.Length']* pca_df['Sepal.Length'][0] + X['Sepal.Width']*
pca_df['Sepal.Width'][0]+ X['Petal.Length']*
pca_df['Petal.Length'][0]+X['Petal.Width']* pca_df['Petal.Width'][0]

# Let us calculate PC2
X['PC2'] = X['Sepal.Length']* pca_df['Sepal.Length'][1] + X['Sepal.Width']*
pca_df['Sepal.Width'][1]+ X['Petal.Length']*
pca_df['Petal.Length'][1]+X['Petal.Width']* pca_df['Petal.Width'][1]

#Let us calculate PC3
X['PC3'] = X['Sepal.Length']* pca_df['Sepal.Length'][2] + X['Sepal.Width']*
pca_df['Sepal.Width'][2]+ X['Petal.Length']*
pca_df['Petal.Length'][2]+X['Petal.Width']* pca_df['Petal.Width'][2]

# Let us calculate PC4
X['PC4'] = X['Sepal.Length']* pca_df['Sepal.Length'][3] + X['Sepal.Width']*
pca_df['Sepal.Width'][3]+ X['Petal.Length']*
pca_df['Petal.Length'][3]+X['Petal.Width']* pca_df['Petal.Width'][3]
```

Now let's print X after the calculation of the PCA components:

| | Sepal.Length | Sepal.Width | Petal.Length | Petal.Width | PC1 | PC2 | PC3 | PC4 |
|---|---|---|---|---|---|---|---|---|
| 0 | 5.1 | 3.5 | 1.4 | 0.2 | 2.818240 | 5.646350 | -0.659768 | 0.031089 |
| 1 | 4.9 | 3.0 | 1.4 | 0.2 | 2.788223 | 5.149951 | -0.842317 | -0.065675 |
| 2 | 4.7 | 3.2 | 1.3 | 0.2 | 2.613375 | 5.182003 | -0.613952 | 0.013383 |
| 3 | 4.6 | 3.1 | 1.5 | 0.2 | 2.757022 | 5.008654 | -0.600293 | 0.108928 |
| 4 | 5.0 | 3.6 | 1.4 | 0.2 | 2.773649 | 5.653707 | -0.541773 | 0.094610 |
| ... | ... | ... | ... | ... | ... | ... | ... | ... |
| 145 | 6.7 | 3.0 | 5.2 | 2.3 | 7.446475 | 5.514485 | -0.454028 | -0.392844 |
| 146 | 6.3 | 2.5 | 5.0 | 1.9 | 7.029532 | 4.951636 | -0.753751 | -0.221016 |
| 147 | 6.5 | 3.0 | 5.2 | 2.0 | 7.266711 | 5.405811 | -0.501371 | -0.103650 |
| 148 | 6.2 | 3.4 | 5.4 | 2.3 | 7.403307 | 5.443581 | 0.091399 | -0.011244 |
| 149 | 5.9 | 3.0 | 5.1 | 1.8 | 6.892554 | 5.044292 | -0.268943 | 0.188390 |

Now let's print the variance ratio and try to understand the implications of using PCA:

```
In [37]: print(pca.explained_variance_ratio_)
         [0.92461872 0.05306648 0.01710261 0.00521218]
```

The variance ratio indicates the following:

- If we choose to replace the original four features with PC1, then we will be able to capture about 92.3% of the variance of the original variables. We will introduce some approximations by not capturing 100% of the variance of the original four features.
- If we choose to replace the original four features with PC1 and PC2, then we will capture an additional 5.3 % of the variance of the original variables.
- If we choose to replace the original four features with PC1, PC2, and PC3, then we will now capture a further 0.017 % of the variance of the original variables.
- If we choose to replace the original four features with four principal components, then we will capture 100% of the variance of the original variables (92.4 + 0.053 + 0.017 + 0.005), but replacing four original features with four principal components is meaningless as we did not reduce the dimensions at all and achieved nothing.

# Limitations of PCA

The following are the limitations of PCA:

- PCA can only be used for continuous variables and is not relevant for category variables.
- While aggregating, PCA approximates the component variables; it simplifies the problem of dimensionality at the expense of accuracy. This trade-off should be carefully studied before using PCA.

# Association rules mining

Patterns in a particular dataset are the treasure that needs to be discovered, understood, and mined for the information they contain. There is an important set of algorithms that try to focus on the pattern analysis in a given dataset. One of the more popular algorithms in this class of algorithm is called the **association rules mining** algorithm, which provides us with the following capabilities:

- The ability to measure the frequency of a pattern
- The ability to establish *cause*-and-*effect* relationship among the patterns.
- The ability to quantify the usefulness of patterns by comparing their accuracy to random guessing

# Examples of use

Association rules mining is used when we are trying to investigate the cause-and-effect relationships between different variables of a dataset. The following are example questions that it can help to answer:

- Which values of humidity, cloud cover, and temperature can lead to rain tomorrow?
- What type of insurance claim can indicate fraud?
- What combinations of medicine may lead to complications for patients?

# Market basket analysis

In this book, recommendation engines are discussed in `Chapter 8`, *Neural Network Algorithms*. Basket analysis is a simpler way of learning recommendations. In basket analysis, our data contains only the information regarding what items were bought together. It does not have any information about the user or whether the user enjoyed individual items. Note that it is much easier to get this data than it is to get ratings data.

For example, this kind of data is generated when we shop at Walmart, and no special technique is required to get the data. This data, when collected over a period of time, is called **transnational data**. When association rules analysis is applied to transnational data sets of the shopping carts being used in convenience stores, supermarkets, and fast-food chains, it is called **market basket analysis**. It measures the conditional probability of buying a set of items together, which helps to answer the following questions:

- What is the optimal placement of items on the shelf?
- How should the items appear in the marketing catalog?
- What should be recommended, based on a user's buying patterns?

As market basket analysis can estimate how items are related to each other, it is often used for mass-market retail, such as supermarkets, convenience stores, drug stores, and fast-food chains. The advantage of market basket analysis is that the results are almost self-explanatory, which means that they are easily understood by the business users.

Let's look at a typical superstore. All the unique items that are available in the store can be represented by a set, $\pi = \{item_1, item_2, \ldots, item_m\}$. So, if that superstore is selling 500 distinct items, then $\pi$ will be a set of size 500.

People will buy items from this store. Each time someone buys an item and pays at the counter, it is added to a set of the items in a particular transaction, called an **itemset**. In a given period of time, the transactions are grouped together in a set represented by $\triangle$, where $\triangle = \{t_1, t_2, \ldots, t_n\}$.

Let's look at the following simple transaction data consisting of only four transactions. These transactions are summarized in the following table:

| t1 | Wickets, pads |
|----|----------------|
| t2 | Bat, wickets, pads, helmet |
| t3 | Helmet, ball |
| t4 | Bat, pads, helmet |

Let's look at this example in more detail:

$\pi$ = {bat , wickets, pads, helmet, ball }, which represents all the unique items available at the store.

Let's consider one of the transactions, t3, from $\triangle$. Note that items bought in t3 can be represented in the itemset$_{t3}$= {helmet,ball}, which indicates that a customer purchased two items. As there are two items in this itemset, the size of itemset$_{t5}$ is said to be two.

# Association rules

An association rule mathematically describes the relationship items involved in various transactions. It does this by investigating the relationship between two itemsets in the form $X \Rightarrow Y$, where $X \subset \pi$, $Y \subset \pi$. In addition, $X$ and $Y$ are nonoverlapping itemsets; which means that $X \cap Y = \varnothing$ .

An association rule could be described in the following form:

{helmet,balls}$\Rightarrow$ {bike}

Here, {helmet,ball} is $X$ and {ball} is $Y$.

# Types of rule

Running associative analysis algorithms will typically result in the generation of a large number of rules from a transaction dataset. Most of them are useless. To pick rules that can result in useful information, we can classify them as one of the following three types:

- Trivial
- Inexplicable
- Actionable

Let's look at each of these types in more detail.

## Trivial rules

Among the large numbers of rules generated, many that are derived will be useless as they summarize common knowledge about the business. They are called trivial rules. Even if the confidence in the trivial rules is high, they remain useless and cannot be used for any data-driven decision making. We can safely ignore all trivial rules.

The following are examples of trivial rules:

- Anyone who jumps from a high-rise building is likely to die.
- Working harder leads to better scores in exams.
- The sales of heaters increase as the temperature drops
- Driving a car over the speed limit on a highway leads to a higher chance of an accident.

## Inexplicable rules

Among the rules that are generated after running the association rules algorithm, the ones that have no obvious explanation are the trickiest to use. Note that a rule can only be useful if it can help us discover and understand a new pattern that is expected to eventually lead toward a certain course of action. If that is not the case, and we cannot explain why event *X* led to event *Y*, then it is an inexplicable rule, because it's just a mathematical formula that ends up exploring the pointless relationship between two events that are unrelated and independent.

The following are examples of inexplicable rules:

- People who wear red shirts tend to score better in exams.
- Green bicycles are more likely to be stolen.
- People who buy pickles end up buying diapers as well.

## Actionable rules

Actionable rules are the golden rules we are looking for. They are understood by the business and lead to insights. They can help us to discover the possible causes of an event when presented to an audience familiar with the business domain—for example, actionable rules may suggest the best placement in a store for a particular product based on current buying patterns. They may also suggest which items to place together to maximize their chances of selling as users tend to buy them together.

The following are examples of actionable rules and their corresponding actions:

- **Rule 1:** Displaying ads to users' social media accounts results in a higher likelihood of sales.

  **Actionable item:** Suggests alternative ways of advertising a product

- **Rule 2:** Creating more price points increases the likelihood of sales.

  **Actionable item:** One item may be advertised in a sale, while the price of another item is raised.

# Ranking rules

Association rules are measured in three ways:

- Support (frequency) of items
- Confidence
- Lift

Let's look at them in more detail.

# Support

The support measure is a number that quantifies how frequent the pattern we are looking for is in our dataset. It is calculated by first counting the number of occurrences of our pattern of interest and then dividing it by the total number of all the transactions.

Let's look at the following formula for a particular *itemset$_a$*:

$$numItemset_a = Number\ of\ transactions\ that\ contain\ itemset_a$$

$$num_{total} = Total\ number\ of\ transactions$$

$$support(itemset_a) = \frac{numItemset_a}{num_{total}}$$

By just looking at the support, we can get an idea of how rare the occurrence of a pattern is. A low support means that we are looking for a rare event.

For example, if *itemset$_a$* = {helmet, ball} appears in two transactions out of six, then support (itemset$_a$) = 2/6 = 0.33.

# Confidence

The confidence is a number that quantifies how strongly we can associate the left side $(X)$ with the right side $(Y)$ by calculating the conditional probability. It calculates the probability that event $X$ will lead toward the event $Y$, given that event $X$ occurred.

Mathematically, consider the rule $X \Rightarrow Y$.

The confidence of this rule is represented as confidence$(X \Rightarrow Y)$ and is measured as follows:

$$confidence(X \Rightarrow Y) = \frac{support(X \cup Y)}{support(X)}$$

Let's look at an example. Consider the following rule:

$$\{helmet, ball\} \Rightarrow \{wickets\}$$

The confidence of this rule is calculated by the following formula:

$$confidence(helmet, ball \Rightarrow wickets) = \frac{support(helmet, ball \cup wickets)}{support(helmet, ball)} = \frac{\frac{1}{6}}{\frac{2}{6}} = 0.5$$

This means that if someone has {helmet, balls} in the basket, then there is 0.5 or 50 percent probability that they will also have wickets to go with it.

# Lift

Another way to estimate the quality of a rule is by calculating the lift. The lift returns a number that quantifies how much improvement has been achieved by a rule at predicting the result compared to just assuming the result at the right-hand side of the equation. If the $X$ and $Y$ itemsets were independent, then the lift is calculated as follows:

$$Lift(X \Rightarrow Y) = \frac{support(X \cup Y)}{support(X) \times support(Y)}$$

# Algorithms for association analysis

In this section, we will explore the following two algorithms that can be used for association analysis:

- **Apriori algorithm**: Proposed by Agrawal, R. and Srikant in 1994.
- **FP-growth algorithm**: An improvement suggested by Han et al. in 2001.

Let's look at each of these algorithms.

# Apriori Algorithm

The apriori algorithm is an iterative and multiphase algorithm used to generate association rules. It is based on a generation-and-test approach.

Before executing the apriori algorithm, we need to define two variables: $support_{threshold}$ and $Confidence_{threshold}$.

The algorithm consists of the following two phases:

- **Candidate-generation phase**: It generates the candidate itemsets, which contain sets of all itemsets above $support_{threshold}$.
- **Filter phase**: It filters out all rules below the expected $confidence_{threshold}$.

After filtering, the resulting rules are the answer.

### Limitations of the apriori algorithm

The major bottleneck in the apriori algorithm is the generation of candidate rules in Phase 1—for example, $\pi = \{item_1, item_2, \ldots, item_m\}$ can produce $2^m$ possible itemsets. Because of its multiphase design, it first generates these itemsets and then works toward finding the frequent itemsets. This limitation is a huge performance bottleneck and makes the apriori algorithm unsuitable for larger items.

# FP-growth algorithm

The **frequent pattern growth** (**FP-growth**) algorithm is an improvement on the apriori algorithm. It starts by showing the frequent transaction FP-tree, which is an ordered tree. It consists of two steps:

- Populating the FP-tree
- Mining frequent patterns

Let's look at these steps one by one.

## Populating the FP-tree

Let's consider the transaction data shown in the following table. Let's first represent it as a sparse matrix:

| ID | Bat | Wickets | Pads | Helmet | Ball |
|----|-----|---------|------|--------|------|
| 1 | 0 | 1 | 1 | 0 | 0 |
| 2 | 1 | 1 | 1 | 1 | 0 |
| 3 | 0 | 0 | 0 | 1 | 1 |
| 4 | 1 | 0 | 1 | 1 | 0 |

Let's calculate the frequency of each item and sort them in descending order by frequency:

| Item | Frequency |
|------|-----------|
| pads | 3 |
| helmet | 3 |
| bat | 2 |
| wicket | 2 |
| ball | 1 |

Now let's rearrange the transaction-based data based on the frequency:

| ID | Original Items | Reordered Items |
|----|----------------|-----------------|
| t1 | Wickets, pads | Pads, wickets |
| t2 | Bat, wickets, pads, helmet | Helmet, pads, wickets, bat |
| t3 | Helmet, ball | Helmet, ball |
| t4 | Bat, pads, helmet | Helmet, pads, bat |

To build the FP-tree, let's start with the first branch of the FP-tree. The FP-tree starts with a **Null** as the root. To build the tree, we can represent each item with a node, as shown in the following diagram (the tree representation of $t_i$ is shown here). Note that the label of each node is the name of the item and its frequency is appended after the colon. Also, note that the **pads** item has a frequency of 1:

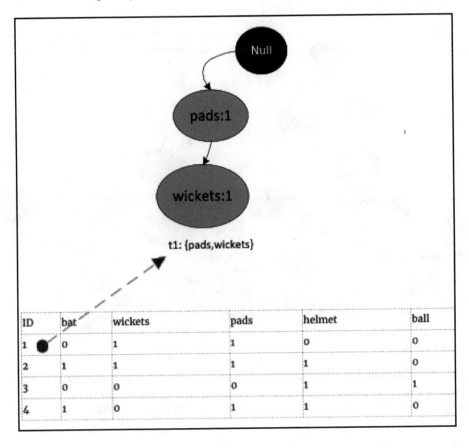

t1: {pads,wickets}

| ID | bat | wickets | pads | helmet | ball |
|----|-----|---------|------|--------|------|
| 1 | 0 | 1 | 1 | 0 | 0 |
| 2 | 1 | 1 | 1 | 1 | 0 |
| 3 | 0 | 0 | 0 | 1 | 1 |
| 4 | 1 | 0 | 1 | 1 | 0 |

Using the same pattern, let's draw all four transactions, resulting in the full FP-tree. The FP-tree has four leaf nodes, each representing the itemset associated with the four transactions. Note that we need to count the frequencies of each item and need to increase it when used multiple times—for example, when adding $t_2$ to the FP-tree, the frequency of **helmet** was increased to two. Similarly, while adding $t_4$, it was increased again to three. The resulting tree is shown in the following diagram:

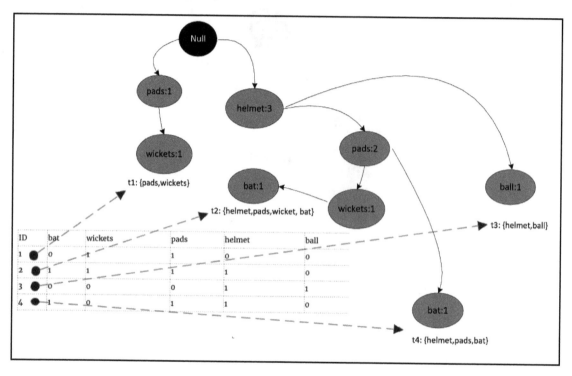

Note that the FP-tree generated in the preceding diagram is an ordered tree.

## Mining Frequent Patterns

The second phase of the FP-growth tree involves mining the frequent patterns from the FP-tree. By creating an ordered tree, the intention is to create an efficient data structure that can be easily navigated to search for frequent patterns.

We start from a leaf node (that is, the end node) and move upward—for example, let's start from one of the leaf node items, **bat**. Then we need to calculate the conditional pattern base for **bat**. The conditional pattern base is calculated by specifying all the paths from the leaf item node to the top. The conditional pattern base for **bat** will be as follows:

| Wicket: 1 | Pads: 1 | Helmet: 1 |
|-----------|---------|-----------|
| Pad: 1 | Helmet: 1 | |

The **frequent pattern** for **bat** will be as follows:

*{wicket, pads, helmet} : bat*

*{pad,helmet} : bat*

## Code for using FP-growth

Let's see how we can generate association rules using the FP-growth algorithm in Python. For this, we will be using the `pyfpgrowth` package. First, if we have never used `pyfpgrowth` before, let's install it first:

```
!pip install pyfpgrowth
```

Then, let's import the packages that we need to use to implement this algorithm:

```
import pandas as pd
import numpy as np
import pyfpgrowth as fp
```

Now we will create the input data in the form of `transactionSet`:

```
dict1 = {
  'id':[0,1,2,3],
  'items':[["wickets","pads"],
  ["bat","wickets","pads","helmet"],
  ["helmet","pad"],
  ["bat","pads","helmet"]]

}
transactionSet = pd.DataFrame(dict1)
```

Once the input data is generated, we will generate patterns that will be based on the parameters that we passed in the `find_frequent_patterns()`. Note that the second parameter passed to this function is the minimum support, which is 1 in this case:

```
patterns = fp.find_frequent_patterns(transactionSet['items'],1)
```

The patterns have been generated. Now let's print the patterns. The patterns list the combinations of items with their supports:

```
In [39]:  patterns
Out[39]:  {('pad',): 1,
           ('helmet', 'pad'): 1,
           ('wickets',): 2,
           ('pads', 'wickets'): 2,
           ('bat', 'wickets'): 1,
           ('helmet', 'wickets'): 1,
           ('bat', 'pads', 'wickets'): 1,
           ('helmet', 'pads', 'wickets'): 1,
           ('bat', 'helmet', 'wickets'): 1,
           ('bat', 'helmet', 'pads', 'wickets'): 1,
           ('bat',): 2,
           ('bat', 'helmet'): 2,
           ('bat', 'pads'): 2,
           ('bat', 'helmet', 'pads'): 2,
           ('pads',): 3,
           ('helmet',): 3,
           ('helmet', 'pads'): 2}
```

Now let's generate the rules:

```
In [22]:  rules = fp.generate_association_rules(patterns,0.3)
          rules
Out[22]:  {('helmet',): (('pads',), 0.6666666666666666),
           ('pad',): (('helmet',), 1.0),
           ('pads',): (('helmet',), 0.6666666666666666),
           ('wickets',): (('bat', 'helmet', 'pads'), 0.5),
           ('bat',): (('helmet', 'pads'), 1.0),
           ('bat', 'pads'): (('helmet',), 1.0),
           ('bat', 'wickets'): (('helmet', 'pads'), 1.0),
           ('pads', 'wickets'): (('bat', 'helmet'), 0.5),
           ('helmet', 'pads'): (('bat',), 1.0),
           ('helmet', 'wickets'): (('bat', 'pads'), 1.0),
           ('bat', 'helmet'): (('pads',), 1.0),
           ('bat', 'helmet', 'pads'): (('wickets',), 0.5),
           ('bat', 'helmet', 'wickets'): (('pads',), 1.0),
           ('bat', 'pads', 'wickets'): (('helmet',), 1.0),
           ('helmet', 'pads', 'wickets'): (('bat',), 1.0)}
```

Each rule has a left-hand side and a right-hand side, separated by a colon (:). It also gives us the support of each of the rules in our input dataset.

# Practical application– clustering similar tweets together

Unsupervised machine learning algorithms can also be applied in real time to cluster similar tweets together. They will do the following:

- STEP 1- **Topic Modeling**: Discover various topics from a given set of tweets
- STEP 2- **Clustering**: Associate each of the tweets with one of the discovered topics

This use of unsupervised learning is shown in the following diagram:

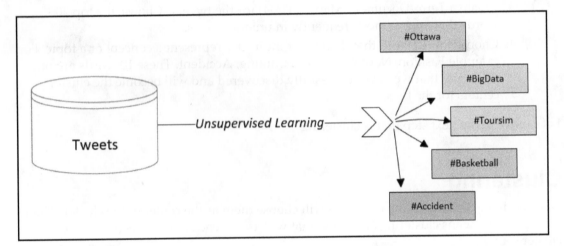

 Note that this example requires real-time processing of input data.

Let's look into these steps one by one.

# Topic modeling

Topic Modeling is the process of discovering the concepts in a set of documents that can be used to differentiate them. In the context of tweets, it is about finding which are the most appropriate topics in which a set of tweets can be divided. Latent Dirichlet Allocation is a popular algorithm that is used for topic modeling. Because each of the tweet are short 144 character document usually about a very particular topic, we can write a simpler algorithm for topic modeling purposes. The algorithm is described as following:

1. Tokenize tweets.
2. Preprocess the data. Remove stopwords, numbers, symbols and perform stemming
3. Create a Term-Document-Matrix (TDM) for the tweets. Choose the top 200 words that appear most frequently in unique tweets.
4. Choose top 10 word that directly or indirectly represent a concept or a topic. For example Fashion, New York, Programming, Accident. These 10 words are now the topics that we have successfully discovered and will become the cluster centers for the tweets.

Let's move to the next step that is clustering

# Clustering

Once we have discovered the topics we will choose them as the center of the cluster. Then we can run k-means clustering algorithm that will assign each of the tweets to one of the cluster center.

So, this the practical example that how a set of tweets can be clustered into topics discovered.

# Anomaly-detection algorithms

The dictionary definition of an *anomaly* is something that is different, abnormal, peculiar, or not easily classified. It is a deviation from the common rule. In the context of data science, an anomaly is a data point that deviates a lot from the expected pattern. Techniques to find such data points are called anomaly-detection techniques.

Now let's see some applications of anomaly-detection algorithms:

- Credit card fraud
- Finding a malignant tumor in a **magnetic resonance imaging (MRI)** scan
- Fault prevention in clusters
- Impersonation in exams
- Accidents on a highway

In the upcoming sections, we will see various anomaly-detection techniques.

# Using clustering

Clustering algorithms such as k-means can be used to group similar data points together. A threshold can be defined and any point beyond that threshold can be classified as an anomaly. The problem with this approach is that the grouping created by k-means clustering may itself be biased because of the presence of anomalous data points and may affect the usefulness and accuracy of the approach.

# Using density-based anomaly detection

A density-based approach tries to find dense neighborhoods. The **k-nearest neighbors (KNN)** algorithm can be used for this purpose. Abnormalities that are far away from the discovered dense neighborhoods are marked as anomalies.

# Using support vector machines

The **Support Vector Machine (SVM)** algorithm can be used to learn the boundaries of the data points. Any points beyond those discovered boundaries are identified as anomalies.

# Summary

In this chapter, we looked at the various unsupervised machine learning techniques. We looked at the circumstances in which it is a good idea to try to reduce the dimensionality of the problem we are trying to solve and the different methods of doing this. We also studied the practical examples where unsupervised machine learning techniques can be very helpful, including market basket analysis and anomaly detection.

In the next chapter, we will look at the various supervised learning techniques. We will start with linear regression and then we will look at more sophisticated supervised machine learning techniques, such as decision-tree-based algorithms, SVM, and XGBoast. We will also study the naive Bayes algorithm, which is best suited for unstructured textual data.

# 7

# Traditional Supervised Learning Algorithms

In this chapter, we will focus on supervised machine learning algorithms, which are one of the most important types of modern algorithms. The distinguishing characteristic of a supervised machine learning algorithm is the use of labeled data to train a model. In this book, supervised machine learning algorithms are divided into two chapters. In this chapter, we will present all the traditional supervised machine learning algorithms, excluding neural networks. The next chapter is all about implementing supervised machine learning algorithms using neural networks. The truth is that with so much ongoing development in this field, neural networks are a comprehensive topic that deserves a separate chapter in this book.

So, this chapter is the first of two parts about supervised machine learning algorithms. First, we will introduce the fundamental concepts of supervised machine learning. Next, we will present two types of supervised machine models—classifiers and regressors. In order to demonstrate the abilities of classifiers, we will first present a real-world problem as a challenge. Then, we will present six different classification algorithms that are used to solve the problem. Then, we will focus on regression algorithms, first by presenting a similar problem to be solved for the regressors. Next, we will present three regression algorithms and use them to solve the problem. Finally, we will compare the results to help us summarize the concepts presented in this chapter.

The overall objective of this chapter is for you to understand the different types of supervised machine learning techniques and know what the best supervised machine learning techniques are for certain classes of problems.

The following concepts are discussed in this chapter:

- Understanding supervised machine learning
- Understanding classification algorithms
- The methods for evaluating the performance of classifiers
- Understanding regression algorithms
- The methods for evaluating the performance of regression algorithms

Let's start by looking at the basic concepts behind supervised machine learning.

# Understanding supervised machine learning

Machine learning focuses on using data-driven approaches to create autonomous systems that can help us to make decisions with or without human supervision. In order to create these autonomous systems, machine learning uses a group of algorithms and methodologies to discover and formulate repeatable patterns in data. One of the most popular and powerful methodologies used in machine learning is the supervised machine learning approach. In supervised machine learning, an algorithm is given a set of inputs, called **features**, and their corresponding outputs, called **target variables**. Using a given dataset, a supervised machine learning algorithm is used to train a model that captures the complex relationship between the features and target variables represented by a mathematical formula. This trained model is the basic vehicle that is used for predictions.

Predictions are made by generating the target variable of an unfamiliar set of features through the trained model.

The ability to learn from existing data in supervised learning is similar to the ability of the human brain to learn from experience. This learning ability in supervised learning uses one of the attributes of the human brain and is a fundamental way of opening the gates to bring decision-making power and intelligence to machines.

Let's consider an example where we want to use supervised machine learning techniques to train a model that can categorize a set of emails into legitimate ones (called **legit**) and unwanted ones (called **spam**). First of all, in order to get started, we need examples from the past so that the machine can learn what sort of content of emails should be classified as spam. This content-based learning task for text data is a complex process and is achieved through one of the supervised machine learning algorithms. Some examples of supervised machine learning algorithms that can be used to train the model in this example include decision trees and naive Bayes classifiers, which we will discuss later in this chapter.

# Formulating supervised machine learning

Before going deeper into the details of supervised machine learning algorithms, let's define some of the basic supervised machine learning terminologies:

| Terminology | Explanation |
|---|---|
| Target variable | The target variable is the variable that we want our model to predict. There can be only one target variable in a supervised machine learning model. |
| Label | If the target variable we want to predict is a category variable, it is called a label. |
| Features | The set of input variables used to predict the label is called the features. |
| Feature engineering | Transforming features to prepare them for the chosen supervised machine learning algorithm is called feature engineering. |
| Feature vector | Before providing an input to a supervised machine learning algorithm, all the features are combined in a data structure called a feature vector. |
| Historical data | The data from the past that is used to formulate the relationship between the target variable and the features is called historical data. Historical data comes with examples. |
| Training/testing data | Historical data with examples is divided into two parts—a larger dataset called the training data and a smaller dataset called the testing data. |
| Model | A mathematical formulation of the patterns that best capture the relationship between the target variable and the features. |
| Training | Creating a model using training data. |
| Testing | Evaluating the quality of the trained model using testing data. |
| Prediction | Using a model to predict the target variable. |

 A trained supervised machine learning model is capable of making predictions by estimating the target variable based on the features.

Let's introduce the notation that we will be using in this chapter to discuss the machine learning techniques:

| Variable | Meaning |
|----------|---------|
| $y$ | Actual label |
| $\hat{y}$ | Predicted label |
| $d$ | Total number of examples |
| $b$ | Number of training examples |
| $c$ | Number of testing examples |

Now, let's see how some of these terminologies are formulated practically.

As we discussed, a feature vector is defined as a data structure that has all the features stored in it.

If the number of features is $n$ and the number of training examples is $b$, then X_train represents the training feature vector. Each example is a row in the feature vector.

For the training dataset, the feature vector is represented by X_train. If there are $b$ examples in the training dataset, then X_train will have $b$ rows. If there are $n$ variables in the training dataset, then it will have $n$ columns. So, the training dataset will have a dimension of $n$ x $b$, as represented in the following diagram:

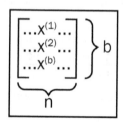

Now, let's assume that there are $b$ training examples and $c$ testing examples. A particular training example is represented by $(X, y)$.

We use superscript to indicate which training example is which within the training set.

So, our labeled dataset is represented by $D = \{(X^{(1)}, y^{(1)}), (X^{(2)}, y^{(2)}), \ldots, (X^{(d)}, y^{(d)})\}$.

We divide that into two parts—$D_{train}$ and $D_{test}$.

So, our training set can be represented by $D_{train} = \{(X^{(1)}, y^{(1)}), (X^{(2)}, y^{(2)}), \ldots, (X^{(b)}, y^{(b)})\}$.

The objective of training a model is that for any $i^{th}$ example in the training set, the predicted value of the target value should be as close to the actual value in the examples as possible. In other words, $\acute{y}(i) \approx y(i); for 1 \leq i \leq b$.

So, our testing set can be represented by $D_{test} = \{X^{(1)}, y^{(1)}), (X^{(2)}, y^{(2)}), ..... , (X^{(c)}, y^{(c)})\}$.

The values of the target variable are represented by a vector, $Y$:

$$Y = \{ y^{(1)}, y^{(2)}, ....., y^{(m)}\}$$

# Understanding enabling conditions

Supervised machine learning is based on the ability of an algorithm to train a model using examples. A supervised machine learning algorithm needs certain enabling conditions to be met in order to perform. These enabling conditions are as follows:

- **Enough examples**: Supervised machine learning algorithms need enough examples to train a model.
- **Patterns in historical data**: The examples used to train a model need to have patterns in it. The likelihood of the occurrence of our event of interest should be dependent on a combination of patterns, trends, and events. Without these, we are dealing with random data that cannot be used to train a model.
- **Valid assumptions**: When we train a supervised machine learning model using examples, we expect that the assumptions that apply to the examples will also be valid in the future. Let's look at an actual example. If we want to train a machine learning model for the government that can predict the likelihood of whether a visa will be granted to a student, the understanding is that the laws and policies will not change when the model is used for predictions. If new policies or laws are enforced after training the model, the model may need to be retrained to incorporate this new information.

# Differentiating between classifiers and regressors

In a machine learning model, the target variable can be a category variable or a continuous variable. The type of target variable determines what type of supervised machine learning model we have. Fundamentally, we have two types of supervised machine learning models:

- **Classifiers**: If the target variable is a category variable, the machine learning model is called a classifier. Classifiers can be used to answer the following type of business questions:
  - Is this abnormal tissue growth a malignant tumor?
  - Based on the current weather conditions, will it rain tomorrow?
  - Based on the profile of a particular applicant, should their mortgage application be approved?
- **Regressors**: If the target variable is a continuous variable, we train a regressor. Regressors can be used to answer the following types of business questions:
  - Based on the current weather condition, how much will it rain tomorrow?
  - What will the price of a particular home be with given characteristics?

Let's look at both classifiers and regressors in more detail.

# Understanding classification algorithms

In supervised machine learning, if the target variable is a category variable, the model is categorized as a classifier:

- The target variable is called a **label**.
- The historical data is called **labeled data**.
- The production data, which the label needs to be predicted for, is called **unlabeled data**.

The ability to accurately label unlabeled data using a trained model is the real power of classification algorithms. Classifiers predict labels for unlabeled data to answer a particular business question.

Before we present the details of classification algorithms, let's first present a business problem that we will use as a challenge for classifiers. We will then use six different algorithms to answer the same challenge, which will help us compare their methodology, approach, and performance.

# Presenting the classifiers challenge

We will first present a common problem, which we will use as a challenge to test six different classification algorithms. This common problem is referred to as the classifier challenge in this chapter. Using all the six classifiers to solve the same problem will help us in two ways:

- All the input variables need to be processed and assembled as a complex data structure, called a feature vector. Using the same feature vector helps us avoid repeating data preparation for all six algorithms.
- We can compare the performance of various algorithms as we are using the same feature vector for input.

The classifiers challenge is about predicting the likelihood of a person making a purchase. In the retail industry, one of the things that can help maximize sales is better understanding the behavior of the customers. This can be done by analyzing the patterns found in historical data. Let's state the problem, first.

## The problem statement

Given the historical data, can we train a binary classifier that can predict whether a particular user will eventually buy a product based on their profile?

First, let's explore the historical labeled data set available to solve this problem:

$x \in \Re^b, y \in \{0,1\}$

For a particular example, when $y = 1$, we call it a positive class and when $y = 0$, we call it a negative class.

 Although the level of the positive and negative class can be chosen arbitrarily, it is good practice to define the positive class as the event of interest. If we are trying to flag the fraudulent transaction for a bank, then the positive class (that is, $y = 1$ ) should be the fraudulent transaction, not the other way around.

Now, let's look at the following:

- The actual label, denoted by $y$
- The predicted label, denoted by $y`$

Note that for our classifiers challenge, the actual value of the label found in examples is represented by $y$. If, in our example, someone has purchased an item, we say $y = 1$. The predicted values are represented by $y`$. The input feature vector, $x$, has a dimension of 4. We want to determine what the probability is that a user will make a purchase, given a particular input.

So, we want to determine the probability that $y = 1$ is, given a particular value of feature vector $x$. Mathematically, we can represent this as follows:

$$\acute{y} = P(y = 1|x) : where; x \in \Re^{n_x}$$

Now, let's look at how we can process and assemble different input variables in the feature vector, $x$. The methodology to assemble different parts of $x$ using the processing pipeline is discussed in more detail in the following section.

# Feature engineering using a data processing pipeline

Preparing data for a chosen machine learning algorithm is called **feature engineering** and is a crucial part of the machine learning life cycle. Feature engineering is done in different stages or phases. The multi-stage processing code used to process data is collectively known as a **data pipeline**. Making a data pipeline using standard processing steps, wherever possible, makes it reusable and decreases the effort needed to train the models. By using more well-tested software modules, the quality of the code is also enhanced.

Let's see design a reusable processing pipeline for the classifiers challenge. As mentioned, we will prepare data once and then use it for all the classifiers.

## Importing data

The historical data for this problem is stored in a file called `dataset` in `.csv` format. We will use the `pd.read_csv` function from pandas to import the data as a data frame:

```
dataset = pd.read_csv('Social_Network_Ads.csv')
```

## Feature selection

The process of selecting features that are relevant to the context of the problem that we want to solve is called **feature selection**. It is an essential part of feature engineering.

Once the file is imported, we drop the User ID column, which is used to identify a person and should be excluded when training a model:

```
dataset = dataset.drop(columns=['User ID'])
```

Now let's preview the dataset:

```
dataset.head(5)
```

The dataset looks like this:

|   | Gender | Age | Estimated Salary | Purchased |
|---|--------|-----|------------------|-----------|
| 0 | Male   | 19  | 19,000           | 0         |
| 1 | Male   | 35  | 20,000           | 0         |
| 2 | Female | 26  | 43,000           | 0         |
| 3 | Female | 27  | 57,000           | 0         |
| 4 | Male   | 19  | 76,000           | 0         |

Now, let's look at how we can further process the input dataset.

## One-hot encoding

Many machine learning algorithms require all the features to be continuous variables. It means that if some of the features are category variables, we need to find a strategy to convert them into continuous variables. One-hot encoding is one of the most effective ways of performing this transformation. For this particular problem, the only category variable we have is Gender. Let's convert that into a continuous variable using one-hot encoding:

```
enc = sklearn.preprocessing.OneHotEncoder()
enc.fit(dataset.iloc[:,[0]])
onehotlabels = enc.transform(dataset.iloc[:,[0]]).toarray()
genders = pd.DataFrame({'Female': onehotlabels[:, 0], 'Male':
onehotlabels[:, 1]})
result = pd.concat([genders,dataset.iloc[:,1:]], axis=1, sort=False)
result.head(5)
```

Once it's converted, let's look at the dataset again:

| | Female | Male | Age | Estimated Salary | Purchased |
|---|---|---|---|---|---|
| 0 | 0.0 | 1.0 | 19 | 19,000 | 0 |
| 1 | 0.0 | 1.0 | 35 | 20,000 | 0 |
| 2 | 1.0 | 0.0 | 26 | 43,000 | 0 |
| 3 | 1.0 | 0.0 | 27 | 57,000 | 0 |
| 4 | 0.0 | 1.0 | 19 | 76,000 | 0 |

Notice that in order to convert a variable from a category variable into a continuous variable, one-hot encoding has converted Gender into two separate columns—Male and Female.

## Specifying the features and label

Let's specify the features and labels. We will use y through this book to represent the label and X to represent the feature set:

```
y=result['Purchased']
X=result.drop(columns=['Purchased'])
```

X represents the feature vector and contains all the input variables that we need to use to train the model.

## Dividing the dataset into testing and training portions

Now, let's divide the training dataset into 25% testing and 75% training portions using sklearn.model_selection import train_test_split:

```
#from sklearn.cross_validation import train_test_split
X_train, X_test, y_train, y_test = train_test_split(X, y, test_size = 0.25,
random_state = 0)
```

This has created the following four data structures:

- X_train: A data structure containing the features of the training data
- X_test: A data structure containing the features of the training test
- y_train: A vector containing the values of the label in the training dataset
- y_test: A vector containing the values of the label in the testing dataset

## Scaling the features

For many machine learning algorithms, it's good practice to scale the variables from 0 to 1. This is also called **feature normalization**. Let's apply the scaling transformation to achieve this:

```
from sklearn.preprocessing import StandardScaler
sc = StandardScaler()
X_train = sc.fit_transform(X_train)
X_test = sc.transform(X_test)
```

After we scale the data, it is ready to be used as input to the different classifiers that we will present in the subsequent sections.

# Evaluating the classifiers

Once the model is trained, we need to evaluate its performance. To do that, we will use the following process:

1. We will divide the labeling dataset into two parts—a training partition and a testing partition. We will use the testing partition to evaluate the trained model.
2. We will use the features of our testing partition to generate labels for each row. This is our set of predicted labels.
3. We will compare the set of predicted labels with the actual labels to evaluate the model.

 Unless we are trying to solve something quite trivial, there will be some misclassifications when we evaluate the model. How we interpret these misclassifications to determine the quality of the model depends on which performance metrics we choose to use.

Once we have both the set of actual labels and the predicted labels, a bunch of performance metrics can be used to evaluate the models. The best metric to quantify the model will depend on the requirements of the business problem that we want to solve, as well as the characteristics of the training dataset.

# Confusion matrix

A confusion matrix is used to summarize the results of the evaluation of a classifier. The confusion matrix for a binary classifier looks as follows:

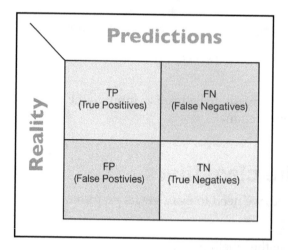

 If the label of the classifier we are training has two levels, it is called a **binary classifier**. The first critical use case of supervised machine learning—specifically, a binary classifier—was during the First World War to differentiate between an aircraft and flying birds.

The classification can be divided into the following four categories:

- **True positives (TP)**: The positive classifications that were correctly classified
- **True Negatives (TN)**: The negative classifications that were correctly classified
- **False Positives (FP)**: The positive classifications that were actually negative
- **False Negatives (FN)**: The negative classifications that were actually positive

Let's see how we can use these four categories to create various performance metrics.

# Performance metrics

Performance metrics are used to quantify the performance of the trained models. Based on this, let's define the following four metrics:

| Metric | Formula |
|---|---|
| Accuracy | $$\frac{TP+TN}{TP+TN+FP+FN}$$ |
| Recall | $$\frac{TP}{TP+FN}=\frac{CorrectlyFlagged}{CorrectlyFlagged+Misses}$$ |
| Precision | $$\frac{TP}{TP+FP}=\frac{CorrectlyFlagged}{CorrectlyFlagged+WronglyFlagged}$$ |
| F1 score | $$2\left(\frac{Precision*Recall}{Precision+Recall}\right)$$ |

Accuracy is the proportion of correction classifications among all predictions. While calculating accuracy, we do not differentiate between TP and TN. Evaluating a model through accuracy is straightforward, but in certain situations, it will not work.

Let's look at the situations where we need more than accuracy to quantify the performance of a model. One of these situations is when we use a model to predict a rare event, such as in the following examples:

- A model to predict the fraudulent transactions in a banks transactional database
- A model to predict the likelihood of mechanical failure of an engine part of an aircraft

In both of these examples, we are trying to predict a rare event. Two additional measures become more important than accuracy in these situations—recall and precision. Let's look at them one by one:

- **Recall**: This calculates the hit rate. In the first of the preceding examples, it is the proportion of fraudulent documents successfully flagged by the model out of all the fraudulent documents. If, in our testing dataset, we had 1 million transactions, out of which 100 were known to be fraudulent, the model was able to identify 78 of them. In this case, the recall value would be 78/100.
- **Precision**: The precision measures how many of the transactions flagged by the model were actually bad. Instead of focusing on the bad transactions that the model failed to flag, we want to determine how precise the bad bins flagged by the model really is.

Note that the F1 score brings both the recall and precision together. If a model has perfect scores for both precision and recall, then its F1 score will be perfect. A high F1 score means that we have trained a high-quality model that has high recall and precision.

# Understanding overfitting

If a machine learning model performs great in a development environment but degrades noticeably in a production environment, we say the model is overfitted. This means the trained model too closely follows the training dataset. It is an indication there are too many details in the rules created by the model. The trade-off between model variance and bias best captures the idea. Let's look at these concepts one by one.

## Bias

Any machine learning model is trained based on certain assumptions. In general, these assumptions are the simplistic approximations of some real-world phenomena. These assumptions simplify the actual relationships between features and their characteristics and make a model easier to train. More assumptions means more bias. So, while training a model, more simplistic assumptions = high bias, and realistic assumptions that are more representative of actual phenomena = low bias.

In linear regression, the non-linearity of the features is ignored and they are approximated as linear variables. So, linear regression models are inherently vulnerable to exhibiting high bias.

## Variance

Variance quantifies how accurately a model estimates the target variable if a different dataset is used to train the model. It quantifies whether the mathematical formulation of our model is a good generalization of the underlying patterns.

Specific overfitted rules based on specific scenarios and situations = high variance, and rules that are generalized and applicable to a variety of scenarios and situations = low variance.

Our goal in machine learning is to train models that exhibit low bias and low variance. Achieving this goal is not always easy and usually keeps data scientists awake at night.

## Bias-variance trade-off

When training a particular machine learning model, it is tricky to decide the right level of generalization for the rules that comprise a trained model. The struggle to come up with the right level of generalization is captured by the bias-variance trade-off.

Note that more simplistic assumptions = more generalization = low variance = high variance.

This trade-off between bias and variance is determined by the choice of algorithm, the characteristics of the data, and various hyperparameters. It is important to achieve the right compromise between the bias and variance based on the requirements of the specific problem you are trying to solve.

# Specifying the phases of classifiers

Once the labeled data is prepared, the development of the classifiers involves training, evaluation, and deployment. These three phases of implementing a classifier are shown in the **CRISP-DM (Cross-Industry Standard Process for Data Mining)** life cycle in the following diagram (the CRISP-DM life cycle was explained in more detail in Chapter 5, *Graph Algorithms*)

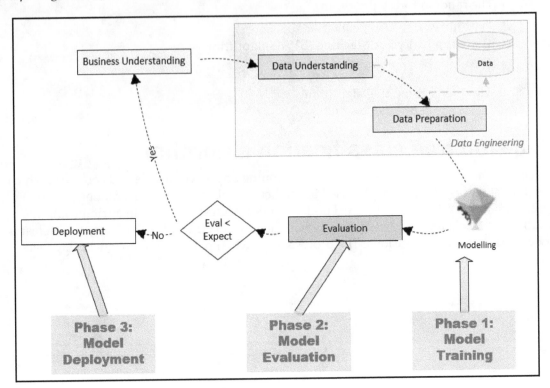

In the first two phases of implementing a classifier—the testing and training phases—we use labeled data. The labeled data is divided into two partitions—a larger partition called the training data and a smaller partition called the testing data. A random sampling technique is used to divide the input labeled data into training and testing partitions to make sure that both partitions contain consistent patterns. Note that, as the preceding diagram shows, first, there is a training phase, where training data is used to train a model. Once the training phase is over, the trained model is evaluated using the testing data. Different performance matrices are used to quantify the performance of the trained model. Once the model is evaluated, we have the model deployment phase, where the trained model is deployed and used for inference to solve real-world problems by labeling unlabeled data.

Now, let's look at some classification algorithms.

We will look at the following classification algorithms in the subsequent sections:

- The decision tree algorithm
- The XGBoost algorithm
- The random forest algorithm
- The logistic regression algorithm
- The **Support Vector Machine** (**SVM**) algorithm
- The naive Bayes algorithm

Let's start with the decision tree algorithm.

# Decision tree classification algorithm

A decision tree is based on the recursive partitioning approach (divide and conquer), which generates a set of rules that can be used to predict a label. It starts with a root node and splits into multiple branches. Internal nodes represent a test on a certain attribute and the result of the test is represented by a branch to the next level. The decision tree ends in leaf nodes that contain the decisions. The process stops when partitioning no longer improves the outcome.

# Understanding the decision tree classification algorithm

The distinguishing feature of decision tree classification is the generation of the human-interpretable hierarchy of rules that are used to predict the label at runtime. The algorithm is recursive in nature. Creating this hierarchy of rules involves the following steps:

1. **Find the most important feature**: Out of all of the features, the algorithm identifies the feature that best differentiates between the data points in the training dataset with respect to the label. The calculation is based on metrics such as information gain or Gini impurity.

2. **Bifurcate**: Using the most identified important feature, the algorithm creates a criterion that is used to divide the training dataset into two branches:
   - Data points that pass the criterion
   - Data points that fail the criterion

3. **Check for leaf nodes**: If any resultant branch mostly contains labels of one class, the branch is made final, resulting in a leaf node.

4. **Check the stopping conditions and repeat**: If the provided stopping conditions are not met, then the algorithm will go back to *step 1* for the next iteration. Otherwise, the model is marked as trained and each node of the resultant decision tree at the lowest level is labeled as a leaf node. The stopping condition can be as simple as defining the number of iterations, or the default stopping condition can be used, where the algorithm stops as soon it reaches a certain homogeneity level for each of the leaf nodes.

The decision tree algorithm can be explained by the following diagram:

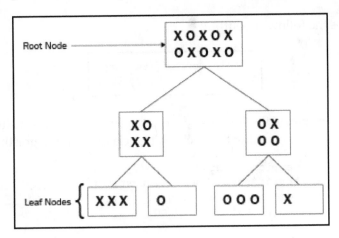

In the preceding diagram, the root contains a bunch of circles and crosses. The algorithm creates a criterion that tries to separate the circles from the crosses. At each level, the decision tree creates partitions of the data, which are expected to be more and more homogeneous from level 1 upward. A perfect classifier has leaf nodes that only contain circles or crosses. Training perfect classifiers is usually difficult due to the inherent randomness of the training dataset.

# Using the decision tree classification algorithm for the classifiers challenge

Now, let's use the decision tree classification algorithm for the common problem that we previously defined to predict whether a customer ends up purchasing a product:

1. To do, first, let's instantiate the decision tree classification algorithm and train a model using the training portion of the data that we prepared for our classifiers:

```
classifier = sklearn.tree.DecisionTreeClassifier(criterion = 'entropy', random_state = 100, max_depth=2)
classifier.fit(X_train, y_train)
```

2. Now, let's use our trained model to predict the labels for the testing portion of our labeled data. Let's generate a confusion matrix that can summarize the performance of our trained model:

```
import sklearn.metrics as metrics
y_pred = classifier.predict(X_test)
cm = metrics.confusion_matrix(y_test, y_pred)
cm
```

This gives the following output:

```
Out[22]:  array([[64,  4],
                 [ 2, 30]])
```

3. Now, let's calculate the accuracy, recall, and precision values for the created classifier by using the decision tree classification algorithm:

```
accuracy= metrics.accuracy_score(y_test,y_pred)
recall = metrics.recall_score(y_test,y_pred)
precision = metrics.precision_score(y_test,y_pred)
print(accuracy,recall,precision)
```

4. Running the preceding code will produce the following output:

```
0.94 0.9375 0.8823529411764706
```

The performance measures help us compare different training modeling techniques with each other.

# The strengths and weaknesses of decision tree classifiers

In this section, let's look at the strengths and weaknesses of using the decision tree classification algorithm.

## Strengths

The following are the strengths of decision tree classifiers:

- The rules of the models created by using a decision tree algorithm are interpretable by humans. Models such as this are called **whitebox models**. Whitebox models are a requirement whenever transparency is needed to trace the details and reasons for decisions that are made by the model. This transparency is essential in applications where we want to prevent bias and protect vulnerable communities. For example, a whitebox model is generally a requirement for critical use cases in government and insurance industries.
- Decision tree classifiers are designed to extract information from discrete problem space. This means that most of the features are category variables, so using a decision tree to train the model is a good choice.

## Weaknesses

The following are the weaknesses of decision tree classifiers:

- If the tree generated by the decision tree classifier goes too deep, the rules capture too many details, resulting in an overfitted model. While using a decision tree algorithm, we need to be aware that decision trees are vulnerable to overfitting and so we need to prune the tree, whenever necessary, to prevent this.
- A weakness of decision tree classifiers is their inability to capture non-linear relationships in the rules that they create.

# Use cases

In this section, let's look at the use cases that the decision tree algorithm is used for.

## Classifying records

Decision trees classifiers can be used to classify data points, such as in the following examples:

- **Mortgage applications**: To train a binary classifier to determine whether an applicant is likely to default.
- **Customer segmentation**: To categorize customers into high-worth, medium-worth, and low-worth customers so that marketing strategies can be customized for each category.
- **Medical diagnosis**: To train a classifier that can categorize a benign or malignant growth.
- **Treatment-effectiveness analysis**: To train a classifier that can flag patients that have reacted positively to a particular treatment.

## Feature selection

The decision tree classification algorithm selects a small subset of features to create rules for. That feature selection can be used to select the features for another machine learning algorithm when you have a large number of features.

# Understanding the ensemble methods

An ensemble is a method, in machine learning, of creating more than one slightly different model using different parameters and then combining them into an aggregate model. In order to create effective ensembles, we need to find what our aggregation criterion is to generate the resultant model. Let's look at some ensemble algorithms.

# Implementing gradient boosting with the XGBoost algorithm

XGBoost was created in 2014 and is based on gradient-boosting principles. It has become one of the most popular ensemble classification algorithms. It generates a bunch of interrelated trees and uses gradient descent to minimize the residual error. This makes it a perfect fit for distributed infrastructures, such as Apache Spark, or for cloud computing, such as Google Cloud or **Amazon Web Services** (**AWS**).

Let's now see how we can implement gradient boosting with the XGBoost algorithm:

1. First, we will instantiate the XGBClassfier classifier and train the model using the training portion of the data:

```
In [20]:  from xgboost import XGBClassifier
          classifier = XGBClassifier()
          classifier.fit(X_train, y_train)

Out[20]:  XGBClassifier(base_score=0.5, booster='gbtree', colsample_bylevel=1,
                        colsample_bynode=1, colsample_bytree=1, gamma=0,
                        learning_rate=0.1, max_delta_step=0, max_depth=3,
                        min_child_weight=1, missing=None, n_estimators=100, n_jobs=1,
                        nthread=None, objective='binary:logistic', random_state=0,
                        reg_alpha=0, reg_lambda=1, scale_pos_weight=1, seed=None,
                        silent=None, subsample=1, verbosity=1)
```

2. Then, we will generate predictions based on the newly trained model:

```
y_pred = classifier.predict(X_test)
cm = metrics.confusion_matrix(y_test, y_pred)
cm
```

The produces the following output :

```
Out[21]:  array([[64,  4],
                 [ 3, 29]])
```

3. Finally, we will quantify the performance of the model:

```
accuracy= metrics.accuracy_score(y_test,y_pred)
recall = metrics.recall_score(y_test,y_pred)
precision = metrics.precision_score(y_test,y_pred)
print(accuracy,recall,precision)
```

This gives us the following output:

```
0.93 0.90625 0.8787878787878788
```

Next, let's look at the random forest algorithm.

# Using the random forest algorithm

Random forest is a type of ensemble method that works by combining several decision trees to decrease both the bias and the variance.

### Training a random forest algorithm

In training, this algorithm takes $N$ samples from the training data and creates $m$ subsets of our overall data. These subsets are created by randomly selecting some of the rows and columns of the input data. The algorithm builds $m$ independent decision trees. These classification trees are represented by $C_1$ to $C_m$.

### Using random forest for predictions

Once the model is trained, it can be used to label new data. Each of the individual trees generates a label. The final prediction is determined by voting these individual predictions, as shown:

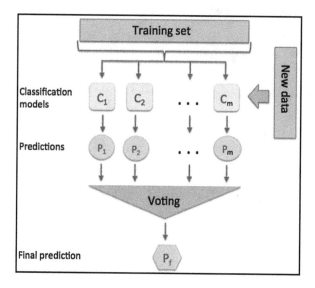

Note that in the preceding diagram, *m* trees are trained, which is represented by $C_1$ to $C_m$. That is Trees = $\{C_1,..,C_m\}$

Each of the trees generates a prediction that is represented by a set:

Individual predictions = P= $\{P_1,..., P_m\}$

The final prediction is represented by $P_f$. It is determined by the majority of the individual predictions. The mode function can be used to find the majority decision (mode is the number that repeats most often and is in the majority). The individual prediction and the final prediction are linked, as follows:

$P_f$ = mode (P)

## Differentiating the random forest algorithm from ensemble boosting

Each of the trees generated by the random forest algorithm is totally independent of each other. It is not aware of any of the details of the other trees in the ensemble. This differentiates it from other techniques, such as ensemble boosting.

# Using the random forest algorithm for the classifiers challenge

Let's instantiate the random forest algorithm and use it to train our model using the training data.

There are two key hyperparameters that we'll be looking at here:

- n_estimators
- max_depth

The n_estimators hyperparameter controls how many individual decision trees are built and the max_depth hyperparameter controls how deep each of these individual decision trees can go.

So, in other words, a decision tree can keep splitting and splitting until it has a node that represents every given example in the training set. By setting `max_depth`, we constrain how many levels of splits it can make. This controls the complexity of the model and determines how closely it fits the training data. If we refer to the following output, `n_estimators` controls the width of the random forest model and `max_depth` controls the depth of the model:

```
from sklearn.ensemble import RandomForestClassifier
classifier = RandomForestClassifier(n_estimators = 10, max_depth = 4,criterion = 'entropy', random_state = 0)
classifier.fit(X_train, y_train)
```
```
Out[9]:  RandomForestClassifier(bootstrap=True, class_weight=None, criterion='entropy',
                    max_depth=4, max_features='auto', max_leaf_nodes=None,
                    min_impurity_decrease=0.0, min_impurity_split=None,
                    min_samples_leaf=1, min_samples_split=2,
                    min_weight_fraction_leaf=0.0, n_estimators=10,
                    n_jobs=None, oob_score=False, random_state=0, verbose=0,
                    warm_start=False)
```

Once the random forest model is trained, let's use it for predictions:

```
y_pred = classifier.predict(X_test)
cm = metrics.confusion_matrix(y_test, y_pred)
cm
```

Which gives the output as:

```
Out[10]:  array([[64,  4],
                 [ 3, 29]])
```

Now, let's quantify how good our model is:

```
accuracy= metrics.accuracy_score(y_test,y_pred)
recall = metrics.recall_score(y_test,y_pred)
precision = metrics.precision_score(y_test,y_pred)
print(accuracy,recall,precision)
```

We will observe the following output:

```
0.93 0.90625 0.8787878787878788
```

Next, let's look into logistic regression.

# Logistic regression

Logistic regression is a classification algorithm used for binary classification. It uses a logistic function to formulate the interaction between the input features and the target variable. It is one of the simplest classification techniques that is used to model a binary dependent variable.

## Assumptions

Logistic regression assumes the following:

- The training dataset does not have a missing value.
- The label is a binary category variable.
- The label is ordinal—in other words, a categorical variable with ordered values.
- All features or input variables are independent of each other.

## Establishing the relationship

For logistic regression, the predicted value is calculated as follows:

$\acute{y} = \sigma(wX + j)$

Let's suppose that $z = wX + j$.

So now:

$$\sigma(z) = \frac{1}{1 + e^{-z}}$$

The preceding relationship can be graphically shown as follows:

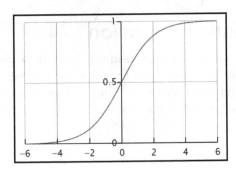

Note that if $z$ is large, $\sigma(z)$ will equal 1. If $z$ is very small or a large negative number, $\sigma(z)$ will equal 0. So, the objective of logistic regression is to find the correct values for $w$ and $j$.

Logistic regression is named after the function that is used to formulate it, called the **logistic** or **sigmoid function**.

## The loss and cost functions

The `loss` function defines how we want to quantify an error for a particular example in our training data. The `cost` function defines how we want to minimize an error in our entire training dataset. So, the `loss` function is used for one of the examples in the training dataset and the `cost` function is used for the overall cost that quantifies the overall deviation of the actual and predicted values. It is dependent on the choice of $w$ and $h$.

The `loss` function used in logistic regression is as follows:

$$Loss\ (\hat{y}^{(i)},\ y^{(i)}) = - (y^{(i)} log\ \hat{y}^{(i)} + (1 - y^{(i)})\ log\ (1 - \hat{y}^{(i)})$$

Note that when $y^{(i)} = 1$, $Loss(\hat{y}^{(i)}, y^{(i)}) = - log\hat{y}^{(i)}$. Minimizing the loss will result in a large value of $\hat{y}^{(i)}$. Being a sigmoid function, the maximum value will be 1.

If $y^{(i)} = 0$, $Loss\ (\hat{y}^{(i)}, y^{(i)}) = - log\ (1 - \hat{y}^{(i)})$. Minimizing the loss will result in $\hat{y}^{(i)}$ being as small as possible, which is 0.

The cost function of logistic regression is as follows:

$$Cost(w, b) = \frac{1}{b} \sum Loss(\hat{y}^{(i)}, y^{(i)})$$

## When to use logistic regression

Logistic regression works great for binary classifiers. Logistic regression doesn't do very well when the data is huge but the quality of the data is not great. It can capture relationships that aren't too complex. While it doesn't usually generate the greatest performance, it does set a very nice benchmark to start.

# Using the logistic regression algorithm for the classifiers challenge

In this section, we will see how we can use the logistic regression algorithm for the classifiers challenge:

1. First, let's instantiate a logistic regression model and train it using the training data:

```
from sklearn.linear_model import LogisticRegression
classifier = LogisticRegression(random_state = 0)
classifier.fit(X_train, y_train)
```

2. Let's predict the values of the test data and create a confusion matrix:

```
y_pred = classifier.predict(X_test)
cm = metrics.confusion_matrix(y_test, y_pred)
cm
```

We get the following output upon running the preceding code:

```
Out[11]: array([[65,  3],
                 [ 6, 26]])
```

3. Now, let's look at the performance metrics:

```
accuracy= metrics.accuracy_score(y_test,y_pred)
recall = metrics.recall_score(y_test,y_pred)
precision = metrics.precision_score(y_test,y_pred)
print(accuracy,recall,precision)
```

4. We get the following output upon running the preceding code:

```
0.91 0.8125 0.896551724137931
```

Next, let's look at **SVM**.

# The SVM algorithm

Now, let's look at SVM. SVM is a classifier that finds an optimal hyperplane that maximizes the margin between two classes. In SVMs, our optimization objective is to maximize the margin. The margin is defined as the distance between the separating hyperplane (the decision boundary) and the training samples that are closest to this hyperplane, called the **support vectors**. So, let's start with a very basic example with only two dimensions, $X1$ and $X2$. We want a line to separate the circles from the crosses. This is shown in the following diagram:

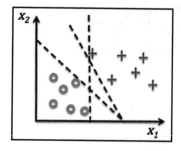

We have drawn two lines and both perfectly separate the crosses from the circles. However, there has to be an optimal line, or decision boundary, that gives us the best chance to correctly classify most of the additional examples. A reasonable choice may be a line that is evenly spaced between these two classes to give a little bit of a buffer for each class, as shown:

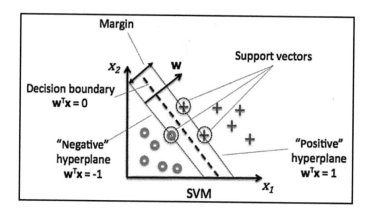

Now, let's see how we can use SVM to train a classifier for our challenge.

# Using the SVM algorithm for the classifiers challenge

1. First, let's instantiate the SVM classifier and then use the training portion of the labeled data to train it. The `kernel` hyperparameter determines the type of transformation that is applied to the input data in order to make it linearly separable.:

```
from sklearn.svm import SVC
classifier = SVC(kernel = 'linear', random_state = 0)
classifier.fit(X_train, y_train)
```

2. Once trained, let's generate some predictions and look at the confusion matrix:

```
y_pred = classifier.predict(X_test)
cm = metrics.confusion_matrix(y_test, y_pred)
cm
```

3. Observe the following output:

```
Out[9]: array([[66,  2],
               [ 9, 23]])
```

4. Now, let's look at the various performance metrics:

```
accuracy= metrics.accuracy_score(y_test,y_pred)
recall = metrics.recall_score(y_test,y_pred)
precision = metrics.precision_score(y_test,y_pred)
print(accuracy,recall,precision)
```

After running the preceding code, we get the following values as our output:

```
0.89 0.71875 0.92
```

# Understanding the naive Bayes algorithm

Based on probability theory, naive Bayes is one of the simplest classification algorithms. If used properly, it can come up with accurate predictions. The Naive Bayes Algorithm is s0-named for two reasons:

- It is based on a naive assumption that there is independence between the features and the input variable.
- It is based on Bayes, theorem.

This algorithm tries to classify instances based on the probabilities of the preceding attributes/instances, assuming complete attribute independence.

There are three types of events:

- **Independent** events do not affect the probability of another event occurring (for example, receiving an email offering you free entry to a tech event *and* a re-organization occurring in your company).
- **Dependent** events affect the probability of another event occurring; that is, they are linked in some way (for example, the probability of you getting to a conference on time could be affected by an airline staff strike or flights that may not run on time).
- **Mutually exclusive** events cannot occur simultaneously (for example, the probability of rolling a three and a six on a single dice roll is 0—these two outcomes are mutually exclusive).

# Bayes, theorem

Bayes, theorem is used to calculate the conditional probability between two independent events, $A$ and $B$. The probability of events $A$ and $B$ happening is represented by $P(A)$ and $P(B)$. The conditional probability is represented by $P(B|A)$, which is the conditional probability that event $B$ will happen given that event $A$ has occurred:

$$P(A|B) = \frac{P(B|A)P(A)}{P(B)}$$

# Calculating probabilities

Naive Bayes is based on probability fundamentals. The probability of a single event occurring (the observational probability) is calculated by taking the number of times the event occurred and dividing it by the total number of processes that could have led to that event. For example, a call center receives over 100 support calls per day, 50 times over the course of a month. You want to know the probability that a call is responded to in under 3 minutes based on the previous times it was responded to. If the call center manages to match this time record on 27 occasions, then the observational probability of 100 calls being answered in under 3 minutes is as follows:

*P(100 support calls in under 3 mins) = (27 / 50) = 0.54 (54%)*

100 calls can be responded to in under 3 minutes in about half the time, based on records of the 50 times it occurred in the past.

## Multiplication rules for AND events

To calculate the probability of two or more events occurring simultaneously, consider whether events are independent or dependent. If they are independent, the simple multiplication rule is used:

*P(outcome 1 AND outcome 2) = P(outcome 1) \* P(outcome 2)*

For example, to calculate the probability of receiving an email with free entry to a tech event *and* re-organization occurring in your workplace, this simple multiplication rule would be used. The two events are independent as the occurrence of one does not affect the chance of the other occurring

If receiving the tech event email has a probability of 31% and the probability of staff re-organization is 82%, then the probability of both occurring is calculated as follows:

P(email AND re-organization) = P(email) \* P(re-organization) = (0.31) \* (0.82) = 0.2542 (25%)

## The general multiplication rule

If two or more events are dependent, the general multiplication rule is used. This formula is actually valid in both cases of independent and dependent events:

*P(outcome 1 AND outcome 2)=P(outcome 1)\*P(outcome 2 | outcome 1)*

Note that `P(outcome 2 | outcome 1)` refers to the conditional probability of `outcome 2` occurring given `outcome 1` has already occurred. The formula incorporates the dependence between the events. If the events are independent, then the conditional probability is irrelevant as one outcome does not influence the chance of the other occurring, and `P(outcome 2 | outcome 1)` is simply `P(outcome 2)`. Note that the formula in this case just becomes the simple multiplication rule.

## Addition rules for OR events

When calculating the probability of either one event or the other occurring (mutually exclusive), the following simple addition rule is used:

*P(outcome 1 OR outcome 2) = P(outcome 1) + P(outcome 2)*

For example, what is the probability of rolling a 6 or a 3? To answer this question, first, note that both outcomes cannot occur simultaneously. The probability of rolling a 6 is (1 / 6) and the same can be said for rolling a 3:

*P(6 OR 3) = (1 / 6) + (1 / 6) = 0.33 (33%)*

If the events are not mutually exclusive and can occur simultaneously, use the following general addition formula, which is always valid in both cases of mutual exclusiveness and of non-mutual exclusiveness:

*P(outcome 1 OR outcome 2) = P(outcome 1) + P(outcome 2) P(outcome 1 AND outcome 2)*

# Using the naive Bayes algorithm for the classifiers challenge

Now, let's use the naive Bayes algorithm to solve the classifiers challenge:

1. First, we import the `GaussianNB()` function and use it to train the model:

```
from sklearn.naive_bayes import GaussianNB
classifier = GaussianNB()
classifier.fit(X_train, y_train)
```

2. Now, let's use the trained model to predict the results. We will use it to predict the labels for our test partition, which is `X_test`:

```
Predicting the Test set results
y_pred = classifier.predict(X_test)
cm = metrics.confusion_matrix(y_test, y_pred)
cm
```

3. Now, let's print the confusion matrix:

```
Out[10]: array([[66,  2],
                 [ 6, 26]])
```

4. Now, let's print the performance matrices to quantify the quality of our trained model:

```
accuracy= metrics.accuracy_score(y_test,y_pred)
recall = metrics.recall_score(y_test,y_pred)
precision = metrics.precision_score(y_test,y_pred)
print(accuracy,recall,precision)
```

Which gives the output as:

```
0.92 0.8125 0.9285714285714286
```

# For classification algorithms, the winner is...

Let's look at the performance metrics of the various algorithms we have presented. This is summarized in the following table:

| Algorithm | Accuracy | Recall | Precision |
|---|---|---|---|
| Decision tree | 0.94 | 0.93 | 0.88 |
| XGBoost | 0.93 | 0.90 | 0.87 |
| Random forest | 0.93 | 0.90 | 0.87 |
| Logistic regression | 0.91 | 0.81 | 0.89 |
| SVM | 0.89 | 0.71 | 0.92 |
| Naive Bayes | 0.92 | 0.81 | 0.92 |

Looking at the preceding table, we can observe that the decision tree classifier performs the best in terms of accuracy and recall. If we are looking for precision, then there is a tie between SVM and naive Bayes, so either one will work for us.

# Understanding regression algorithms

The supervised machine learning model uses one of the regression algorithms if the target variable is a continuous variable. In this case, the machine learning model is called a regressor.

In this section, we will present various algorithms that can be used to train a supervised machine learning regression model—or simply, regressors. Before we go into the details of the algorithms, let's first create a challenge for these algorithms to test their performance, abilities, and effectiveness on.

# Presenting the regressors challenge

Similar to the approach that we used with the classification algorithms, we will first present a problem to be solved as a challenge for all regression algorithms. We will call this common problem as the regressors challenge. Then, we will use three different regression algorithms to address the challenge. This approach of using a common challenge for different regression algorithms has two benefits:

- We can prepare the data once and used the prepared data on all three regression algorithms.
- We can compare the performance of three regression algorithms in a meaningful way as we will use them to solve the same problem.

Let's look at the problem statement of the challenge.

# The problem statement of the regressors challenge

Predicting the mileage of different vehicles is important these days. An efficient vehicle is good for the environment and is also cost-effective. The mileage can be estimated from the power of the engine and the characteristics of the vehicle. Let's create a challenge for regressors to train a model that can predict the **Miles Per Gallon** (**MPG**) of a vehicle based on its characteristics.

Let's look at the historical dataset that we will use to train the regressors.

### Exploring the historical dataset

The following are the features of the historical dataset data that we have:

| Name | Type | Description |
|---|---|---|
| NAME | Category | Identifies a particular vehicle |
| CYLINDERS | Continuous | The number of cylinders (between 4 and 8) |
| DISPLACEMENT | Continuous | The displacement of the engine in cubic.inches |
| HORSEPOWER | Continuous | The horsepower of the engine |
| ACCELERATION | Continuous | The time it takes to accelerate from 0 to 60 mph (in seconds) |

The target variable for this problem is a continuous variable, MPG, that specifies the mpg for each of the vehicles.

Let's first design the data processing pipeline for this problem.

# Feature engineering using a data processing pipeline

Let's see how we can design a reusable processing pipeline to address the regressors challenge. As mentioned, we will prepare the data once and then use it in all the regression algorithms. Let's follow these steps:

1. We start by importing the dataset, as follows:

```
dataset = pd.read_csv('auto.csv')
```

2. Let's now preview the dataset:

```
dataset.head(5)
```

This is how the dataset will look:

| | NAME | CYLINDERS | DISPLACEMENT | HORSEPOWER | WEIGHT | ACCELERATION | MPG |
|---|---|---|---|---|---|---|---|
| 0 | chevrolet chevelle malibu | 8 | 307.0 | 130 | 3504 | 12.0 | 18.0 |
| 1 | buick skylark 320 | 8 | 350.0 | 165 | 3693 | 11.5 | 15.0 |
| 2 | plymouth satellite | 8 | 318.0 | 150 | 3436 | 11.0 | 18.0 |
| 3 | amc rebel sst | 8 | 304.0 | 150 | 3433 | 12.0 | 16.0 |
| 4 | ford torino | 8 | 302.0 | 140 | 3449 | 10.5 | 17.0 |

3. Now, let's proceed on to feature selection. Let's drop the NAME column as it is only an identifier that is needed for cars. Columns that are used to identify the rows in our dataset are not relevant for training the model. Let's drop this column:

```
dataset=dataset.drop(columns=['NAME'])
```

4. Let's convert all of the input variables and impute all the null values:

```
dataset=dataset.drop(columns=['NAME'])
dataset= dataset.apply(pd.to_numeric, errors='coerce')
dataset.fillna(0, inplace=True)
```

Imputation improves the quality of the data and prepares it to be used to train the model. Now, let's see the final step:

5. Let's divide the data into testing and training partitions:

```
from sklearn.model_selection import train_test_split
#from sklearn.cross_validation import train_test_split
```

```
X_train, X_test, y_train, y_test = train_test_split(X, y, test_size
= 0.25, random_state = 0)
```

This has created the following four data structures:

- X_train: A data structure containing the features of the training data
- X_test: A data structure containing the features of the training test
- y_train: A vector containing the values of the label in the training dataset
- y_test: A vector containing the values of the label in the testing dataset

Now, let's use the prepared data on three different regressors so that we can compare their performance.

# Linear regression

Of all the supervised machine learning techniques, the linear regression algorithm is the easiest one to understand. We will first look at simple linear regression and then we will expand the concept to multiple linear regression.

## Simple linear regression

In its simplest form, linear regression formulates the relationship between a single continuous independent variable and a single continuous independent variable. A (simple) regression is used to show the extent that changes in a dependent variable (shown on the y-axis) can be attributed to changes in an explanatory variable (shown on the x-axis). It can be represented as follows:

$$\acute{y} = (X)w + \alpha$$

This formula can be explained as follows:

- $y$ is the dependent variable.
- $X$ is the independent variable.
- $w$ is the slope that indicates how much the line rises for each increase in $X$.
- $\alpha$ is the intercept that indicates the value of $y$ when $X = 0$.

Some examples of relationships between a single continuous dependent variable and a single continuous independent variable are as follows:

- A person's weight and their calories intake
- The price of a house and its area in square feet in a particular neighborhood
- The humidity in the air and the likelihood of rain

For linear regression, both the input (independent) variable and the target (dependent) variable must be numeric. The best relationship is found by minimizing the sum of the squares of the vertical distances of each point from a line drawn through all the points. It is assumed that the relationship is linear between the predictor variable and the target variable. For example, the more money invested in research and development, the higher the sales.

Let's look at a specific example. Let's try to formulate the relationship between marketing expenditures and sales for a particular product. They are found to be directly relational to each other. The marketing expenditures and sales are drawn on a two-dimensional graph and are shown as blue diamonds. The relationship can best be approximated by drawing a straight line, as in the following graph:

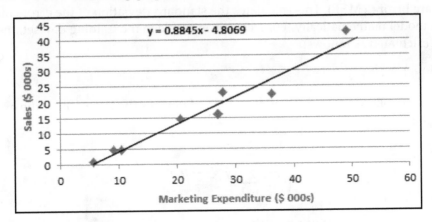

Once the linear line is drawn, we can see the mathematical relationship between the marketing expenditure and sales.

# Evaluating the regressors

The linear line that we drew is an approximation of the relationship between the dependent and independent variables. Even the best line will have some deviation from the actual values, as shown:

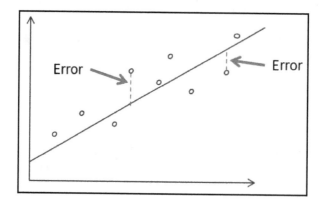

A typical way of quantifying the performance of linear regression models is by using **Root Mean Square Error** (**RMSE**). This calculates the standard deviation of the errors made by the trained model mathematically. For a certain example in the training dataset, the `loss` function is calculated as follows:

Loss $(ý^{(i)}, y^{(i)}) = 1/2(ý^{(i)} - y^{(i)})^2$

This leads to the following `cost` function, which minimizes the loss of all of the examples in the training set:

$$\sqrt{\frac{1}{n}\sum_{i=1}^{n}(ý^{(i)} - y^i)^2}$$

Let's try to interpret RMSE. If RMSE is $50 for our example model that predicts the price of a product, this means that around 68.2% of the predictions will fall within $50 of the true value (that is, $\alpha$). It also means that 95% of the predictions will fall within $100 (that is, $2\alpha$) of the actual value. Finally, 99.7% of the predictions will fall within $150 of the actual value.

# Multiple regression

The fact is that most real-world analyses have more than one independent variable. Multiple regression is an extension of simple linear regression. The key difference is that there are additional beta coefficients for the additional predictor variables. When training a model, the goal is to find the beta coefficients that minimize the errors of the linear equation. Let's try to mathematically formulate the relationship between the dependent variable and the set of independent variables (features).

Similar to a simple linear equation, the dependent variable, $y$, is quantified as the sum of an intercept term plus the product of the $\beta$ coefficients multiplied by the $x$ value for each of the $i$ features:

$$y = \alpha + \beta_1 x_1 + \beta_2 x2 + ... + \beta_i x_i + \varepsilon$$

The error is represented by $\varepsilon$ and indicates that the predictions are not perfect.

The $\beta$ coefficients allow each feature to have a separate estimated effect on the value of $y$ because of $y$ changes by an amount of $\beta_i$ for each unit increase in $x_i$. Moreover, the intercept ($\alpha$) indicates the expected value of $y$ when the independent variables are all 0.

Note that all the variables in the preceding equation can be represented by a bunch of vectors. The target and predictor variables are now vectors with a row and the regression coefficients, $\beta$, and errors, $\varepsilon$, are also vectors.

# Using the linear regression algorithm for the regressors challenge

Now, let's train the model using the training portion of the dataset:

1. Let's start by importing the linear regression package:

```
from sklearn.linear_model import LinearRegression
```

2. Then, let's instantiate the linear regression model and train it using the training dataset:

```
regressor = LinearRegression()
regressor.fit(X_train, y_train)
```

3. Now, let's predict the results using the test portion of the dataset:

```
y_pred = regressor.predict(X_test)
from sklearn.metrics import mean_squared_error
from math import sqrt
sqrt(mean_squared_error(y_test, y_pred))
```

4. The output generated by running the preceding code will generate the following:

```
Out[10]: 4.36214129677179
```

As discussed in the preceding section, RMSE is the standard deviation of the error. It indicates that 68.2% of predictions will fall within 4.36 of the value of the target variable.

# When is linear regression used?

Linear regression is used to solve many real-world problems, including the following:

- Sales forecasting
- Predicting optimum product prices
- Quantifying the causal relationship between an event and the response, such as in clinical drug trials, engineering safety tests, or marketing research
- Identifying patterns that can be used to forecast future behavior, given known criteria—for example, predicting insurance claims, natural disaster damage, election results, and crime rates

# The weaknesses of linear regression

The weaknesses of linear regression are as follows:

- It only works with numerical features.
- Categorical data needs to be preprocessed.
- It does not cope well with missing data.
- It makes assumptions about the data.

# The regression tree algorithm

The regression tree algorithm is similar to the classification tree algorithm, except the target variable is a continuous variable, not a category variable.

## Using the regression tree algorithm for the regressors challenge

In this section, we will see how a regression tree algorithm can be used for the regressors challenge:

1. First, we train the model using a regression tree algorithm:

```
In [43]:  from sklearn.tree import DecisionTreeRegressor
          regressor = DecisionTreeRegressor(max_depth=3)
          regressor.fit(X_train, y_train)

Out[43]:  DecisionTreeRegressor(criterion='mse', max_depth=4, max_features=None,
                        max_leaf_nodes=None, min_impurity_decrease=0.0,
                        min_impurity_split=None, min_samples_leaf=1,
                        min_samples_split=2, min_weight_fraction_leaf=0.0,
                        presort=False, random_state=None, splitter='best')
```

2. Once the regression tree model is trained, we use the trained model to predict the values:

```
y_pred = regressor.predict(X_test)
```

3. Then, we calculate RMSE to quantify the performance of the model:

```
from sklearn.metrics import mean_squared_error
from math import sqrt
sqrt(mean_squared_error(y_test, y_pred))
```

We get the following output:

```
Out[45]:  5.2771702288377
```

# The gradient boost regression algorithm

Let's now look at the gradient boost regression algorithm. It uses an ensemble of decision trees in an effort to better formulate the underlying patterns in data.

## Using gradient boost regression algorithm for the regressors challenge

In this section, we will see how we can use the gradient boost regression algorithm for the regressors challenge:

1. First, we train the model using the gradient boost regression algorithm:

```
In [5]:  from sklearn import ensemble
         params = {'n_estimators': 500, 'max_depth': 4, 'min_samples_split': 2,
                   'learning_rate': 0.01, 'loss': 'ls'}
         regressor = ensemble.GradientBoostingRegressor(**params)

         regressor.fit(X_train, y_train)

Out[5]:  GradientBoostingRegressor(alpha=0.9, criterion='friedman_mse', init=None,
                     learning_rate=0.01, loss='ls', max_depth=4,
                     max_features=None, max_leaf_nodes=None,
                     min_impurity_decrease=0.0, min_impurity_split=None,
                     min_samples_leaf=1, min_samples_split=2,
                     min_weight_fraction_leaf=0.0, n_estimators=500,
                     n_iter_no_change=None, presort='auto',
                     random_state=None, subsample=1.0, tol=0.0001,
                     validation_fraction=0.1, verbose=0, warm_start=False)
```

2. Once the gradient regression algorithm model is trained, we use it to predict the values:

```
y_pred = regressor.predict(X_test)
```

3. Finally, we calculate RMSE to quantify the performance of the model:

```
from sklearn.metrics import mean_squared_error
from math import sqrt
sqrt(mean_squared_error(y_test, y_pred))
```

4. Running this will give us the output value, as follows:

```
Out[7]:  4.034836373089085
```

# For regression algorithms, the winner is...

Let's look at the performance of the three regression algorithms that we used on the same data and exactly the same use case:

| Algorithm | RMSE |
|---|---|
| Linear regression | 4.36214129677179 |
| Regression tree | 5.2771702288377 |
| Gradient boost regression | 4.034836373089085 |

Looking at the performance of all the regression algorithms, it is obvious that the performance of gradient boost regression is the best as it has the lowest RMSE. This is followed by linear regression. The regression tree algorithm performed the worst for this problem.

# Practical example – how to predict the weather

Let's see how we can use the concepts developed in this chapter to predict the weather. Let's assume that we want to predict whether it will rain tomorrow based on the data collected over a year for a particular city.

The data available to train this model is in the CSV file called weather.csv:

1. Let's import the data as a pandas data frame:

```
import numpy as np
import pandas as pd
df = pd.read_csv("weather.csv")
```

2. Let's look at the columns of the data frame:

```
In [63]:  df.columns

Out[63]:  Index(['Date', 'MinTemp', 'MaxTemp', 'Rainfall', 'Evaporation', 'Sunshine',
                  'WindGustDir', 'WindGustSpeed', 'WindDir9am', 'WindDir3pm',
                  'WindSpeed9am', 'WindSpeed3pm', 'Humidity9am', 'Humidity3pm',
                  'Pressure9am', 'Pressure3pm', 'Cloud9am', 'Cloud3pm', 'Temp9am',
                  'Temp3pm', 'RainToday', 'RISK_MM', 'RainTomorrow'],
                 dtype='object')
```

3. Next, let's look at the header of the first 13 columns of the `weather.csv` data:

```
In [124]:  df.iloc[:,0:12].head()
Out[124]:
```

|   | Date | MinTemp | MaxTemp | Rainfall | Evaporation | Sunshine | WindGustDir | WindGustSpeed | WindDir9am | WindDir3pm | WindSpeed9am | WindSpeed3pm |
|---|------|---------|---------|----------|-------------|----------|-------------|---------------|------------|------------|--------------|--------------|
| 0 | 2007-11-01 | 8.0 | 24.3 | 0.0 | 3.4 | 6.3 | 7 | 30.0 | 12 | 7 | 6.0 | 20 |
| 1 | 2007-11-02 | 14.0 | 26.9 | 3.6 | 4.4 | 9.7 | 1 | 39.0 | 0 | 13 | 4.0 | 17 |
| 2 | 2007-11-03 | 13.7 | 23.4 | 3.6 | 5.8 | 3.3 | 7 | 85.0 | 3 | 5 | 6.0 | 6 |
| 3 | 2007-11-04 | 13.3 | 15.5 | 39.8 | 7.2 | 9.1 | 7 | 54.0 | 14 | 13 | 30.0 | 24 |
| 4 | 2007-11-05 | 7.6 | 16.1 | 2.8 | 5.6 | 10.6 | 10 | 50.0 | 10 | 2 | 20.0 | 28 |

4. Now, let's look at the last 10 columns of the `weather.csv` data:

```
In [127]:  df.iloc[:,12:25].head()
Out[127]:
```

|   | Humidity9am | Humidity3pm | Pressure9am | Pressure3pm | Cloud9am | Cloud3pm | Temp9am | Temp3pm | RainToday | RISK_MM | RainTomorrow |
|---|-------------|-------------|-------------|-------------|----------|----------|---------|---------|-----------|---------|--------------|
| 0 | 68 | 29 | 1019.7 | 1015.0 | 7 | 7 | 14.4 | 23.6 | 0 | 3.6 | 1 |
| 1 | 80 | 36 | 1012.4 | 1008.4 | 5 | 3 | 17.5 | 25.7 | 1 | 3.6 | 1 |
| 2 | 82 | 69 | 1009.5 | 1007.2 | 8 | 7 | 15.4 | 20.2 | 1 | 39.8 | 1 |
| 3 | 62 | 56 | 1005.5 | 1007.0 | 2 | 7 | 13.5 | 14.1 | 1 | 2.8 | 1 |
| 4 | 68 | 49 | 1018.3 | 1018.5 | 7 | 7 | 11.1 | 15.4 | 1 | 0.0 | 0 |

5. Let's use `x` to represent the input features. We will drop the `Date` field for the feature list as it is not useful in the context of predictions. We will also drop the `RainTomorrow` label:

```
x = df.drop(['Date','RainTomorrow'],axis=1)
```

6. Let's use `y` to represent the label:

```
y = df['RainTomorrow']
```

7. Now, let's divide the data into `train_test_split`:

```
from sklearn.model_selection import train_test_split
train_x , train_y ,test_x , test_y = train_test_split(x,y ,
test_size = 0.2, random_state = 2)
```

8. As the label is a binary variable, we are training a classifier. So, logistic regression will be a good choice here. First, let's instantiate the logistic regression model:

```
model = LogisticRegression()
```

9. Now, we can use `train_x` and `test_x` to train the model:

```
model.fit(train_x , test_x)
```

10. Once the model is trained, let's use it for predictions:

```
predict = model.predict(train_y)
```

11. Now, let's find the accuracy of our trained model:

```
In [89]:  predict = model.predict(train_y)

In [90]:  from sklearn.metrics import accuracy_score

In [91]:  accuracy_score(predict , test_y)

Out[91]:  0.9696969696969697
```

Now, this binary classifier can be used to predict whether it will rain tomorrow.

# Summary

In this chapter, we started by looking at the basics of supervised machine learning. Then, we looked at various classification algorithms in more detail. Next, we looked at different methods to evaluate the performance of classifiers and studied various regression algorithms. We also looked at the different methods that can be used to evaluate the performance of the algorithms that we studied.

In the next chapter, we will look at neural networks and deep learning algorithms. We will look at the methods used to train a neural network and we will also look at the various tools and frameworks available for evaluating and deploying a neural network.

# 8
# Neural Network Algorithms

A combination of various factors has made **Artificial Neural Networks** (**ANNs**) one of the most important machine learning techniques available today. These factors include the need to solve increasingly complex problems, the explosion of data, and the emergence of technologies, such as readily available cheap clusters, that provide the computing power necessary to design very complex algorithms.

In fact, this is the research area that is rapidly evolving and is responsible for most of the major advances claimed by leading-edge tech fields such as robotics, natural language processing, and self-driving cars.

Looking into the structure of an ANN, its basic unit is a neuron. The real strength of the ANN lies in its ability to use the power of multiple neurons by organizing them in a layered architecture. An ANN creates a layered architecture by chaining neurons together in various layers. A signal passes through these layers and is processed in different ways in each of the layers until the final required output is generated. As we will see in this chapter, the hidden layers used by ANNs act as layers of abstraction, enabling deep learning, which is extensively used in realizing powerful applications such as Amazon's Alexa, Google's image search, and Google Photos.

This chapter first introduces the main concepts and components of a typical neural network. Then, it presents the various types of neural networks and explains the different kinds of activation functions used in these neural networks. Then, the backpropagation algorithm is discussed in detail, which is the most widely used algorithm for training a neural network. Next, the transfer learning technique is explained, which can be used to greatly simplify and partially automate the training of models. Finally, how to use deep learning to flag fraudulent documents is looked at by way of a real-world example application.

The following are the main concepts discussed in this chapter:

- Understanding ANNs
- The evolution of ANNs
- Training a neural network
- Tools and frameworks
- Transfer learning
- Case study: using deep learning for fraud detection

Let's start by looking at the basics of ANNs.

# Understanding ANNs

Inspired by the working of neurons in the human brain, the concept of neural networks was proposed by Frank Rosenblatt in 1957. To understand the architecture fully, it is helpful to briefly look at the layered structure of neurons in the human brain. (Refer to the following diagram to get an idea of how the neurons in the human brain are chained together.)

In the human brain, **dendrites** act as sensors that detect a signal. The signal is then passed on to an **axon**, which is a long, slender projection of a nerve cell. The function of the axon is to transmit this signal to muscles, glands, and other neurons. As shown in the following diagram, the signal travels through interconnecting tissue called a **synapse** before being passed on to other neurons. Note that through this organic pipeline, the signal keeps traveling until it reaches the target muscle or gland, where it causes the required action. It typically takes seven to eight milliseconds for the signal to pass through the chain of neurons and reach its destination:

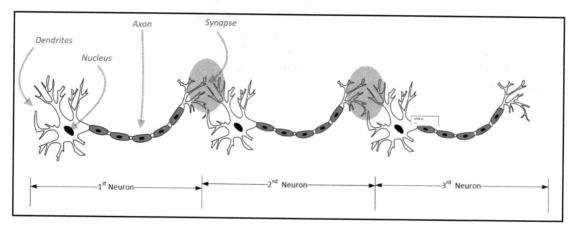

Inspired by this natural architectural masterpiece of signal processing, Frank Rosenblatt devised a technique that would mean digital information could be processed in layers to solve a complex mathematical problem. His initial attempt at designing a neural network was quite simple and looked similar to a linear regression model. This simple neural network did not have any hidden layers and was named a *perceptron*. The following diagram illustrates it:

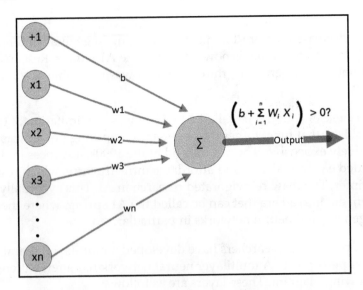

Let's try to develop the mathematical representation of this perceptron. In the preceding diagram, the input signals are shown on the left-hand side. It is a weighted sum of inputs because each of the inputs $(x_1, x_2..x_n)$ gets multiplied by a corresponding weight $(w_1, w_2... w_n)$ and then summed up:

$$\left(b + \sum_{i=1}^{n} w_i x_i\right) > 0?$$

Note that it is a binary classifier because the final output from this perceptron is true or false depending on the output of the aggregator (shown as $\Sigma$ in the diagram). The aggregator will produce a true signal if it can detect a valid signal from at least one of the inputs.

Let's now look into how neural networks have evolved over time.

# The Evolution of ANNs

In the preceding section, we looked into a simple neural network without any layers called a perceptron. The perceptron was found to have serious limitations, and in 1969, Marvin Minsky and Seymour Papert worked on research that led to the conclusion that a perceptron is incapable of learning any complex logic.

In fact, they showed that it would be a struggle to learn even logical functions as simple as XOR. That led to a decrease in interest in machine learning in general, and neural networks in particular, and started an era that is now known as the **AI winter**. Researchers around the world would not take AI seriously, thinking that it was incapable of solving any complex problems.

One of the primary reasons for the so-called AI winter was the limitation of the hardware capabilities available at that time. Either the necessary computing power was not available or it was prohibitively expensive. Toward the end of the 1990s, advances in distributed computing provided easily available and affordable infrastructure, which resulted in the thaw of the AI winter. The thaw reinvigorated research in AI. This eventually resulted in turning the current era into an era that can be called the **AI spring**, where there is so much interest in AI in general and neural networks in particular.

For more complex problems, researchers have developed a multilayer neural network called a **multilayer perceptron**. A multilayer neural network has a few different layers, as shown in the following diagram. These layers are as follows:

- Input layer
- Hidden layer(s)
- Output layer:

 A deep neural network is a neural network with one or more hidden layers. Deep learning is the process of training an ANN.

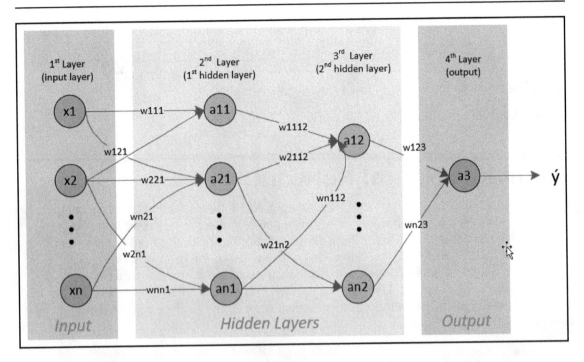

An important thing to note is that the neuron is the basic unit of this network, and each neuron of a layer is connected to all neurons of the next layer. For complex networks, the number of these interconnections explodes, and we will explore different ways of reducing these interconnections without sacrificing too much quality.

First, let's try to formulate the problem we are trying to solve.

The input is a feature vector, x, of dimensions n.

We want the neural network to predict values. The predicted values are represented by ý.

Mathematically, we want to determine, given a particular input, the probability that a transaction is fraudulent. In other words, given a particular value of x, what is the probability that y = 1? Mathematically, we can represent this as follows:

$$\acute{y} = P(y = 1|x) : where; x \in \Re^{n_x}$$

Note that x is an $n_x$-dimensional vector, where $n_x$ is the number of input variables.

This neural network has four layers. The layers between the input and the output are the hidden layers. The number of neurons in the first hidden layer is denoted by $n_h^{[l]}$. The links between various nodes are multiplied by parameters called *weights*. Training a neural network is all about finding the right values for the weights.

Let's see how we can train a neural network.

# Training a Neural Network

The process of building a neural network using a given dataset is called training a neural network. Let's look into the anatomy of a typical neural network. When we talk about training a neural network, we are talking about calculating the best values for the weights. The training is done iteratively by using a set of examples in the form of training data. The examples in the training data have the expected values of the output for different combinations of input values. The training process for neural networks is different from the way traditional models are trained (which were discussed in Chapter 7, *Traditional Supervised Learning Algorithms*).

# Understanding the Anatomy of a Neural Network

Let's see what a neural network consists of:

- **Layers:** Layers are the core building blocks of a neural network. Each layer is a data-processing module that acts as a filter. It takes one or more inputs, processes it in a certain way, and then produces one or more outputs. Each time data passes through a layer, it goes through a processing phase and shows patterns that are relevant to the business question we are trying to answer.
- **Loss function:** A loss function provides the feedback signal that is used in the various iterations of the learning process. The loss function provides the deviation for a single example.
- **Cost function:** The cost function is the loss function on a complete set of examples.
- **Optimizer:** An optimizer determines how the feedback signal provided by the loss function will be interpreted.
- **Input data:** Input data is the data that is used to train the neural network. It specifies the target variable.

- **Weights:** The weights are calculated by training the network. Weights roughly correspond to the importance of each of the inputs. For example, if a particular input is more important than other inputs, after training, it is given a greater weight value, acting as a multiplier. Even a weak signal for that important input will gather strength from the large weight value (that acts as a multiplier). Thus weight ends up turning each of the inputs according to their importance.
- **Activation function:** The values are multiplied by different weights and then aggregated. Exactly how they will be aggregated and how their value will be interpreted will be determined by the type of the chosen activation function.

Let's now have a look at a very important aspect of neural network training.

While training neural networks, we take each of the examples one by one. For each of the examples, we generate the output using our under-training model. We calculate the difference between the expected output and the predicted output. For each individual example, this difference is called the **loss**. Collectively, the loss across the complete training dataset is called the **cost**. As we keep on training the model, we aim to find the right values of weights that will result in the smallest loss value. Throughout the training, we keep on adjusting the values of the weights until we find the set of values for the weights that results in the minimum possible overall cost. Once we reach the minimum cost, we mark the model as trained.

# Defining Gradient Descent

The purpose of training a neural network model is to find the right values for weights. We start training a neural network with random or default values for the weights. Then, we iteratively use an optimizer algorithm, such as gradient descent, to change the weights in such a way that our predictions improve.

The starting point of a gradient descent algorithm is the random values of weights that need to be optimized as we iterate through the algorithm. In each of the subsequent iterations, the algorithm proceeds by changing the values of the weights in such a way that the cost is minimized.

The following diagram explains the logic of the gradient descent algorithm:

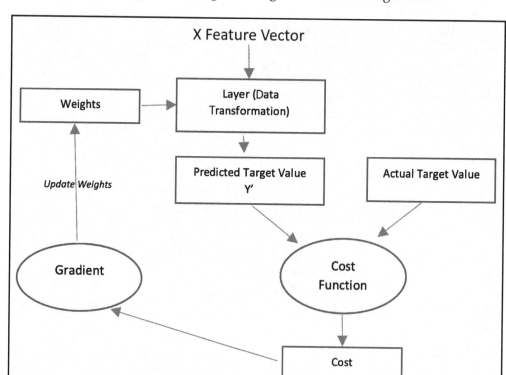

In the preceding diagram, the input is the feature vector **X**. The actual value of the target variable is **Y** and the predicted value of the target variable is **Y'**. We determine the deviation of the actual value from the predicted values. We update the weights and repeat the steps until the cost is minimized.

How to vary the weight in each iteration of the algorithm will depend on the following two factors:

- **Direction:** Which direction to go in to get the minimum of the loss function
- **Learning Rate:** How big the change should be in the direction we have chosen

A simple iterative process is shown in the following diagram:

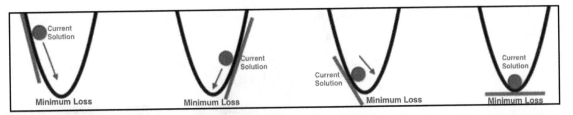

The diagram shows how, by varying the weights, gradient descent tries to find the minimum cost. The learning rate and chosen direction will determine the next point on the graph to explore.

 Selecting the right value for the learning rate is important. If the learning rate is too small, the problem may take a lot of time to converge. If the learning rate is too high, the problem will not converge. In the preceding diagram, the dot representing our current solution will keep oscillating between the two opposite lines of the graph.

Now, let's see how to minimize a gradient. Consider only two variables, $x$ and $y$. The gradient of $x$ and $y$ is calculated as follows:

$$gradient = \frac{\triangle y}{\triangle x}$$

To minimize the gradient, the following approach can be used:

```
while(gradient!=0):
    if (gradient < 0); move right
    if (gradient > 0); move left
```

This algorithm can also be used to find the optimal or near-optimal values of weights for a neural network.

Note that the calculation of gradient descent proceeds backward throughout the network. We start by calculating the gradient of the final layer first, and then the second-to-last one, and then the one before that, until we reach the first layer. This is called backpropagation, which was introduced by Hinton, Williams, and Rumelhart in 1985.

Next, let's look into activation functions.

# Activation Functions

An activation function formulates how the inputs to a particular neuron will be processed to generate an output.

As shown in the following diagram, each of the neurons in a neural network has an activation function that determines how inputs will be processed:

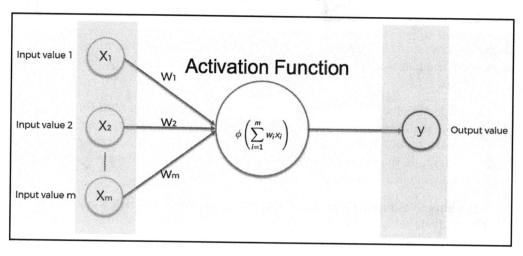

In the preceding diagram, we can see that the results generated by an activation function are passed on to the output. The activation function sets the criteria that how the values of the inputs are supposed to be interpreted to generate an output.

For exactly the same input values, different activation functions will produce different outputs. Understanding how to select the right activation function is important when using neural networks to solve problems.

Let's now look into these activation functions one by one.

# Threshold Function

The simplest possible activation function is the threshold function. The output of the threshold function is binary: 0 or 1. It will generate 1 as the output if any of the input is greater than 1. This can be explained in the following diagram:

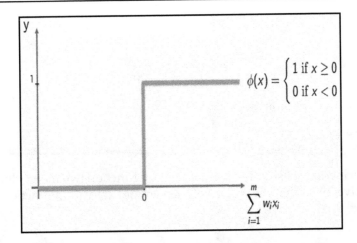

$$\phi(x) = \begin{cases} 1 \text{ if } x \geq 0 \\ 0 \text{ if } x < 0 \end{cases}$$

$$\sum_{i=1}^{m} w_i x_i$$

Note that as soon as there are any signs of life detected in the weighted sums of inputs, the output ($y$) becomes 1. This makes the threshold activation function very sensitive. It is quite vulnerable to being wrongly triggered by the slightest signal in the input due to a glitch or some noise.

## Sigmoid

The sigmoid function can be thought of as an improvement of the threshold function. Here, we have control over the sensitivity of the activation function:

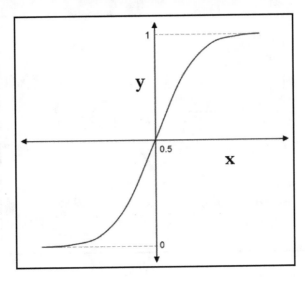

The sigmoid function, $y$, is defined as follows:

$$y = f(x) = \frac{1}{1 + e^{-x}}$$

It can be implemented in Python as follows:

```
def sigmoidFunction(z):
        return 1/ (1+np.exp(-z))
```

Note that by reducing the sensitivity of the activation function, we make glitches in the input less disruptive. Note that the output of the sigmoid activation function is still binary, that is, 0 or 1.

# Rectified linear unit (ReLU)

The output for the first two activation functions presented in this chapter was binary. That means that they will take a set of input variables and convert them into binary outputs. ReLU is an activation function that takes a set of input variables as input and converts them into a single continuous output. In neural networks, ReLU is the most popular activation function and is usually used in the hidden layers, where we do not want to convert continuous variables into category variables.

The following diagram summarizes the ReLU activation function:

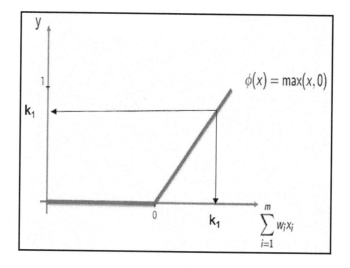

Note that when $x \leq 0$, that means $y = 0$. This means that any signal from the input that is zero or less than zero is translated into a zero output:

$$y = f(x) = 0; \text{ for } x < 0$$

$$y = f(x) = x \text{ for } x >= 0$$

As soon as $x$ becomes more than zero, it is $x$.

The ReLU function is one of the most used activation functions in neural networks. It can be implemented in Python as follows:

```
def ReLU(x):
if x<0:
    return 0
else:
    return x
```

Now let's look into Leaky ReLU, which is based on ReLU.

# Leaky ReLU

In ReLU, a negative value for $x$ results in a zero value for $y$. It means that some information is lost in the process, which makes training cycles longer, especially at the start of training. The Leaky ReLU activation function resolves this issue. The following applies for Leaky ReLu:

$$y = f(x) = \text{ß}x \text{ ; for } x < 0$$

$$y = f(x) = x \text{ for } x >= 0$$

This is shown in the following diagram:

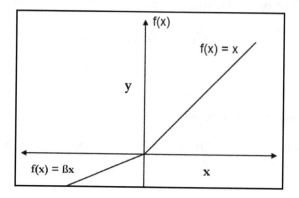

Here, $\beta$ is a parameter with a value less than one.

It can be implemented in Python as follows:

```
def leakyReLU(x,beta=0.01):
    if x<0:
        return (beta*x)
    else:
        return x
```

There are three ways of specifying the value for ß:

- We can specify a default value of ß.
- We can make ß a parameter in our neural network and we can let the neural network decide the value (this is called **parametric ReLU**).
- We can make ß a random value (this is called **randomized ReLU**).

# Hyperbolic tangent (tanh)

The tanh function is similar to the sigmoid function, but it has the ability to give a negative signal as well. The following diagram illustrates this:

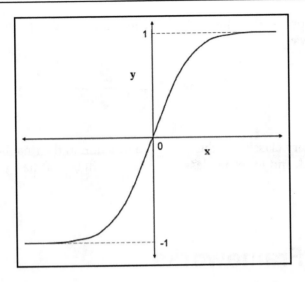

The $y$ function is as follows:

$$y = f(x) = \frac{1 - e^{-2x}}{1 + e^{-2x}}$$

It can be implemented by the following Python code:

```
def tanh(x):
    numerator = 1-np.exp(-2*x)
    denominator = 1+np.exp(-2*x)
    return numerator/denominator
```

Now let's look at the softmax function.

# Softmax

Sometimes we need more than two levels for the output of the activation function. Softmax is an activation function that provides us with more than two levels for the output. It is best suited to multiclass classification problems. Let's assume that we have $n$ classes. We have input values. The input values map the classes as follows:

$$x = \{x^{(1)}, x^{(2)}, \dots x^{(n)}\}$$

Softmax operates on probability theory. The output probability of the $e^{th}$ class of the softmax is calculated as follows:

$$prob^{(s)} = \frac{e^{x^s}}{\sum_{i=1}^{n} e^{x^i}}$$

For binary classifiers, the activation function in the final layer will be sigmoid, and for multiclass classifiers it will be softmax.

# Tools and Frameworks

In this section, we will look at the frameworks and tools available for implementing neural networks in detail.

Over time, many different frameworks have been developed to implement neural networks. Different frameworks have their own strengths and weaknesses. In this section, we will focus on Keras with a TensorFlow backend.

# Keras

Keras is one of the most popular and easy-to-use neural network libraries and is written in Python. It was written with ease of use in mind and provides the fastest way to implement deep learning. Keras only provides high-level blocks and is considered at the model level.

## Backend Engines of Keras

Keras needs a lower-level deep learning library to perform tensor-level manipulations. This lower level deep-learning library is called the *backend engine*. Possible backend engines for Keras include the following:

- **TensorFlow** (www.tensorflow.org): This is the most popular framework of its kind and is open sourced by Google.
- **Theona** (deeplearning.net/software/theano): This was developed at the MILA lab at Université de Montréal.
- **Microsoft Cognitive Toolkit** (**CNTK**): This was developed by Microsoft.

The format of this modular deep learning technology stack is shown in the following diagram:

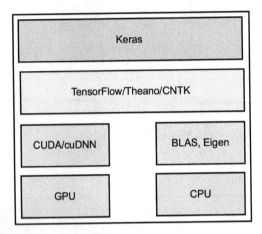

The advantage of this modular deep learning architecture is that the backend of Keras can be changed without rewriting any code. For example, if we find TensorFlow better than Theona for a particular task, we can simply change the backend to TensorFlow without rewriting any code.

## Low-level layers of the deep learning stack

The three backend engines we just mentioned can all run both on CPUs and GPUs using the low-level layers of the stack. For CPUs, a low-level library of tensor operations called **Eigen** is used. For GPUs, TensorFlow uses NVIDIA's **CUDA Deep Neural Network** (**cuDNN**) library.

## Defining hyperparameters

As discussed in `Chapter 6`, *Unsupervised Machine Learning Algorithms*, a hyperparameter is a parameter whose value is chosen before the learning process starts. We start with common-sense values and then try to optimize them later. For neural networks, the important hyperparameters are these:

- The activation function
- The learning rate
- The number of hidden layers
- The number of neurons in each hidden layer

Let's look into how we can define a model using Keras.

# Defining a Keras model

There are three steps involved in defining a complete Keras model:

1. **Define the layers**.

   We can build a model using Keras in two possible ways:

   - **The Sequential API:** This allows us to architect models for a linear stack of layers. It is used for relatively simple models and is the usual choice for building models:

---

**Import Packages**

```
[ ]  import tensorflow as tf
     from tensorflow.keras.models import Sequential
     from tensorflow.keras.layers import Dense, Activation, Dropout
     from tensorflow.keras.datasets import mnist
```

**Load Data**

Let us load the mnist dataset

```
[ ]  (x_train, y_train), (x_test, y_test) = mnist.load_data()
```

```
[→]  Downloading data from https://storage.googleapis.com/tensorflow/tf-keras-datasets/mnist.npz
     11493376/11490434 [==============================] - 0s 0us/step
```

```
[ ]  model = tf.keras.models.Sequential([
         tf.keras.layers.Flatten(),
         tf.keras.layers.Dense(128, activation='relu'),
         tf.keras.layers.Dropout(0.15),
         tf.keras.layers.Dense(128, activation='relu'),
         tf.keras.layers.Dropout(0.15),
         tf.keras.layers.Dense(10, activation='softmax'),
     ])
```

---

Note that, here, we have created three layers – the first two layers have the ReLU activation function and the third layer has softmax as the activation function.

- **The Functional API:** This allows us to architect models for acyclic graphs of layers. More complex models can be created using the Functional API.

```
inputs = tf.keras.Input(shape=(128,128))
x = tf.keras.layers.Flatten()(inputs)
x = tf.keras.layers.Dense(512, activation='relu',name='d1')(x)
x = tf.keras.layers.Dropout(0.2)(x)
predictions = tf.keras.layers.Dense(10,activation=tf.nn.softmax, name='d2')(x)
model = tf.keras.Model(inputs=inputs, outputs=predictions)
```

Note that we can define the same neural network using both the Sequential and Functional APIs. From the point of view of performance, it does not make any difference which approach you take to define the model.

2. **Define the learning process.**

In this step, we define three things:

- The optimizer
- The loss function
- The metrics that will quantify the quality of the model:

```
optimiser = tf.keras.optimizers.RMSprop
model.compile (optimizer= optimiser, loss='mse', metrics = ['accuracy'])
```

Note that we use the `model.compile` function to define the optimizer, loss function, and metrics.

3. **Train the model.**

Once the architecture is defined, it is time to train the model:

```
model.fit(x_train, y_train, batch_size=128, epochs=10)
```

Note that parameters such as `batch_size` and `epochs` are configurable parameters, making them hyperparameters.

# Choosing sequential or functional model

The sequential model creates the ANN as a simple stack of layer. The sequential model is easy and straightforward to understand and implement, but its simplistic architecture also has a major restriction. Each layer is connected to exactly one input and output tensor. This means that if our model has multiple inputs or multiple outputs either at the input or output or at any of the hidden layers, then we cannot use a sequential model. In this case, we will have to use the functional model.

# Understanding TensorFlow

TensorFlow is one of the most popular libraries for working with neural networks. In the preceding section, we saw how we can use it as the backend engine of Keras. It is an open source, high-performance library that can actually be used for any numerical computation. If we look at the stack, we can see that we can write TensorFlow code in a high-level language such as Python or C++, which gets interpreted by the TensorFlow distributed execution engine. This makes it quite useful for and popular with developers.

The way TensorFlow works is that you create a **Directed Graph** (**DG**) to represent your computation. Connecting the nodes are the edges, the input, and the output of the mathematical operations. Also, they represent arrays of data.

# Presenting TensorFlow's Basic Concepts

Let's take a brief look at TensorFlow concepts such as scalars, vectors, and matrices. We know that a simple number, such as three or five, is called a **scalar** in traditional mathematics. Moreover, in physics, a **vector** is something with magnitude and direction. In terms of TensorFlow, we use a vector to mean one-dimensional arrays. Extending this concept, a two-dimensional array is a **matrix**. For a three-dimensional array, we use the term **3D tensor**. We use the term **rank** to capture the dimensionality of a data structure. As such, a **scalar** is a **rank 0** data structure, a **vector** is a **rank 1** data structure, and a **matrix** is a **rank 2** data structure. These multi-dimensional structures are known as **tensors** and are shown in the following diagram:

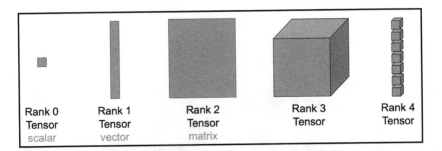

As we can see in the preceding diagram, the rank defines the dimensionality of a tensor.

Let's now look at another parameter, shape. shape is a tuple of integers specifying the length of an array in each dimension. The following diagram explains the concept of shape:

Rank 1 tensor; a vector with shape [3]

Rank 2 tensor; a matrix with shape [2, 3]

```
[1., 2., 3.]

[[1., 2., 3.], [4., 5., 6.]]

[[[1., 2., 3.]], [[7., 8., 9.]]]
```

Rank 3 tensor with shape [2, 1, 3]

Using shape and rank, we can specify the details of tensors.

## Understanding Tensor Mathematics

Let's now look at different mathematical computations using tensors:

- Let's define two scalars and try to add and multiply them using TensorFlow:

```
In [13]:  print("Define constant tensors")
          a = tf.constant(2)
          print("a = %i" % a)
          b = tf.constant(3)
          print("b = %i" % b)

          Define constant tensors
          a = 2
          b = 3
```

- We can add and multiply them and display the results:

```
In [14]:  print("Running operations, without tf.Session")
          c = a + b
          print("a + b = %i" % c)
          d = a * b
          print("a * b = %i" % d)

          Running operations, without tf.Session
          a + b = 5
          a * b = 6
```

- We can also create a new scalar tensor by adding the two tensors:

```
In [16]:  c = a + b
          print("a + b = %s" % c)

          a + b = Tensor("add:0", shape=(2, 2), dtype=float32)
```

- We can also perform complex tensor functions:

```
In [17]:  d = tf.matmul(a, b)
          print("a * b = %s" % d)

          a * b = Tensor("MatMul:0", shape=(2, 2), dtype=float32)
```

# Understanding the Types of Neural Networks

There is more than one way that neural networks can be built. If every neuron in each layer is connected to each of the neurons in another layer, then we call it a dense or fully connected neural network. Let's look at some other forms of neural networks.

# Convolutional Neural Networks

**Convolution Neural Networks (CNNs)** are typically used to analyze multimedia data. In order to learn more about how a CNN is used to analyze image-based data, we need to have a grasp of the following processes:

- Convolution
- Pooling

Let's explore them one by one.

## Convolution

The process of convolution emphasizes a pattern of interest in a particular image by processing it with another smaller image called a **filter** (also called a **kernel**). For example, if we want to find the edges of objects in an image, we can convolve the image with a particular filter to get them. Edge detection can help us in object detection, object classification, and other applications. So, the process of convolution is about finding characteristics and features in an image.

The approach to finding patterns is based on finding patterns that can be reused on different data. The reusable patterns are called filters or kernels.

## Pooling

An important part of processing multimedia data for the purpose of machine learning is downsampling it. This provides two benefits:

- It reduces the overall dimensionality of the problem, decreasing the time needed to train the model in a major way.
- Through aggregation, we abstract the unnecessary details in the multimedia data, making it more generic and more representative of similar problems.

Downsampling is performed as follows:

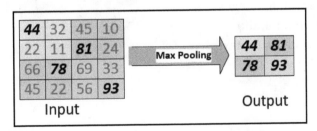

Note that we have replaced every block of four pixels with one pixel, choosing the highest value of the four pixels to be the value of that one pixel. This means that we have downsampled by a factor of four. As we have chosen the maximum value in each block, this process is called **max pooling**. We could have chosen the average value; in that case, it would be average pooling.

# Recurrent Neural Networks

**Recurrent Neural Networks (RNNs)** are a special type of neural network that are based on looped architecture. This is why they are called *recurrent*. The important thing to note is that RNNs have memory. This means that they have the ability to store information from recent iterations. They are used in areas such as analyzing sentence structures to predict the next word in a sentence.

# Generative Adversarial Networks

**Generative Adversarial Networks (GANs)** are a type of neural network that generate synthetic data. They were created in 2014 by Ian Goodfellow and his colleagues. They can be used to generate photographs of people that have never existed. More importantly, they are used to generate synthetic data to augment training datasets.

In the upcoming section, we will see what transfer learning is.

# Transfer Learning

Over the years, many organizations, research groups, and individuals within the open source community have perfected some complex models trained using gigantic amounts of data for generic use cases. In some cases, they have invested years of effort in optimizing these models. Some of these open source models can be used for the following applications:

- Object detection in video
- Object detection in images
- Transcription for audio
- Sentiment analysis for text

Whenever we start working on training a new machine learning model, the question to ask ourselves is this: instead of starting from scratch, can we simply customize a well-established pre-trained model for our purposes? In other words, can we transfer the learning of existing models to our custom model so that we can answer our business question? If we can do that, it will provide three benefits:

- Our model training efforts will be given a jump-start.
- By using a well-tested and well-established model, the overall quality of our model is likely to improve.
- If we do not have enough data for the problem we are working on, using a pre-trained model through transfer learning may help.

Let's look into two actual examples where this would be useful:

- When training a robot, we could first use a simulation game to train a neural network model. In that simulation, we could create all those rare events that are very hard to find in the real world. Once trained, we could use transfer learning ;to train the model for the real world.
- Let's assume that we want to train a model that can classify Apple And Windows laptops from a video feed. There are already well-established object detection models available as open source that can accurately classify various objects in a video feed. We can use these models as a starting point and identify objects as laptops. Once we have identified the objects as laptops, we can further train the model to differentiate between Apple and Windows laptops.

In the next section, we will apply the concepts that we have covered in this chapter to building a fraudulent document classifying neural network.

# Case study – using deep learning for fraud detection

Using **Machine Learning** (**ML**) techniques to identify fraudulent documents is an active and challenging field of research. Researchers are investigating to what extent the pattern recognition power of neural networks can be exploited for this purpose. Instead of manual attribute extractors, raw pixels can be used for several deep learning architectural structures.

# Methodology

The technique presented in this section uses a type of neural network architecture called **Siamese neural networks**, which features two branches that share identical architectures and parameters. The use of Siamese neural networks to flag fraudulent documents is shown in the following diagram:

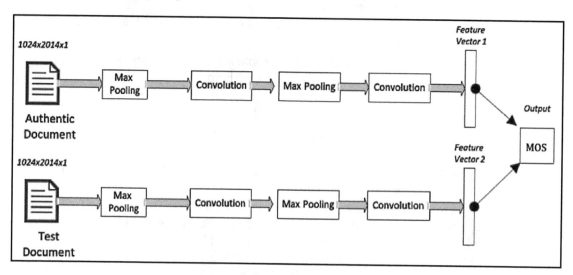

When a particular document needs to be verified for authenticity, we first classify the document based on its layout and type, and then we compare it against its expected template and pattern. If it deviates beyond a certain threshold, it is flagged as a fake document; otherwise, it is considered an authentic or true document. For critical use cases, we can add a manual process for borderline cases where the algorithm cannot conclusively classify a document as authentic or fake.

To compare a document against its expected template, we use two identical CNNs in our Siamese architecture. CNNs have the advantage of learning optimal shift-invariant local feature detectors and can build representations that are robust to geometric distortions of the input image. This is well suited to our problem since we aim to pass authentic and test documents through a single network, and then compare their outcomes for similarity. To achieve this goal, we implement the following steps.

Let's assume that we want to test a document. For each class of document, we perform the following steps:

1. Get the stored image of the authentic document. We call it the **true document**. The test document should look like the true document.

2. The true document is passed through the neural network layers to create a feature vector, which is the mathematical representation of the patterns of the true document. We call it F**eature Vector 1**, as shown in the preceding diagram.

3. The document that needs to be tested is called the **test document**. We pass this document through a neural network similar to the one that was used to create the feature vector for the true document. The feature vector of the test document is called F**eature Vector 2**.

4. We use the Euclidean distance between feature vector 1 and feature vector 2 to calculate the similarity score between the true document and the test document. This similarity score is called the **Measure Of Similarity** (**MOS**). The MOS is a number between 0 and 1. A higher number represents a lower distance between the documents and a greater likelihood that the documents are similar.

5. If the similarity score calculated by the neural network is below a pre-defined threshold, we flag the document as fraudulent.

Let's see how we can implement Siamese neural networks using Python:

1. First, let's import the Python packages that are required:

```
import random
import numpy as np
import tensorflow as tf
```

2. Next, we will define the neural network that will be used to process each of the branches of the Siamese network:

```
def createTemplate():
    return tf.keras.models.Sequential([
        tf.keras.layers.Flatten(),
        tf.keras.layers.Dense(128, activation='relu'),
        tf.keras.layers.Dropout(0.15),
        tf.keras.layers.Dense(128, activation='relu'),
        tf.keras.layers.Dropout(0.15),
        tf.keras.layers.Dense(64, activation='relu'),
    ])
```

Note that, in order to reduce overfitting, we have also specified a dropout rate of 0.15.

3. To implement Siamese networks, we will use MNIST images. MNIST images are ideal for testing the effectiveness of our approach. Our approach entails preparing the data in such a way that each sample will have two images and a binary similarity flag. This flag is an indicator that they are from the same class. Let's now implement the function named `prepareData`, which can prepare the data for us:

```
def prepareData(inputs: np.ndarray, labels: np.ndarray):
        classesNumbers = 10
        digitalIdx = [np.where(labels == i)[0] for i in
range(classesNumbers)]
        pairs = list()
        labels = list()
        n = min([len(digitalIdx[d]) for d in range(classesNumbers)])
 - 1
        for d in range(classesNumbers):
          for i in range(n):
              z1, z2 = digitalIdx[d][i], digitalIdx[d][i + 1]
              pairs += [[inputs[z1], inputs[z2]]]
              inc = random.randrange(1, classesNumbers)
              dn = (d + inc) % classesNumbers
              z1, z2 = digitalIdx[d][i], digitalIdx[dn][i]
              pairs += [[inputs[z1], inputs[z2]]]
              labels += [1, 0]
        return np.array(pairs), np.array(labels, dtype=np.float32)
```

Note that `prepareData()` will result in an equal number of samples across all digits.

4. We will now prepare the training and testing datasets:

```
(x_train, y_train), (x_test, y_test) =
tf.keras.datasets.mnist.load_data()
x_train = x_train.astype(np.float32)
x_test = x_test.astype(np.float32)
x_train /= 255
x_test /= 255
input_shape = x_train.shape[1:]
train_pairs, tr_labels = prepareData(x_train, y_train)
test_pairs, test_labels = prepareData(x_test, y_test)
```

5. Now, let's create the two halves of the Siamese system:

```
input_a = tf.keras.layers.Input(shape=input_shape)
enconder1 = base_network(input_a)
input_b = tf.keras.layers.Input(shape=input_shape)
enconder2 = base_network(input_b)
```

6. Now, we will implement the **measure of similarity (MOS)**, which will quantify the distance between two documents that we want to compare:

```
distance = tf.keras.layers.Lambda(
    lambda embeddings: tf.keras.backend.abs(embeddings[0] -
embeddings[1])) ([enconder1, enconder2])
measureOfSimilarity = tf.keras.layers.Dense(1,
activation='sigmoid') (distance)
```

Now, let's train the model. We will use 10 epochs to train this model:

```
[10] # Build the model
model = tf.keras.models.Model([input_a, input_b], measureOfSimilarity)
# Train
model.compile(loss='binary_crossentropy',optimizer=tf.keras.optimizers.Adam(),metrics=['accuracy'])

model.fit([train_pairs[:, 0], train_pairs[:, 1]], tr_labels,
        batch_size=128,epochs=10,validation_data=([test_pairs[:, 0], test_pairs[:, 1]], test_labels))

Epoch 1/10
847/847 [==============================] - 6s 7ms/step - loss: 0.3459 - accuracy: 0.8500 - val_loss: 0.2652 - val_accuracy: 0.9105
Epoch 2/10
847/847 [==============================] - 6s 7ms/step - loss: 0.1773 - accuracy: 0.9337 - val_loss: 0.1685 - val_accuracy: 0.9508
Epoch 3/10
847/847 [==============================] - 6s 7ms/step - loss: 0.1215 - accuracy: 0.9563 - val_loss: 0.1301 - val_accuracy: 0.9610
Epoch 4/10
847/847 [==============================] - 6s 7ms/step - loss: 0.0956 - accuracy: 0.9665 - val_loss: 0.1087 - val_accuracy: 0.9685
Epoch 5/10
847/847 [==============================] - 6s 7ms/step - loss: 0.0790 - accuracy: 0.9724 - val_loss: 0.1104 - val_accuracy: 0.9669
Epoch 6/10
847/847 [==============================] - 6s 7ms/step - loss: 0.0649 - accuracy: 0.9770 - val_loss: 0.0949 - val_accuracy: 0.9715
Epoch 7/10
847/847 [==============================] - 6s 7ms/step - loss: 0.0568 - accuracy: 0.9803 - val_loss: 0.0895 - val_accuracy: 0.9722
Epoch 8/10
847/847 [==============================] - 6s 7ms/step - loss: 0.0513 - accuracy: 0.9823 - val_loss: 0.0807 - val_accuracy: 0.9770
Epoch 9/10
847/847 [==============================] - 6s 7ms/step - loss: 0.0439 - accuracy: 0.9847 - val_loss: 0.0916 - val_accuracy: 0.9737
Epoch 10/10
847/847 [==============================] - 6s 7ms/step - loss: 0.0417 - accuracy: 0.9853 - val_loss: 0.0835 - val_accuracy: 0.9749
<tensorflow.python.keras.callbacks.History at 0x7ff1218297b8>
```

Note that we reached an accuracy of 97.49% using 10 epochs. Increasing the number of epochs will further improve the level of accuracy.

# Summary

In this chapter, we first looked at the details of neural networks. We started by looking at how neural networks have evolved over the years. We studied different types of neural networks. Then, we looked at the various building blocks of neural networks. We studied in depth the gradient descent algorithm, which is used to train neural networks. We discussed various activation functions and studied the applications of activation functions in a neural network. We also looked at the concept of transfer learning. Finally, we looked at a practical example of how a neural network can be used to train a machine learning model that can be deployed to flag forged or fraudulent documents.

Looking ahead, in the next chapter, we will look into how we can use such algorithms for natural language processing. We will also introduce the concept of web embedding and will look into the use of recurrent networks for natural language processing. Finally, we will also look into how to implement sentiment analysis.

# 9
# Algorithms for Natural Language Processing

This chapter introduces algorithms for **natural language processing** (**NLP**). This chapter proceeds from the theoretical to the practical in a progressive manner. It will first introduce the fundamentals of NLP, followed by the basic algorithms. Then, it will look at one of the most popular neural networks that is widely used to design and implement solutions for important use cases for textual data. We will then look at the limitations of NLP before finally learning how we can use NLP to train a machine learning model that can predict the polarity of movie reviews.

This chapter will consist of the following sections:

- Introducing NLP
- Bag-of-words-based (BoW-based) NLP
- Introduction to word embedding
- Use of recurrent neural networks for NLP
- Using NLP for sentiment analysis
- Case study: movie review sentiment analysis

By the end of this chapter, you will understand the basic techniques that are used for NLP. You should be able to understand how NLP can be used to solve some interesting real-world problems.

Let's start with the basic concepts.

# Introducing NLP

NLP is used to investigate methodologies to formalize and formulate the interactions between computers and human (natural) languages. NLP is a comprehensive subject, and involves using computer linguistics algorithms and human–computer interaction technologies and methodologies to process complex unstructured data. NLP can be used for a variety of cases, including the following:

- **Topic identification**: To discover topics in a text repository and classify the documents in the repository according to the discovered topics
- **Sentiment analysis**: To classify the text according to the positive or negative sentiments that it contains
- **Machine translation**: To translate the text from one spoken human language to another
- **Text to speech**: To convert spoken words into text
- **Subjective interpretation**: To intelligently interpret a question and answer it using the information available
- **Entity recognition**: To identify entities (such as a person, place, or thing) from text
- **Fake news detection**: To flag fake news based on the content

Let's start by looking at some of the terminology that is used when discussing NLP.

# Understanding NLP terminology

NLP is a comprehensive subject. In the literature surrounding a certain field, we will observe that, sometimes, different terms are used to specify the same thing. We will start by looking at some of the basic terminology related to NLP. Let's start with normalization, which is one of the basic kinds of NLP processing, usually performed on the input data.

# Normalization

Normalization is performed on the input text data to improve its quality in the context of training a machine learning model. Normalization usually involves the following processing steps:

- Converting all text to uppercase or lowercase
- Removing punctuation
- Removing numbers

Note that although the preceding processing steps are typically needed, the actual processing steps depend on the problem that we want to solve. They will vary from use case to use case—for example, if the numbers in the text represent something that may have some value in the context of the problem that we are trying to solve, then we may not need to remove the numbers from the text in the normalization phase.

# Corpus

The group of input documents that we are using to solve the problem in question is called the **corpus**. The corpus acts as the input data for the NLP problem.

# Tokenization

When we are working with NLP, the first job is to divide the text into a list of tokens. This process is called **tokenization**. The granularity of the resulting tokens will vary based on the objective—for example, each token can consist of the following:

- A word
- A combination of words
- A sentence
- A paragraph

# Named entity recognition

In NLP, there are many use cases where we need to identify certain words and numbers from unstructured data as belonging to predefined categories, such as phone numbers, postal codes, names, places, or countries. This is used to provide a structure to the unstructured data. This process is called **named entity recognition** (NER).

# Stopwords

After word-level tokenization, we have a list of words that are used in the text. Some of these words are common words that are expected to appear in almost every document. These words do not provide any additional insight into the documents that they appear in. These words are called **stopwords**. They are usually removed in the data-processing phase. Some examples of stopwords are *was*, *we*, and *the*.

# Sentiment analysis

Sentimental analysis, or opinion mining, is the process of extracting positive or negative sentiments from the text.

# Stemming and lemmatization

In textual data, most words are likely to be present in slightly different forms. Reducing each word to its origin or stem in a family of words is called **stemming**. It is used to group words based on their similar meanings to reduce the total number of words that need to be analyzed. Essentially, stemming reduces the overall conditionality of the problem.

For example, {use, used, using, uses} => use.

The most common algorithm for stemming English is the Porter algorithm.

Stemming is a crude process that can result in chopping off the ends of words. This may result in words that are misspelled. For many use cases, each word is just an identifier of a level in our problem space, and misspelled words do not matter. If correctly spelled words are required, then lemmatization should be used instead of stemming.

 Algorithms lack common sense. For the human brain, treating similar words the same is straightforward. For an algorithm, we have to guide it and provide the grouping criteria.

Fundamentally, there are three different ways of implementing NLP. These three techniques, which are different in terms of sophistication, are as follows:

- **Bag-of-words**-based (BoW-based) NLP
- Traditional NLP classifiers
- Using deep learning for NLP

# NLTK

The **Natural Language Toolkit** (**NLTK**) is the most widely utilized package for handling NLP tasks in Python. NLTK is one of the oldest and most popular Python libraries used for NLP. NLTK is great because it basically provides a jumpstart to building any NLP process by giving you the basic tools that you can then chain together to accomplish your goal rather than building all those tools from scratch. A lot of tools are packaged into NLTK, and in the next section, we will download the package and explore some of those tools.

Let's look at BoW-based NLP.

# BoW-based NLP

The representation of input text as a bag of tokens is called **BoW-based processing**. The drawback of using BoW is that we discard most of the grammar and tokenization, which sometimes results in losing the context of the words. In the BoW approach, we first quantify the importance of each word in the context of each document that we want to analyze.

Fundamentally, there are three different ways of quantifying the importance of the words in the context of each document:

- **Binary**: A feature will have a value of 1 if the word appears in the text or 0 otherwise.
- **Count**: A feature will have the number of times the word appears in the text as its value or 0 otherwise.
- **Term frequency/Inverse document frequency**: The value of the feature will be a ratio of how unique a word is in a single document to how unique it is in the entire corpus of documents. Obviously, for common words such as the, in, and so on (known as stop words), the **term frequency–inverse document frequency** (**TF-IDF**) score will be low. For more unique words—for instance, domain-specific terms—the score will be higher.

Note that by using BoW, we are throwing away information—namely, the order of the words in our text. This often works, but may lead to reduced accuracy.

Let's look at a specific example. We will train a model that can classify the reviews of a restaurant as negative or positive. The input file is a strutted file where the reviews will be classified as positive or negative.

For this, let's first process the input data.

The processing steps are defined in the following diagram:

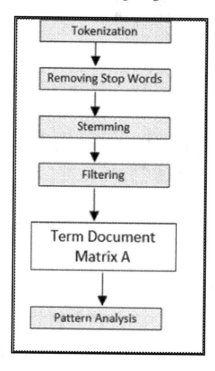

Let's implement this processing pipeline by going through the following steps:

1. First, we import the packages that we need:

```
import numpy as np
import pandas as pd
```

2. Then we import the dataset from a CSV file:

```
In [2]:  # Importing the dataset
         dataset = pd.read_csv('Restaurant_Reviews.tsv', delimiter = '\t', quoting = 3)
         dataset.head()
```

Out[2]:

|   | Review | Liked |
|---|---|---|
| 0 | Wow... Loved this place. | 1 |
| 1 | Crust is not good. | 0 |
| 2 | Not tasty and the texture was just nasty. | 0 |
| 3 | Stopped by during the late May bank holiday of... | 1 |
| 4 | The selection on the menu was great and so wer... | 1 |

3. Next, we clean the data:

```
# Cleaning the texts
import re
import nltk
nltk.download('stopwords')
from nltk.corpus import stopwords
from nltk.stem.porter import PorterStemmer
corpus = []
for i in range(0, 1000):
    review = re.sub('[^a-zA-Z]', ' ', dataset['Review'][i])
    review = review.lower()
    review = review.split()
    ps = PorterStemmer()
    review = [ps.stem(word) for word in review if not word in
set(stopwords.words('english'))]
    review = ' '.join(review)
    corpus.append(review)
```

4. Now let's define the features (represented by y) and the label (represented by X):

```
from sklearn.feature_extraction.text import CountVectorizer
cv = CountVectorizer(max_features = 1500)
X = cv.fit_transform(corpus).toarray()
y = dataset.iloc[:, 1].values
```

5. Let's divide the data into testing and training data:

```
from sklearn.model_selection import train_test_split
X_train, X_test, y_train, y_test = train_test_split(X, y, test_size
= 0.20, random_state = 0)
```

6. For training the model, we are using the naive Bayes algorithm:

```
from sklearn.naive_bayes import GaussianNB
classifier = GaussianNB()
classifier.fit(X_train, y_train)
```

7. Let's predict the test set results:

```
y_pred = classifier.predict(X_test)
```

8. The confusion matrix looks like this:

```
In [18]:  # Making the Confusion Matrix
          from sklearn.metrics import confusion_matrix
          cm = confusion_matrix(y_test, y_pred)

In [19]:  cm

Out[19]:  array([[55, 42],
                 [12, 91]])
```

Looking at the confusion matrix, we can estimate the misclassification.

# Introduction to word embedding

In the preceding section, we studied how we can perform NLP by using BoW as the abstraction for the input text data. One of the major advancements in NLP is our ability to create a meaningful numeric representation of words in the form of dense vectors. This technique is called word embedding. Yoshua Bengio first introduced the term in his paper *A Neural Probabilistic Language Model*. Each word in an NLP problem can be thought of as a categorical object. Mapping each of the words to a list of numbers represented as a vector is called word embedding. In other words, the methodologies that are used to convert words into real numbers are called word embedding. A differentiating feature of embedding is that it uses a dense vector, instead of using traditional approaches that use sparse matrix vectors.

There are basically two problems with using BoW for NLP:

- **Loss of semantic context**: When we tokenize the data, its context is lost. A word may have different meanings based on where it is used in the sentence; this becomes even more important when interpreting complex human expressions, such as humor or satire.
- **Sparse input**: When we tokenize, each word becomes a feature. As we saw in the preceding example, each word is a feature. It results in sparse data structures.

# The neighborhood of a word

A key insight into how to present textual data (specifically, individual words, or lexemes) to an algorithm comes from linguistics. In word embedding, we pay attention to the neighborhood of each word and use it to establish its meaning and importance. Neighbourhood of a word is the set of words surrounds a particular word. The context of a word is determined by its neighborhood.

Note that in BoW, a word loses its context, as its context is from the neighborhood that it is in.

# Properties of word embeddings

Good word embeddings exhibit the following four properties:

- **They are dense**: In fact, embeddings are essentially factor models. As such, each component of the embedding vector represents a quantity of a (latent) feature. We typically do not know what that feature represents; however, we will have very few—if any—zeros that will cause a sparse input.
- **They are low dimensional**: An embedding has a predefined dimensionality (chosen as a hyperparameter). We saw earlier that in the BoW representation we needed $|V|$ inputs for each word, so that the total size of the input was $|V| * n$ where $n$ is the number of words we use as input. With word embeddings, our input size will be $d * n$, where $d$ is typically between 50 and 300. Considering the fact that large text corpora are often much larger than 300 words, this means that we have large savings in input size, which we saw can lead to better accuracy for a smaller total number of data instances.

- **They embed domain semantics**: This property is probably the most surprising, but also the most useful. When properly trained, embeddings learn about the meaning of their domain.
- **Generalize easily**: Finally, web embedding is capable of picking up generalized abstract patterns—for example, we can train on (the embeddings of) cat, deer, dog, and so on, and the model will understand that we mean animals. Note that the model was never trained for sheep, and yet the model will still correctly classify it. By using embedding, we can expect to receive the correct answer.

Now let us explore, how we can use RNNs for Natural Language Processing.

# Using RNNs for NLP

An RNN is a traditional feed-forward network with feedback. A simple way of thinking about an RNN is that it is a neural network with states. RNNs are used with any type of data for generating and predicting various sequences of data. Training an RNN model is about formulating these sequences of data. RNNs can be used for text data as sentences are just sequences of words. When we use RNNs for NLP, we can use them for the following:

- Predicting the next word when typing

- Generating new text, following the style already used in the text:

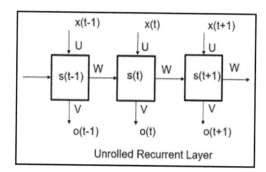

Unrolled Recurrent Layer

Remember the combination of words that resulted in their correct prediction? The learning process of RNNs is based on the text that is found in the corpus. They are trained by reducing the error between the predicted next word and the actual next word.

# Using NLP for sentiment analysis

The approach presented in this section is based on the use case of classifying a high rate of incoming stream tweets. The task at hand is to extract the embedded sentiments within the tweets about a chosen topic. The sentiment classification quantifies the polarity in each tweet in real time and then aggregate the total sentiments from all tweets to capture the overall sentiments about the chosen topic. To face the challenges posed by the content and behavior of Twitter stream data and perform the real-time analytics efficiently, we use NLP by using a trained classifier. The trained classifier is then plugged into the Twitter stream to determine the polarity of each tweet (positive, negative, or neutral), followed by the aggregation and determination of the overall polarity of all tweets about a certain topic. Let's see how this is done step by step.

First, we have to train the classifier. In order to train the classifier, we needed an already-prepared dataset that has historical Twitter data and follows the patterns and trends of the real-time data. Therefore, we used a dataset from the website www.sentiment140.com, which comes with a human-labeled corpus (a large collection of texts upon which the analysis is based) with over 1.6 million tweets. The tweets within this dataset have been labeled with one of three polarities: zero for negative, two for neutral, and four for positive. In addition to the tweet text, the corpus provides the tweet ID, date, flag, and the user who tweeted. Now let's see each of the operations that are performed on the live tweet before it reaches the *trained* classifier:

1. Tweets are first split into individual words called tokens (tokenization).
2. The output from tokenization creates a BoW, which is a collection of individual words in the text.
3. These tweets are further filtered by removing numbers, punctuations, and stop words (stop word removal). Stop words are words that are extremely common, such as *is*, *am*, *are*, and *the*. As they hold no additional information, these words are removed.
4. Additionally, nonalphabetical characters, such as #@ and numbers, are removed using pattern matching, as they hold no relevance in the case of sentiment analysis. Regular expressions are used to match alphabetical characters only and the rest are ignored. This helps to reduce the clutter from the Twitter stream.
5. The outcomes of the prior phase are taken to the stemming phase. In this phase, the derived words are reduced to their roots—for example, a word like *fish* has the same roots as *fishing* and *fishes*. For this, we use the library of standard NLP, which provides various algorithms, such as Porter stemming.

6. Once the data is processed, it is converted into a structure called a **term document matrix** (**TDM**). The TDM represents the term and frequency of each work in the filtered corpus.

7. From the TDM, the tweet reaches the trained classifier (as it is trained, it can process the tweet), which calculates the **sentimental polarity importance** (**SPI**) of each word which is a number from -5 to +5. The positive or negative sign specifies the type of emotions represented by that particular word, and its magnitude represents the strength of sentiment. This means that the tweet can be classified as either positive or negative (refer to the following image). Once we calculate the polarity of the individual tweets, we sum their overall SPI to find the aggregated sentiment of the source—for example, an overall polarity greater than one indicates that the aggregated sentiment of the tweets in our observed period of time is positive.

To retrieve the real-time raw tweets, we use the Scala library *Twitter4J*, a Java library that provides a package for a real-time Twitter streaming API. The API requires the user to register a developer account with Twitter and fill in some authentication parameters. This API allows you to either get random tweets or filter tweets using chosen keywords. We used filters to retrieve tweets related to our chosen keywords.

The overall architecture is shown in the following figure:

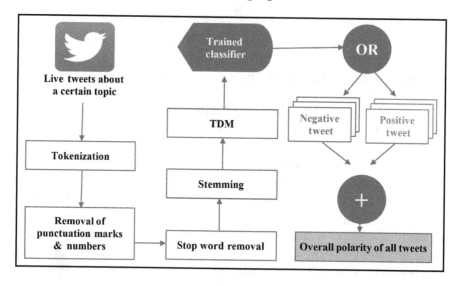

The sentiment analysis have various applications. It can be applied to classify the feedback from customers. Social media polarity analysis can be used by governments to find the effectiveness of their policies. It can also quantify the success of various advertisement campaigns.

In the next section, we will learn how we can actually apply sentiment analysis to predict the sentiments of movie reviews.

# Case study: movie review sentiment analysis

Let's use NLP to conduct a movie review sentiment analysis. For this, we will use some open source movie review data available at `http://www.cs.cornell.edu/people/pabo/movie-review-data/`:

1. First, we will import the dataset that contains the movie reviews:

```
import numpy as np
import pandas as pd
```

2. Now, let us load the movies' data and print the first few rows to observe its structure.

```
df=pd.read_csv("moviereviews.tsv",sep='\t')
df.head()
```

|   | label | review |
|---|-------|--------|
| 0 | neg | how do films like mouse hunt get into theatres... |
| 1 | neg | some talented actresses are blessed with a dem... |
| 2 | pos | this has been an extraordinary year for austra... |
| 3 | pos | according to hollywood movies made in last few... |
| 4 | neg | my first press screening of 1998 and already i... |

```
In [2]: len(df)
Out[2]: 2000
```

Note that the dataset has 2000 movie reviews. Out of these, half are negative and half are positive.

3. Now, let's start preparing the dataset for training the model. First, let us drop any missing values that are in the data

```
df.dropna(inplace=True)
```

4. Now we need to remove the whitespaces as well. Whitespaces are not null but need to be removed. For this, we need to iterate over each row in the input DataFrame. We will use .itertuples() to access every field:

```
blanks=[]

for i,lb,rv in df.itertuples():
    if rv.isspace():
        blanks.append(i)
df.drop(blanks,inplace=True)
```

Note that we have used i, lb, and rv to the index, label, and review columns.

Let's split the data into test and train datasets:

1. The first step is to specify the features and the label and then split the data into the train and test sets:

```
from sklearn.model_selection import train_test_split

X = df['review']
y = df['label']

X_train, X_test, y_train, y_test = train_test_split(X, y,
test_size=0.3, random_state=42)
```

Now we have the testing and training datasets.

2. Now let's divide the sets into train and test:

```
from sklearn.pipeline import Pipeline
from sklearn.feature_extraction.text import TfidfVectorizer
from sklearn.naive_bayes import MultinomialNB

# Naïve Bayes:
text_clf_nb = Pipeline([('tfidf', TfidfVectorizer()),
                        ('clf', MultinomialNB()),
])
```

Note that we are using tfidf to quantify the importance of a datapoint in a collection.

Next, let's train the model using the naive Bayes algorithm, and then test the trained model.

Let's follow these steps to train the model:

1. Now let's train the model using the testing and training datasets that we created:

```
text_clf_nb.fit(X_train, y_train)
```

2. Let us run the predictions and analyze the results:

```
# Form a prediction set
predictions = text_clf_nb.predict(X_test)
```

Let us now look into the performance of our model by printing the confusion matrix. We will also look at *precision, recall, f1-score,* and *accuracy.*

```
In [23]: from sklearn.metrics import confusion_matrix,classification_report,accuracy_score

In [24]: print(confusion_matrix(y_test,predictions))
         [[259  23]
          [102 198]]

In [25]: print(classification_report(y_test,predictions))
                       precision    recall  f1-score   support

                 neg        0.72      0.92      0.81       282
                 pos        0.90      0.66      0.76       300

            accuracy                            0.79       582
           macro avg        0.81      0.79      0.78       582
        weighted avg        0.81      0.79      0.78       582


In [26]: print(accuracy_score(y_test,predictions))
         0.7852233676975945
```

These performance metrics give us a measure of the quality of the predictions. With a **0.78** accuracy, now we have successfully trained a model that can predict what type of review we can predict for that particular movie.

# Summary

In this chapter, we discussed the algorithms related to NLP. First, we looked at the terminology related to NLP. Next, we looked at the BoW methodology of implementing an NLP strategy. Then we looked at the concept of word embedding and the use of neural networks in NLP. Finally, we looked at an actual example where we used the concepts developed in this chapter to predict the sentiments of movie reviews based on their text. Having gone through this chapter, the user should be able to use NLP for text classification and sentiment analysis.

In the next chapter, we will look at recommendation engines. We will study different types of recommendation engine and how they can be used to solve some real-world problems.

# 10
# Recommendation Engines

Recommendation engines are a way of using information available about user preferences and product details to provide informed recommendations. The objective of a recommendation engine is to understand the patterns of similarities among a set of items and/or to formulate the interactions between the users and items.

This chapter starts with presenting the basics of recommendation engines. Then, it discusses various types of recommendation engines. Next, this chapter discusses how recommendation engines are used to suggest items and products to different users and the various limitations of recommendation engines. Finally, we will learn to use recommendation engines to solve a real-world problem.

The following concepts are discussed in this chapter:

- Introducing recommendation engines
- Types of recommendation engines
- Understanding the limitations of recommendation systems
- Areas of practical application
- A practical example—creating a recommendation engine to recommend movies to subscribers

By the end of this chapter, you should be able to understand how to use recommendation engines to suggest various items based on some preference criteria.

Let's start by looking into the background concepts of recommendation engines.

# Introducing recommendation systems

Recommendation systems represent the methods that researchers originally developed to predict items that a user is most likely to be interested in. The ability of recommendation systems to give personalized suggestions on items makes them perhaps the most important technology in the context of the online purchasing world.

When used in e-commerce applications, recommendation engines uses sophisticated algorithms to improve the shopping experience for shoppers and allows service providers to customize products according to the preferences of the users.

 In 2009, Netflix offered 1 million dollars to anyone who could provide an algorithm that could improve its existing recommendation engine (Cinematch) by more than 10%. The prize was won by BellKor's Pragmatic Chaos team.

# Types of recommendation engines

Generally, there are three different types of recommendation engines:

- Content-based recommendation engines
- Collaborative filtering engines
- Hybrid recommendation engines

# Content-based recommendation engines

The basic idea of the content-based recommendation engine is to suggest items similar to those in which the user has preceding shown interest. The effectiveness of content-based recommendation engines is dependent on our ability to quantify the similarity of an item to others.

Let's look into the following diagram. If **User 1** has read **Doc 1**, then we can recommend **Doc 2** to the user, which is similar to **Doc 1**:

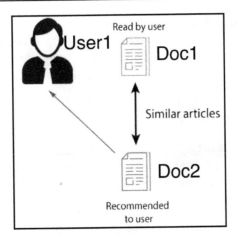

Now, the problem is how to determine which items are similar to each other. Let's look into a couple of methods of finding similarities between different items.

# Finding similarities between unstructured documents

One way of determining the similarities between different documents is by first processing the input documents. The resultant data structure after processing unstructured documents is called a **Term Document Matrix (TDM)**, which is shown in the following diagram:

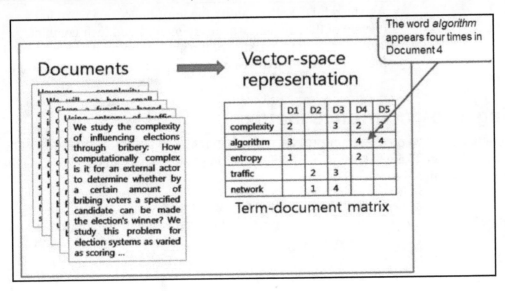

Term-document matrix

A TDM has all of the glossary of words as rows and all of the documents as the columns. It can be used to establish which documents are similar to the other documents based on the selected distance measure. Google News, for example, suggests news to a user based on its similarity to a news item the user has already shown interest in.

Once we have a TDM, there are two ways of quantifying the similarity between the documents:

- **Using frequency counts**: This means that we assume that the importance of a word is directly proportional to the frequency of each word. This is the simplest way of calculating importance.

- **Using TFIDF** (short for **Term Frequency–Inverse Document Frequency**): This is a number that calculates the importance of each word in the context of the problem we are trying to solve. It is a multiple of two terms:
  - **Term Frequency (TF)**: This is the number of times a word or a term appears in a document. Term frequency directly correlates with the importance of a word.
  - **Inverse Document Frequency (IDF)**: First, **Document Frequency (DF)** is the number of documents containing the term we are searching for. As the opposite of DF, IDF gives us the measure of uniqueness a word represents and correlates that with its importance.
  - As TF and IDF both quantify the importance of a word in the context of the problem we are trying to solve, their combination, TF-IDF, is a good measure of the importance of each word and is a more sophisticated alternative to using simple frequency counts.

# Using a co-occurrence matrix

This method is based on the assumption that if two items are bought together most of the time, then they are likely to be similar or at least belong to the same category of items that are usually purchased together.

For example, if people are using shaving gel and a razor together most of the time, then if someone buys a razor, it makes sense to suggest that person will buy shaving gel as well.

Let's analyze the historical buying patterns of these four users:

|  | Razor | Apple | Shaving cream | Bike | Hummus |
|---|---|---|---|---|---|
| Mike | 1 | 1 | 1 | 0 | 1 |
| Taylor | 1 | o | 1 | 1 | 1 |
| Elena | 0 | 0 | 0 | 1 | 0 |
| Amine | 1 | 0 | 1 | 0 | 0 |

This will create the following co-occurrence matrix:

|  | Razor | Apple | Shaving cream | Bike | Hummus |
|---|---|---|---|---|---|
| Razor | - | 1 | 3 | 1 | 1 |
| Apple | 1 | - | 1 | 0 | 1 |
| Shaving cream | 3 | 1 | - | 1 | 2 |
| Bike | 1 | 0 | 1 | - | 1 |
| Hummus | 1 | 1 | 2 | 1 | - |

The preceding co-occurrence matrix summarizes the likelihood of buying two items together. Let's see how we can use it.

# Collaborative filtering recommendation engines

The recommendations from collaborative filtering are based on the analysis of the historical buying patterns of users. The basic assumption is that if two users show interest in mostly the same items, we can classify both users as similar. In other words, we can assume the following:

- If the overlap in the buying history of two users exceeds a threshold, we can classify them as similar users.
- Looking at the history of similar users, the items that do not overlap in the buying history become the basis of future recommendations through collaborative filtering.

For example, let's look at a specific example. We have two users, **Mike** and **Elena**, as shown in the following diagram:

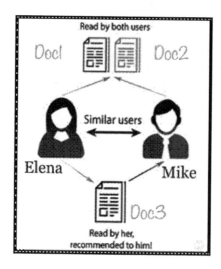

Note the following:

- Both Mike and Elena have shown interest in exactly the same documents, **Doc1** and **Doc2**.
- Based on their similar historical patterns, we can classify both of them as similar users.
- If Elena now reads **Doc3**, then we can suggest **Doc3** to Mike as well.

 Note that this strategy of suggesting items to the users based on their history will not always work.

Let's assume that Elena and Mike showed interest in **Doc1**, which was about photography (because they share a love of photography). Also, both of them showed interest in **Doc2**, which was about cloud computing, again, because both of them have an interest in the subject. Based on collaborative filtering, we classified them as similar users. Now Elena starts reading **Doc3**, which is a magazine on women's fashion. If we follow the collaborative filtering algorithm, we will suggest Mike read it, who may not have much interest in it.

Back in 2012, the American superstore, Target, was experimenting with the use of using collaborative filtering for recommending products to buyers. The algorithm classified a father similar to his teen-aged daughter based on their profiles. Target ended up sending a discount coupon for diapers, baby formula, and crib to the father. He was not aware of his daughter's pregnancy.

Note that the collaborative filtering algorithm does not depend on any other information and is a standalone algorithm, based on the changing behaviors of users and collaborative recommendations.

# Hybrid recommendation engines

So far, we have discussed content-based and collaborative-filtering-based recommendation engines. Both types of recommendation engines can be combined to create a hybrid recommendation engine. To do so, we follow these steps:

- Generate a similarity matrix of the items.
- Generate preference matrices of the users.
- Generate recommendations.

Let's look into these steps one by one.

## Generating a similarity matrix of the items

In hybrid recommendation, we start by creating a similarity matrix of items using content-based recommendation. This can be done by using the co-occurrence matrix or by using any distance measure to quantify the similarities between items.

Let's assume that we currently have five items. Using content-based recommendations, we generate a matrix that captures the similarities between items and looks like this:

|        | Item 1 | Item 2 | Item 3 | Item 4 | Item 5 |
|--------|--------|--------|--------|--------|--------|
| Item 1 | 10     | 5      | 3      | 2      | 1      |
| Item 2 | 5      | 10     | 6      | 5      | 3      |
| Item 3 | 3      | 6      | 10     | 1      | 5      |
| Item 4 | 2      | 5      | 1      | 10     | 3      |
| Item 5 | 1      | 3      | 5      | 3      | 10     |

Let's see how we can combine this similarity matrix with a preference matrix to generate recommendations.

## Generating reference vectors of the users

Based on the history of each of the users of the system, we will produce a preference vector that captures those users' interests.

Let's assume that we want to generate recommendations for an online store named *KentStreetOnline*, which sells 100 unique items. KentStreetOnline is popular and has 1 million active subscribers. It is important to note that we need to generate only one similarity matrix with dimensions of 100 by 100. We also need to generate a preference vector for each of the users; this means that we need to generate 1 million preference vectors for each of the 1 million users.

Each entry of the performance vector represents a preference for an item. The value of the first row means that the preference weight for **Item 1** is **4**. For example, the value of the second row means that there is no preference for **Item 2**.

This is graphically shown in the following figure:

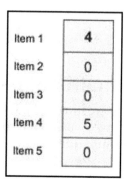

| Item 1 | 4 |
| Item 2 | 0 |
| Item 3 | 0 |
| Item 4 | 5 |
| Item 5 | 0 |

Now, let's look into how we can generate recommendations based on the similarity matrix, S, and the user preference matrix, U.

## Generating recommendations

To make recommendations, we can multiply the matrices. Users are more likely to be interested in an item that co-occurs frequently with an item that they gave a high rating to:

*Matrix[S] x Matrix[U] = Matrix[R]*

This calculation is shown graphically in the following diagram:

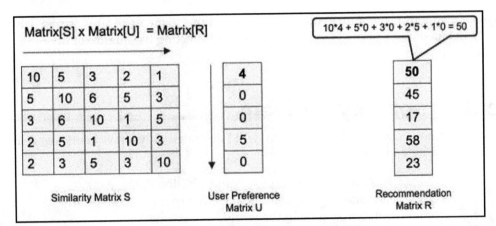

A separate resultant matrix is generated for each of the users. The numbers in the recommendation matrix, *Matrix[R]*, quantify the predicted interest of a user in each of the items. For example, in the resultant matrix the fourth item has the highest number, 58. So this item is highly recommended for this particular user.

Now, let's look into the limitations of different recommender systems.

# Understanding the limitations of recommender systems

Recommendation engines use predictive algorithms to suggest recommendations to a bunch of users. It is a powerful technology, but we should be aware of its limitations. Let's look into the various limitations of recommendation systems.

## The cold start problem

It is obvious that, for collaborative filtering to work, we need to have historical data about user preferences. For a new user, we may not have any data, so our user similarity algorithm will be based on assumptions that may not be accurate. For content-based recommendations, we may not have the details about the new items right away. This requirement of having data about items and users to generate high-quality recommendations is called the **cold start problem**.

## Metadata requirements

Content-based methods require explicit item descriptions to measure similarity. Such explicitly-detailed descriptions may not be available, affecting the quality of the predictions.

## The data sparsity problem

Across an enormous number of items, a user will have rated only a few items, resulting in a very sparse user/item rating matrix.

 Amazon has around a billion users and a billion items. Amazon's recommendation engine is said to have the sparsest data for any recommendation engine in the world.

## Bias due to social influence

Social influence can play an important role in recommenders. Social relations can be seen as an influencing factor on a user's preferences. Friends tend to purchase similar items as well as give similar ratings.

## Limited data

A limited number of reviews makes it difficult for recommender systems to accurately measure user similarities.

## Areas of practical applications

Let's have a look where recommendation systems are applied in the practical world:

- Two-thirds of the movies on Netflix are recommended.
- Thirty-five percent of Amazon's sales come from recommendations.
- On Google News, recommendations generate 38 percent more click-through.
- Attempts to predict a user's preference for an item is based on past ratings of other items.

- They can suggest courses to university students based on their needs and preferences.
- They can match resumes to jobs on online job portals.

Now, let's try to use a recommendation engine to solve a real-world problem.

# Practical example – creating a recommendation engine

Let's build a recommendation engine that can recommend movies to a bunch of users. We will be using data put together by the GroupLens Research research group at the University of Minnesota.

Follow these steps:

1. First, we will import the relevant packages:

   ```
   import pandas as pd
   import numpy as np
   ```

2. Now, let's import the `user_id` and `item_id` datasets:

   ```
   df_reviews = pd.read_csv('reviews.csv')
   df_movie_titles = pd.read_csv('movies.csv',index_col=False)
   ```

3. We merge the two DataFrames by the movie ID:

   ```
   df = pd.merge(df_users, df_movie_titles, on='movieId')
   ```

   The header of the **df** DataFrame, after running the preceding code, looks like the following:

   ```
   Out[5]:
   ```

   |  | userId | movieId | rating | timestamp | title | genres |
   |---|---|---|---|---|---|---|
   | 0 | 1 | 1 | 4.0 | 964982703 | Toy Story (1995) | Adventure\|Animation\|Children\|Comedy\|Fantasy |
   | 1 | 5 | 1 | 4.0 | 847434962 | Toy Story (1995) | Adventure\|Animation\|Children\|Comedy\|Fantasy |
   | 2 | 7 | 1 | 4.5 | 1106635946 | Toy Story (1995) | Adventure\|Animation\|Children\|Comedy\|Fantasy |
   | 3 | 15 | 1 | 2.5 | 1510577970 | Toy Story (1995) | Adventure\|Animation\|Children\|Comedy\|Fantasy |
   | 4 | 17 | 1 | 4.5 | 1305696483 | Toy Story (1995) | Adventure\|Animation\|Children\|Comedy\|Fantasy |

The details of the columns are as follows:

- **userid**: The unique ID of each of the users
- **movieid**: The unique ID of each of the movies
- **rating**: Ratings of each of the movies from 1 to 5
- **timestamp**: The timestamp when the movie was rated
- **title**: The title of the movie
- **genres**: The genre of the movie

4. To look into the summary trends of the input data, let's compute the mean and count of ratings per movie using `groupby` by the `title` and `rating` columns:

```
Out[6]:
```

| title | rating | number_of_ratings |
|---|---|---|
| '71 (2014) | 4.0 | 1 |
| 'Hellboy': The Seeds of Creation (2004) | 4.0 | 1 |
| 'Round Midnight (1986) | 3.5 | 2 |
| 'Salem's Lot (2004) | 5.0 | 1 |
| 'Til There Was You (1997) | 4.0 | 2 |

5. Let's now prepare data for the recommendation engine. For that, we will transform the dataset into a matrix, which will have the following characteristics:

- Movie titles will be columns.
- `User_id` will be the index.
- Ratings will be the value.

We will use the `pivot_table` function of the DataFrame to get it done:

```
movie_matrix = df.pivot_table(index='userId', columns='title',
values='rating')
```

Note that the preceding code will generate a very sparse matrix.

6. Now, let's use this recommendation matrix that we have created to recommend movies. For that, let's consider a particular user who has watched the movie, *Avatar (2009)*. First, we will find all of the users that have shown interest in *Avatar (2009)*:

```
Avatar_user_rating = movie_matrix['Avatar (2009)']
Avatar_user_rating = Avatar_user_rating.dropna()
Avatar_user_rating.head()
```

7. Now, let's try to suggest the movies that correlate with *Avatar (2009)*. For that, we will calculate the correlation of the `Avatar_user_rating` DataFrame with `movie_matrix`, as follows:

```
similar_to_Avatar=movie_matrix.corrwith(Avatar_user_rating)
corr_Avatar = pd.DataFrame(similar_to_Avatar,
columns=['correlation'])
corr_Avatar.dropna(inplace=True)
corr_Avatar = corr_Avatar.join(df_ratings['number_of_ratings'])
corr_Avatar.head()
```

This gives out the following output:

| Out[12]: | | |
|---|---|---|
| **title** | **correlation** | **number_of_ratings** |
| 'burbs, The (1989) | 0.353553 | 17 |
| (500) Days of Summer (2009) | 0.131120 | 42 |
| *batteries not included (1987) | 0.785714 | 7 |
| 10 Things I Hate About You (1999) | 0.265637 | 54 |
| 10,000 BC (2008) | -0.075431 | 17 |

This means that we can use these movies as recommendations for the user.

# Summary

In this chapter, we learned about recommendation engines. We studied the selection of the right recommendation engine based on the problem that we are trying to solve. We also looked into how we can prepare data for recommendation engines to create a similarity matrix. We also learned how recommendation engines can be used to solve practical problems, such as suggesting movies to users based on their past patterns.

In the next chapter, we will focus on the algorithms that are used to understand and process data.

# Section 3: Advanced Topics

3

As the name suggests, we will deal with higher level concepts of algorithms in this section. Cryptography and large scale algorithms are key highlights of this section. The last chapter of this section, and also of the book, explores the practical considerations one should keep in mind while implementing them. The chapters included in this section are:

- Chapter 11, *Data Algorithms*
- Chapter 12, Cryptography
- Chapter 13, *Large Scale Algorithms*
- Chapter 14, *Practical Considerations*

# 11
# Data Algorithms

This chapter is about data-centric algorithms and, in particular, it focuses on three aspects of data-centric algorithms: storage, streaming, and compression. This chapter starts with a brief overview of data-centric algorithms, then we will discuss various strategies that can be used in data storage. Next, how to apply algorithms to streaming data is described, then different methodologies to compress data are discussed. Finally, we will learn how we can use the concepts developed in this chapter to monitor the speeds of cars traveling on a highway using a state-of-the-art sensor network.

By the end of this chapter, you should be able to understand the concepts and trade-offs involved in the design of various data-centric algorithms.

This chapter discusses the following concepts:

- Data classification
- Data storage algorithms
- How to use algorithms to compress data
- How to use algorithms to stream data

Let's first introduce the basic concepts.

## Introduction to data algorithms

Whether we realize it or not, we are living in an era of big data. Just to get an idea about how much data is constantly being generated, just look into some of the numbers published by Google for 2019. As we know, Google Photos is the multimedia repository for storing photos created by Google. In 2019, an average of 1.2 billion photos and videos were uploaded to Google Photos every day. Also, an average of 400 hours of video (amounting to 1 PB of data) were uploaded every minute each day to YouTube. We can safely say the amount of data that is being generated has simply exploded.

The current interest in data-driven algorithms is driven by the fact that data contains valuable information and patterns. If used in the right way, data can become the basis of policy-making decisions, marketing, governance, and trend analysis.

For obvious reasons, algorithms that deal with data are becoming more and more important. Designing algorithms that can process data is an active area of research. There is no doubt that exploring the best ways to use data to provide some quantifiable benefit is the focus of various organizations, businesses, and governments all over the world. But data in its raw form is seldom useful. To mine the information from the raw data, it needs to be processed, prepared, and analyzed.

For that, we first need to store it somewhere. Efficient methodologies to store the data are becoming more and more important. Note that due to the physical storage limitations of single-node systems, big data can only be stored in distributed storage consisting of more than one node connected by high-speed communication links. So, it makes sense that, for learning data algorithms, we start by looking at different data storage algorithms.

First, let's classify data into various categories.

# Data classification

Let's look into how we can classify data in the context of designing data algorithms. As discussed in Chapter 2, *Data Structures Used in Algorithms*, quantifying the volume, variety, and velocity of the data can be used to classify it. This classification can become a basis to design data algorithms that can be used for its storage and processing.

Let's look into these characteristics one by one in the context of data algorithms:

- **Volume** quantifies the amount of data that needs to be stored and processed in an algorithm. As the volume increases, the task becomes data-intensive and requires provisioning enough resources to store, cache, and process data. Big data is a term that vaguely defines a large volume of data that cannot be handled by a single node.
- **Velocity** defines the rate at which new data is being generated. Usually, high-velocity data is called "hot data" or a "hot stream" and low-velocity data is called a "cold stream" or simply "cold data". In many applications, data will be a mix of hot and cold streams that will first need to be prepared and combined into a single table before it can be used with the algorithm.
- **Variety** refers to different types of structured and unstructured data that needs to be combined into a single table before it can be used by the algorithm.

The next section will help us to understand the trade-offs involved and will present various design choices when designing storage algorithms.

# Presenting data storage algorithms

A reliable and efficient data repository is the heart of a distributed system. If this data repository is created for analytics, then it is also called a data lake. A data repository brings together data from different domains into a single location. Let's start with first understanding different issues related to the storage of data in a distributed repository.

## Understanding data storage strategies

In the initial years of digital computing, the usual way of designing a data repository was by using a single node architecture. With the ever-increasing sizes of datasets, distributed storage of data has now become mainstream. The right strategy to store data in a distributed environment depends on the type of data and its expected usage pattern as well as its non-functional requirements. To further analyze the requirements of a distributed data store, let's start with the **Consistency Availability Partition-Tolerance (CAP)** theorem, which provides us with the basis of devising a data storage strategy for a distributed system.

### Presenting the CAP theorem

In 1998, Eric Brewer proposed a theorem that later became famous as the CAP theorem. It highlights the various trade-offs involved in designing a distributed storage system.

To understand the CAP theorem, first, let's define the following three characteristics of distributed storage systems: consistency, availability, and partition tolerance. CAP is, in fact, an acronym made up of these three characteristics:

- **Consistency** (or simply C): The distributed storage consists of various nodes. Any of these nodes can be used to read, write, or update records in the data repository. Consistency guarantees that at a certain time, $t_1$, independent of which node we use to read the data, we will get the same result. Every *read* operation either returns the latest data that is consistent across the distributed repository or gives an error message.
- **Availability** (or simply A): Availability guarantees that any node in the distributed storage system will be able to immediately handle the request with or without consistency.

- **Partition Tolerance** (or simply P): In a distributed system, multiple nodes are connected via a communication network. Partition tolerance guarantees that, in the event of communication failure between a small subset of nodes (one or more), the system remains operational. Note that to guarantee partition tolerance, data needs to be replicated across a sufficient number of nodes.

Using these three characteristics, the CAP theorem carefully summarizes the trade-offs involved in the architecture and design of a distributed system. Specifically, the CAP theorem states that, in a storage system, we can only have two of the following characteristics: consistency or C, availability or A, and partition tolerance or P.

This is shown in the following diagram:

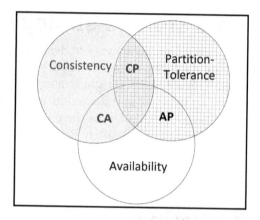

The CAP theorem also means that we can have three types of distributed storage systems:

- A CA system (implementing Consistency-Availability)
- An AP system (implementing Availability-Partition Tolerance)
- A CP system (implementing Consistency-Partition Tolerance)

Let's look into them, one by one.

## CA systems

Traditional single-node systems are CA systems. This is because if we do not have a distributed system, then we do not need to worry about partition tolerance. In that case, we can have a system that has both consistency and availability, that is, a CA system.

Traditional single-node databases such as Oracle or MySQL are all examples of CA systems.

## AP systems

AP systems are the distributed storage systems tuned for availability. Designed as highly-responsive systems, they can sacrifice consistency, if needed, to accommodate high-velocity data. This means that these are distributed storage systems that are designed to immediately handle requests from users. Typical user requests are to read or write fast-changing data. Typical AP systems are used in real-time monitoring systems such as sensor networks.

High-velocity distributed databases, such as Cassandra, are good examples of AP systems.

Let's look into where an AP system can be used. If Transport Canada wants to monitor traffic on one of the highways in Ottawa through a network of sensors installed at different locations on the highway, an AP system is recommended for implementing distributed data storage.

## CP systems

CP systems have both consistency and partition tolerance. This means that these are the distributed storage systems that are tuned to guarantee consistency before a read process can fetch a value.

A typical use case for CP systems is when we want to store document files in JSON format. Document datastores such as MongoDB are CP systems tuned for consistency in a distributed environment.

Distributed data storage is increasingly becoming the most important part of a modern IT infrastructure. Distributed data storage should be carefully designed based on the characteristics of the data and the requirements of the problem we want to solve. Classifying data storage into CA, AP, and CP systems help us to understand the various trade-offs involved when designing data storage systems.

Now, let's look into streaming data algorithms.

# Presenting streaming data algorithms

Data can be categorized as bounded or unbounded. Bounded data is data at rest and is usually processed through a batch process. Streaming is basically data processing on unbounded data. Let's look into an example. Let's assume that we are analyzing fraudulent transactions at a bank. If we want to look for fraud transactions 7 days ago, we have to look at the data at rest; this is an example of a batch process.

n the other hand, if we want to detect fraud in real-time, that is an example of streaming. Hence, streaming data algorithms are those algorithms that deal with processing data streams. The fundamental idea is to divide the input data stream into batches, which are then processed by the processing node. Streaming algorithms need to be fault-tolerant and should be able to handle the incoming velocity of data. As the demand for real-time trend analysis is increasing, the demand for stream processing is also increasing these days. Note that, for streaming to work, data has to be processed fast and while designing algorithms, this needs to be always kept in mind.

## Applications of streaming

There are many applications of streaming data and its utilization in a meaningful way. Some of the applications are as follows:

- Fraud detection
- System monitoring
- Smart order routing
- Live dashboards
- Traffic sensors along highways
- Credit card transactions
- User moves in multi-user online gaming

Now, let's see how we can implement streaming using Python.

# Presenting data compression algorithms

Data compression algorithms are involved in the process of reducing the size of data.

In this chapter, we will delve into a specific data compression algorithm named the lossless compression algorithm.

# Lossless compression algorithms

These are algorithms that are capable of compressing data in such a way that it can be decompressed without any loss of information. They are used when it is important to retrieve the exact original files after decompression. Typical uses of lossless compression algorithms are as follows:

- To compress documents
- To compress and package source code and executable files
- To convert a large number of small files into a small number of large files

# Understanding the basic techniques of lossless compression

Data compression is based on the principle that the majority of data is known to be using more bits than its entropy indicates is optimal. Recall that entropy is a term used to specify the information that the data carries. It means that a more optimal bit representation of the same information is possible. Exploring and formulating more efficient bit representation becomes the basis for devising compression algorithms. Lossless data compression takes advantage of this redundancy to compress data without losing any information. In the late '80s, Ziv and Lempel proposed dictionary-based data compression techniques that can be used to implement lossless data compression. These techniques were an instant hit due to their speed and good compression rate. These techniques were used to create the popular Unix-based *compress* tool. Also, the ubiquitous `gif` image format uses these compression techniques, which proved to be popular as they could be used to represent the same information in a lesser number of bits, saving space and communication bandwidth. These techniques later became the basis of developing the `zip` utility and its variants. The compression standard, V.44, used in modems is also based on it.

Let's now look at the techniques one by one in the upcoming sections.

# Huffman coding

Huffman coding is one of the oldest methods of compressing data and is based on creating a Huffman tree, which is used to both encode and decode data. Huffman coding can represent data content in a more compact form by exploiting the fact that some data (for instance certain characters of the alphabet) appears more frequently in a data stream. By using encodings of different length (shorter for the most frequent characters and longer for the least frequent ones), the data consumes less space.

Now, let's learn a few terminologies related to Huffman coding:

- **Coding**: Coding in the context of data represents the method of representing data from one form to another. We would like the resultant form to be concise.
- **Codeword**: A particular character in encoded form is called a codeword.
- **Fixed-length coding**: This is when each encoded character, that is, codeword, uses the same number of bits.
- **Variable-length coding**: Codewords can use a different number of bits.
- **Evaluation of code**: This is the expected number of bits per codeword.
- **Prefix free codes**: This means that no codeword is a prefix of any other codeword.
- **Decoding**: This means that a variable-length code must be free from any prefix.

For understanding the last two terms, you need to have a look at this table first:

| character | frequency | fixed length code | variable length code |
|---|---|---|---|
| L | .45 | 000 | 0 |
| M | .13 | 001 | 101 |
| N | .12 | 010 | 100 |
| X | .16 | 011 | 111 |
| Y | .09 | 100 | 1101 |
| Z | .05 | 101 | 1100 |

Now, we can infer the following:

- **Fixed length code**: The fixed-length code for this table is 3.
- **Variable length code**: The variable-length code for this table is *45(1) + .13(3) + .12(3) + .16(3) + .09(4) + .05(4) = 2.24*.

The following diagram shows the Huffman tree created from the preceding example:

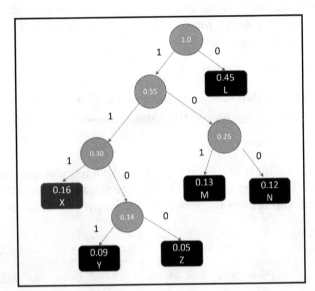

Note that Huffman encoding is about converting data into a Huffman tree that enables compression. Decoding or decompression brings the data back to the original format.

# A practical example – Twitter real-time sentiment analysis

Twitter is said to have almost 7,000 tweets every second on a wide variety of topics. Let's try to build a sentiment analyzer that can capture the emotions of the news from different news sources in real time. We will start by importing the required packages:

1. Import the needed packages:

```
import tweepy, json, time
import numpy as np
import pandas as pd
import matplotlib.pyplot as plt
from vaderSentiment.vaderSentiment import
SentimentIntensityAnalyzer
analyzer = SentimentIntensityAnalyzer()
```

Note that we are using the following two packages:

2. **VADER** sentiment analysis, which stands for **Valence Aware Dictionary and Sentiment Reasoner**. It is one of the popular rule-based sentiment analysis tools that is developed for social media. If you have never used it before, then you will first have to run the following:

```
pip install vaderSentiment
```

3. Tweepy, which is a Python-based API to access Twitter. Again, if you have never used it before, you need to first run this:

```
pip install Tweepy
```

4. The next step is a bit tricky. You need to make a request to create a developer account with Twitter to get access to the live stream of tweets. Once you have the API keys, you can represent them with the following variables:

```
twitter_access_token = <your_twitter_access_token>
twitter_access_token_secret = <your_twitter_access_token_secret>
twitter_consumer_key = <your_consumer_key>
twitter_consumer_secret = <your_twitter_consumer_secret>
```

5. Let's then configure the Tweepy API authentication. For that, we need to provide the previously created variables:

```
auth = tweepy.OAuthHandler(twitter_consumer_key,
twitter_consumer_secret)
auth.set_access_token(twitter_access_token,
twitter_access_token_secret)
api = tweepy.API(auth, parser=tweepy.parsers.JSONParser())
```

6. Now comes the interesting part. We will choose the Twitter handles of the news sources that we want to monitor for sentiment analysis. For this example, we have chosen the following news sources:

```
news_sources = ("@BBC", "@ctvnews", "@CNN","@FoxNews", "@dawn_com")
```

7. Now, let's create the main loop. This loop will start with an empty array called `array_sentiments` to hold the sentiments. Then, we will loop through all five news sources and collect 100 tweets each. Then, for each tweet, we will calculate its polarity:

```
In [12]:  # We start extracting 100 tweets from each of the news sources
          print("...STARTING..... collecting tweets from sources")

          # Let us define an array to hold the sentiments
          array_sentiments = []

          for user in news_sources:
              count_tweet=100  # Setting the twitter count at 100
              print("Start tweets from %s"%user)
              for x in range(5):        # Extracting 5 pages of tweets
                  public_tweets=api.user_timeline(user,page=x)
                  # For each tweet
                  for tweet in public_tweets:
                      #Calculating the compound,+ive,-ive and neutral value for each tweet
                      compound = analyzer.polarity_scores(tweet["text"])["compound"]
                      pos = analyzer.polarity_scores(tweet["text"])["pos"]
                      neu = analyzer.polarity_scores(tweet["text"])["neu"]
                      neg = analyzer.polarity_scores(tweet["text"])["neg"]

                      array_sentiments.append({"Media":user,
                                              "Tweet Text":tweet["text"],
                                              "Compound":compound,
                                              "Positive":pos,
                                              "Negative":neg,
                                              "Neutral":neu,
                                              "Date":tweet["created_at"],
                                              "Tweets Ago":count_tweet})

                      count_tweet-=1

          print("DONE with extracting tweets")
...STARTING..... collecting tweets from sources
Start tweets from @BBC
Start tweets from @ctvnews
Start tweets from @CNN
Start tweets from @FoxNews
Start tweets from @dawn_com
DONE with extracting tweets
```

8. Now, let's create a graph that shows the polarity of the news from these individual news sources:

```
In [21]: for media in source:
             mydf=sentiments_df[sentiments_df["Media"]==media]
             plt.scatter(mydf["Tweets Ago"],mydf["Compound"], marker="o", linewidth=0, alpha=0.8, label=media,
                         facecolors=mydf.Media.map({"BBC": "pink", "ctvnews" : "purple",  "CNN": 'red',
                                                    "FoxNews":"blue","dawn_com":"green"}))

         plt.legend(bbox_to_anchor = (1,1),title="Media Sources")
         plt.title("Sentiment Analysis of Media Tweets (%s)" % (time.strftime("%x")), fontsize=14)
         plt.xlabel("Tweets Ago")
         plt.ylabel("Tweet Polarity")
         plt.xlim(101,0)
         plt.ylim(-1,1)
         plt.grid(True)
         plt.savefig("Output/Sentiment Analysis of Media Tweets.png",bbox_inches='tight')
         plt.show()
```

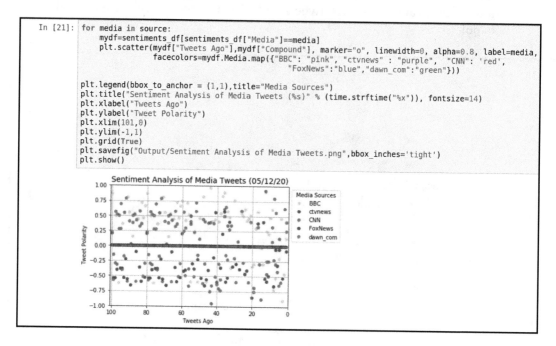

Note that each of the news sources is represented by a different color.

9. Now, let's look at the summary statistics:

```
In [22]: # Calculating the mean for each Media channel and storing to a dataframe
         means_media_trends=sentiments_df.groupby("Media").mean()["Compound"].to_frame()
         #Resetting the index
         means_media_trends.reset_index(inplace=True)

         means_media_trends
```

Out[22]:

|   | Media | Compound |
|---|---|---|
| 0 | BBC | 0.234137 |
| 1 | CNN | 0.057011 |
| 2 | FoxNews | 0.000000 |
| 3 | ctvnews | -0.194618 |
| 4 | dawn_com | -0.025389 |

The preceding numbers summarize the trends of the sentiments. For example, the sentiments of BBC are found to be the most positive, and the Canadian news channel, CTVnews, seems to be carrying the most negative emotions.

# Summary

In this chapter, we looked at the design of data-centric algorithms. We focused on three aspects of data-centric algorithms: storage, compression, and streaming.

We looked into how the characteristics of data can dictate the data storage design. We looked into two different types of data compression algorithms. Then, we studied a practical example of how data streaming algorithms can be used to count words from a stream of textual data.

In the next chapter, we will look at cryptographic algorithms. We will learn how we can use the power of these algorithms to secure exchanged and stored messages.

# 12
# Cryptography

This chapter introduces you to algorithms related to cryptography. We will start by presenting the background, then we will discuss symmetric encryption algorithms. We will then explain the **Message-Digest 5 (MD5)** algorithm and the **Secure Hash Algorithm (SHA)** and present the limitations and weaknesses of implementing symmetric algorithms. Next, we will discuss asymmetric encryption algorithms and how they are used to create digital certificates. Finally, we will present a practical example that summarizes all of these techniques.

By the end of this chapter, you will have a basic understanding of various issues related to cryptography.

The following topics are discussed in this chapter:

- Introduction to cryptography
- Understanding the types of cryptography techniques
- Example – security concerns when deploying a machine learning model

Let's start by looking at the basic concepts.

# Introduction to Cryptography

Techniques to protect secrets have been around for centuries. The earliest attempts to secure and hide data from adversaries date back to ancient inscriptions discovered on monuments in Egypt, where a special alphabet that was known by only a few trusted people was used. This early form of security is called **obscurity** and is still used in different forms today. In order for this method to work, it is critical to protect the secret, which is the meaning of the alphabet. Later in time, finding foolproof ways of protecting important messages was important in both World War One and World War Two. In the late-20$^{th}$ century, with the introduction of electronics and computers, sophisticated algorithms were developed to secure data, giving rise to a whole new field called **cryptography**. This chapter discusses the algorithmic aspects of cryptography. The purpose of these algorithms is to allow secure data exchange between two processes or users. Cryptographic algorithms find strategies of using mathematical functions to ensure the stated security goals.

# Understanding the Importance of the Weakest Link

Sometimes, when architecting the security of digital infrastructure, we put too much emphasis on the security of individual entities and don't pay the necessary attention to end-to-end security. This can result in us overlooking some loopholes and vulnerabilities in the system, which can later be exploited by hackers to access sensitive data. The important point to remember is that a digital infrastructure, as a whole, is only as strong as its **weakest link**. For a hacker, this weakest link can provide backdoor access to the sensitive data in the digital infrastructure. Beyond a certain point, there is not much benefit in fortifying the front door without closing all the back doors.

As the algorithms and techniques for keeping digital infrastructure become more and more sophisticated, attackers keep upgrading their techniques as well. It is always important to remember that one of the easiest ways for attackers to hack digital infrastructure is by exploiting these vulnerabilities to access sensitive information.

In 2014, a cyber attack on a Canadian federal research institute—the **National Research Council (NRC)**—is estimated to have cost hundreds of millions of dollars. The attackers were able to steal decades of research data and intellectual property material. They used a loophole in the Apache software that was used on the web servers to gain access to the sensitive data.

In this chapter, we will highlight the vulnerabilities of various encryption algorithms.

Let's first look at the basic terminology used.

# The Basic Terminology

Let's look at the basic terminology related to cryptography:

- **Cipher**: An algorithm that performs a particular cryptographic function.
- **Plain text**: The plain data, which can be a text file, a video, a bitmap, or a digitized voice. In this chapter, we will represent plain text as $P$.
- **Cipher text**: The scrambled text that is obtained after applying cryptography to the plain text. In this chapter, we will represent this as $C$.
- **Cipher suite**: A set or suite of cryptographic software components. When two separate nodes want to exchange messages using cryptography, they first need to agree on a cipher suite. This is important in ensuring that they use exactly the same implementation of the cryptographic functions.
- **Encryption**: The process of converting plain text, $P$, into cipher text, $C$, is called encryption. Mathematically, it is represented by $encrypt(P) = C$.
- **Decryption**: The process of converting cipher text back into plain text. Mathematically, it is represented by $decrypt(C) = P$.
- **Cryptanalysis**: The methods used to analyze the strength of the cryptographic algorithms. The analyst tries to recover the plain text without access to the secret.
- **Personally Identifiable Information (PII)**: PII is the information that can be used to trace an individual's identity when used alone or with other relevant data. Some examples include protected information, such as a social security number, date of birth, or mother's maiden name.

# Understanding the Security Requirements

It is important to first understand the exact security needs of a system. Understanding this will help us use the correct cryptographic technique and discover the potential loopholes in a system. In order to do this, we first need to better understand the needs of the system. In order to understand the security requirements, we perform the following three steps:

- Identify the entities.
- Establish the security goals.
- Understand the sensitivity of the data.

Let's look at these steps one by one.

# Identifying the Entities

One way to identify the entities is to start by answering the following four questions, which will help us understand the needs of the system in the context of security:

- Which applications need to be protected?
- Who are we protecting the applications from?
- Where should we protect them?
- Why are we protecting them?

Once we better understand these requirements, we can establish the security goals of our digital system.

# Establishing the Security Goals

Cryptographic algorithms are typically used to meet one or more security goals:

- **Authentication**: Simply put, authentication is how we prove that a user is who they claim to be. Through the process of authentication, we ensure that a user's identity is verified. The process of authentication starts by having the user present their identity. This is followed by providing information that is only known by the user and so can only be produced by them.
- **Confidentiality**: Data that needs to be protected is called **sensitive data**. Confidentiality is the concept of restricting sensitive data to authorized users only. To protect the confidentiality of sensitive data during its transit or in storage, you need to render the data so that it is unreadable except by authorized users. This is accomplished by using encryption algorithms, which we will discuss later on in this chapter.
- **Integrity**: Integrity is the process of establishing that data has not been altered in any way during its transit or storage. For example, **TCP/IP (Transmission Control Protocol/Internet Protocol)** uses checksum or **Cyclic Redundancy Check (CRC)** algorithms to verify data integrity.
- **Non-repudiation**: Non-repudiation is the concept of a sender of information receiving confirmation that the data was received and the recipient receiving confirmation of the sender's identity. This provides irrefutable evidence that a message was sent or received, which can be used later to prove the receipt of data and the points of failures in communication.

# Understanding the Sensitivity of the Data

It is important to understand the classified nature of data. We also need to think about how serious the consequences are if the data is compromised. The classification of the data helps us choose the correct cryptographic algorithm. There is more than one way to classify data, based on the sensitivity of the information it contains. Let's look at the typical ways of classifying data:

- **Public data or unclassified data**: Anything that is available for consumption for the public. For example, information found on a company's website or a government's info portal.
- **Internal data or confidential data**: Although not for public consumption, exposing this data to the public may not have damaging consequences. For example, if an employee's emails complaining about their manager are exposed, it may be embarrassing for the company but this may not have damaging consequences.
- **Sensitive data or secret data**: Data that is not supposed to be for public consumption and exposing it to the public has damaging consequences for an individual or an organization. For example, leaking the details of a future iPhone may harm Apple's business goals and can give an advantage to rivals, such as Samsung.
- **Highly sensitive data**: Also called **top-secret data**. This is information that if disclosed, would be extremely damaging to the organization. This can include customer social security numbers, credit card numbers, or other very sensitive information. Top-secret data is protected through multiple layers of security and requires special permission to access.

 In general, more sophisticated security designs are much slower than simple algorithms. It is important to strike the right balance between the security and the performance of the system.

# Understanding the Basic Design of Ciphers

Designing ciphers is about coming up with an algorithm that can scramble sensitive data so that a malicious process or an unauthorized user cannot access it. Although over time ciphers have become more and more sophisticated, the underlying principles that ciphers are based on remain unchanged.

Let's start by looking at some relatively simple ciphers that will help us understand the underlying principles that are used in the design of cryptographic algorithms.

# Presenting Substitution Ciphers

Substitution ciphers have been in use for hundreds of years in various forms. As the name indicates, substitution ciphers are based on a simple concept—substituting characters in plain text with other characters in a predetermined, organized way.

Let's look at the exact steps involved in this:

1.  First, we map each character to a substitute character.
2.  Then, encode and convert the plaintext into cipher text by replacing each character in the plain text with another character in the ciphertext using substitution mapping.
3.  To decode, bring back the plaintext by using substitution mapping.

Let's look at some examples:

*   **Caesar cipher**:

    In Caesar ciphers, the substitution mapping is created by replacing each character with the third character to the right of it. This mapping is described in the following diagram:

    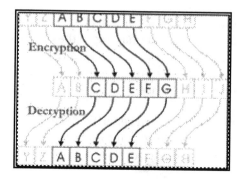

    Let's see how we can implement a Caesar cipher using Python:

    ```
    import string
    rotation = 3
    P = 'CALM'; C=''
    for letter in P:
        C = C+ (chr(ord(letter) + rotation))
    ```

    We can see that we applied a Caesar cipher to the plaintext, CALM.

Let's print the cipher text after encrypting with the Caesar cipher:

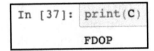

```
In [37]:  print(C)
          FDOP
```

 Caesar ciphers are said to have been used by Julius Caesar to communicate with his advisers.

- **Rotation 13 (ROT13):**

ROT13 is another of the substitution-based encryptions. In ROT13, the substitution mapping is created by replacing each character with the 13th character to the right of it. The following diagram illustrates this:

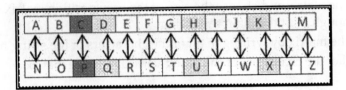

This means that if `ROT13()` is the function that implements ROT13, then the following applies:

```
import codecs
P = 'CALM'
C=''
C=codecs.encode(P, 'rot_13')
```

Now, let's print the encoded value of C:

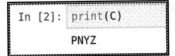

```
In [2]:  print(C)
         PNYZ
```

- **Cryptanalysis of substitution ciphers** :

  Substitution ciphers are simple to implement and understand. Unfortunately, they are also easy to crack. A simple cryptanalysis of substitution ciphers shows that if we use the English language alphabet, then all we need to determine to crack the cipher is how much are we rotating by. We can try each letter of the English alphabet one by one until we are able to decrypt the text. This means that it will take around 25 attempts to reconstruct the plain text.

Now, let's look at another type of simple cipher—transposition ciphers.

# Understanding Transposition Ciphers

In transposition ciphers, the characters of the plain text are transposed. Let's look at the steps involved for this:

1. Create the matrix and choose the size of the transposition matrix. It should be large enough to fit the plain text string.
2. Fill in the matrix by writing in all of the characters of the string horizontally.
3. Read all of the characters of the string vertically in the matrix.

Let's look at an example.

Let's take the `Ottawa Rocks` plain text (*P*).

First, let's encode *P*. For that, we will use a 3 x 4 matrix and write in the plaintext horizontally:

| O | t | t | a |
|---|---|---|---|
| w | a | R | o |
| c | k | s | |

The `read` process will read the string vertically, which will generate the cipher text—`OwctaktRsao`.

The Germans used a cipher named ADFGVX in the First World War, which used both the transposition and substitution ciphers. Years later, it was cracked by George Painvin.

So, these are some of the types of ciphers. Now, let's look at some of the cryptographic techniques that are currently used.

# Understanding the Types of Cryptographic Techniques

Different types of cryptographic techniques use different types of algorithms and are used under different sets of circumstances.

Broadly, cryptographic techniques can be divided into the following three types:

- Hashing
- Symmetric
- Asymmetric

Let's look at them one by one.

# Using the Cryptographic Hash Function

The cryptographic hash function is a mathematical algorithm that can be used to create unique fingerprint of a message. It creates a fixed-sized output, called a **hash**, from plain text.

Mathematically, this looks as follows:

$$C_1 = hashFunction(P_1)$$

This is explained as follows:

- $P_1$ is the plain text representing the input data.
- $C_1$ is a fixed-length hash that is generated by the cryptographic hash function.

This is shown in the following diagram. The variable-length data is converted into a fixed-length hash through a one-way hash function:

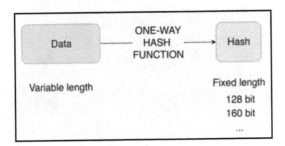

The hash function has the following five characteristics:

- It is deterministic. The same plain text generates the same hash.
- Unique input strings should generate unique output hash values.
- Regardless of the input message, it has a fixed length.
- Even small changes in the plain text generate a new hash.
- It is a one-way function, which means that plain text, $P_1$, cannot be generated from the cipher text, $C_1$.

If we have a situation where each unique message does not have a unique hash, we call it a **collision**. That is, if we have two texts, $P_1$ and $P_2$, in the case of collision, it means $hashFunction(P_1) = hashFunction(P_2)$.

Regardless of the hashing algorithm used, collisions are rare. Otherwise, hashing wouldn't be useful. However, for some applications, collisions cannot be tolerated. In those cases, we need to use a hashing algorithm that is more complex but much less likely to generate hash values that collide.

# Implementing cryptographic hash functions

Cryptographic hash functions can be implemented by using various algorithms. Let's take a deeper look at two of them.

### Understanding MD5-tolerated

MD5 was developed by Poul-Henning Kamp in 1994 to replace MD4. It generates a 128-bit hash. MD5 is a relatively simple algorithm that is vulnerable to collision. In applications where a collision cannot be tolerated, MD5 should not be used.

Let's look at an example. In order to generate an MD5 hash in Python, we will use the `passlib` library, which one of the most popular open source libraries, implementing over 30 password-hashing algorithms. If it is not already installed on your device, install it by using the following code in a Jupyter notebook:

```
!pip install passlib
```

In Python, we can generate the MD5 hash as follows:

```
In [36]:  myHash

Out[36]:  '$1$a6sQqHlF$j5iHhbCzmOzVwrxWDxnUu.'
```

Note that MD5 generates a hash of 128 bits.

As mentioned, we can use this generated hash as a fingerprint of the original text, which was myPassword. Let's see how we can do this in Python:

```
In [37]:  md5_crypt.verify("myPassword", myHash)

Out[37]:  True

In [38]:  md5_crypt.verify("myPassword2", myHash)

Out[38]:  False
```

Note that the generated hash for the myPassword string matched the original hash, which generated a True value. However, it returned False as soon as the plain text was changed to myPassword2.

Now, let's look at another hashing algorithm—**Secure Hash Algorithm (SHA)**.

## Understanding SHA

SHA was developed by the **National Institute of Standards and Technology** (NIST). Let's see how we can use Python to create a hash using the SHA algorithm:

```
from passlib.hash import sha512_crypt
sha512_crypt.using(salt = "qIo0foX5", rounds=5000).hash("myPassword")
```

Note the use of a parameter called salt. Salting is the procedure of adding random characters before hashing.

Running this code will give us the following result:

```
In [13]:  myHash

Out[13]:  '$6$qIo0foX5$a.RA/OyedLnLEnWovzqngCqhyy3EfqRtwacvWKsIoYSvYgRxCRetM3XSwrgMxwdPqZt4KfbXzCp6y
          NyxI5j6o/'
```

Note that when we use the SHA algorithm, the hash generated is of 512 bytes.

# An Application of the Cryptographic Hash Function

Hash functions are used to check the integrity of a file after making a copy of it. To achieve this, when a file is copied from a source to a destination (for example, when downloaded from a web server), a corresponding hash is also copied with it. This original hash, $h_{original}$, acts as a fingerprint of the original file. After copying the file, we generate the hash again from the copied version of the file—that is, $h_{copied}$. If $h_{original} = h_{copied}$—that is, the generated hash matches the original hash—this verifies that the file has not changed and none of the data was lost during the download process. We can use any cryptographic hash function, such as MD5 or SHA, to generate a hash for this purpose.

Now, let's look at symmetric encryption.

# Using Symmetric Encryption

In cryptography, a key is a combination of numbers that is used to encode plain text using an algorithm of our choice. In symmetric encryption, we use the same key for encryption and decryption. If the key used for symmetric encryption is $K$, then for symmetric encryption, the following equation holds:

$$E_K(P) = C$$

Here, $P$ is the plain text and $C$ is the cipher text.

For decryption, we use the same key, $K$, to convert it back to $P$:

$$D_K(C) = P$$

This process is shown in the following diagram:

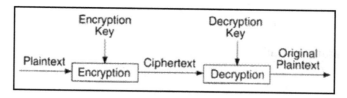

Now, let's look at how we can use symmetric encryption with Python.

# Coding Symmetric Encryption

We will use Python's `cryptography` package, in this section, to demonstrate symmetric encryption. It is a comprehensive package that implements many cryptographic algorithms, such as symmetric ciphers and different message digests. When using it for the first time, we first need to install it using the `pip` command:

```
!pip install cryptography
```

Once installed, we can now use the package to implement symmetric encryption, as follows:

1. First, let's import the packages we need:

   ```
   import cryptography as crypt
   from cryptography.fernet import Fernet
   ```

2. Let's generate the key:

   ```
   In [29]:  key = Fernet.generate_key()
             print(key)

             b'NbzXiNqKR25SEv_O8EpuW2Lr_QO2vDStTDV4ex4WA5U='
   ```

3. Now, let's open the key:

   ```
   file = open('mykey.key', 'wb')
   file.write(key)
   file.close()
   ```

4. Using the key, let's now try to encrypt the message:

   ```
   file = open('mykey.key', 'rb')
   key = file.read()
   file.close()
   ```

5. Now, let's decrypt the message using the same key:

   ```
   from cryptography.fernet import Fernet
   message = "Ottawa is really cold".encode()

   f = Fernet(key)
   encrypted = f.encrypt(message)
   ```

6. Let's decrypt the message and assign it to a variable named `decrypt`:

```
decrypted = f.decrypt(encrypted)
```

7. Let's now print the `decrypt` variable to verify whether we are able to get the same message:

```
In [46]:  print(decrypted)
          b'Ottawa is really cold'
```

Let's look at some of the advantages of symmetric encryption.

## The Advantages of Symmetric Encryption

Although the performance of the symmetric encryption is dependent on the exact algorithm that is used, in general, it is a lot faster than asymmetric encryption.

## The Problems with Symmetric Encryption

When two users or processes plan to use symmetric encryption to communicate, they need to exchange keys using a secure channel. This gives rise to the following two problems:

- **Key protection**: How to protect the symmetric encryption key.
- **Key distribution**: How to share the symmetric encryption key from the source to the destination.

Now, let's look at asymmetric encryption.

## Asymmetric Encryption

In the 1970s, asymmetric encryption was devised to address some of the weaknesses of symmetric encryption that we discussed in the previous section.

The first step in asymmetric encryption is to generate two different keys that look totally different but are algorithmically related. One of them is chosen as the private key, $K_{pr}$, and the other one is chosen as the public key, $K_{pu}$. Mathematically, we can represent this as follows:

$$E_{Kpr}(P) = C$$

Here, *P* is the plain text and *C* is the cipher text.

We can decrypt it as follows:

$$D_{Kpu}(C) = P$$

Public keys are supposed to be freely distributed and private keys are kept secret by the owner of the key pair.

The fundamental principle is that if you encrypt with one of the keys, the only way to decrypt it is by using the other key. For example, if we encrypt the data using the public key, we will need to decrypt it using the other key—that is, the private key. Now, let's look at one of the fundamental protocols of asymmetric encryption—the **Secure Sockets Layer (SSL)/Transport Layer Security (TLS)** handshake—which is responsible for establishing a connection between two nodes using asymmetric encryption.

## The SSL/TLS Handshaking Algorithm

SSL was originally developed to add security to HTTP. Over time, SSL was replaced with a more efficient and more secure protocol, called TLS. TLS handshakes are the basis of how HTTP creates a secure communication session. A TLS handshake occurs between the two participating entities—the **client** and the **server**. This process is shown in the following diagram:

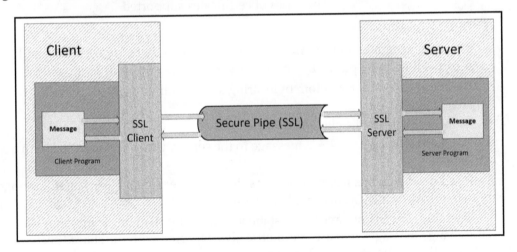

*Cryptography*

A TLS handshake establishes a secure connection between the participating nodes. The following are the steps that are involved in this process:

1. The client sends a `client hello` message to the server. The message also contains the following:
   - The version of TLS that is used
   - The list of cipher suites supported by the client
   - A compression algorithm
   - A random byte string, identified by `byte_client`

2. The server sends a `server hello` message back to the client. The message also contains the following:
   - A cipher suite selected by the server from the list provided by the client
   - A session ID
   - A random byte string, identified by `byte_server`
   - A server digital certificate, identified by `cert_server`, containing the public key of the server
   - If the server requires a digital certificate for client authentication or a client certificate request, the client server request also includes the following:
     - The distinguished names of the acceptable CAs
     - The types of certificates supported

3. The client verifies `cert_server`.
4. The client generates a random byte string, identified by `byte_client2`, and encrypts it with the public key of the server provided through `cert_server`.
5. The client generates a random byte string and identifies encrypts with its own private key.
6. The server verifies the client certificate.
7. The client sends a `finished` message to the server, which is encrypted with a secret key.
8. To acknowledge this from the server side, the server sends a `finished` message to the client, which is encrypted with a secret key.
9. The server and client have now established a secure channel. They can now exchange messages that are symmetrically encrypted with the shared secret key. The entire methodology is shown as follows:

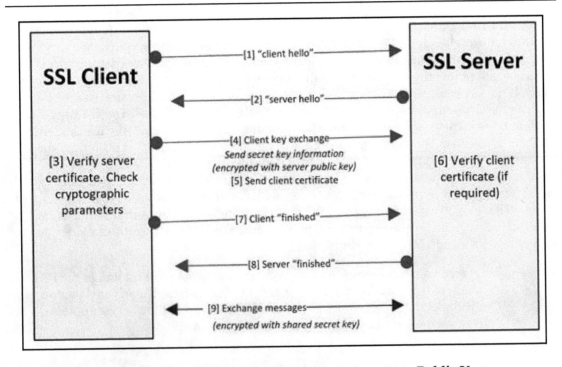

Now, let's discuss how we can use asymmetric encryption to create **Public Key Infrastructure (PKI)**, which is created to meet one or more security goals for an organization.

# Public Key Infrastructure

Asymmetric encryption is used to implement PKI. PKI is one of the most popular and reliable ways to manage encryption keys for an organization. All the participants trust a central trusting authority called a CA. CAs verify the identity of individuals and organizations and then issue them digital certificates (a digital certificate contains a copy of a person or organization's public key and its identity), verifying that the public key associated with that individual or organization actually belongs to that individual or organization.

The way it works is that the CA asks a user to prove their identity, with different standards followed for individuals and organizations. This could involve simply verifying ownership of a domain name, or it could involve a more rigorous process that involves physical proof of identity, depending on the type of digital certificate that a user is trying to obtain. If the CA is satisfied that the user is indeed who they claim to be, the user then provides the CA with their public encryption key over a secure channel. The CA uses this information to create a digital certificate that contains information about the user's identity and their public key. This certificate is digitally signed by the CA. The user can then show their certificate to anyone who wants to verify their identity, without having to send it through a secure channel, as the certificate doesn't contain any sensitive information itself. The person receiving the certificate does not have to verify the user's identity directly. That person can simply verify that the certificate is valid by verifying the CA's digital signature, which validates that the public key contained in the certificate does, in fact, belong to the individual or organization named on the certificate.

 The private key of the CA of an organization is the weakest link in the PKI chain of trust. If an impersonator gets hold of Microsoft's private key, for example, they can install malicious software onto millions of computers around the world by impersonating a Windows update.

# Example – Security Concerns When Deploying a Machine Learning Model

In Chapter 6, *Unsupervised Machine Learning Algorithms*, we looked at the **CRISP-DM (Cross-Industry Standard Process for Data Mining)** life cycle, which specifies the different phases of training and deploying a machine learning model. Once a model is trained and evaluated, the final phase is deployment. If it is a critical machine learning model, then we want to make sure that all of its security goals are met.

Let's analyze the common challenges faced in deploying a model such as this and how we can address those challenges using the concepts discussed in this chapter. We will discuss strategies to protect our trained model against the following three challenges:

- **Man-in-the-Middle (MITM)** attacks
- Masquerading
- Data tempering

Let's look at them one by one.

# MITM attacks

One of the possible attacks that we would want to protect our model against is MITM attacks. A MITM attack occurs when an intruder tries to eavesdrop on a supposedly private communication to deploy a trained machine learning model.

Let's try to understand MITM attacks sequentially using an example scenario.

Let's assume that Bob and Alice want to exchange messages using PKI:

1.  Bob is using {$Pr_{Bob}$, $Pu_{Bob}$} and Alice is using {$Pr_{Alice}$, $Pu_{Alice}$}. Bob has created a message, $M_{Bob}$, and Alice has created a message, $M_{Alice}$. They want to exchange these messages with each other in a secure way.
2.  Initially, they need to exchange their public keys to establish a secure connection with each other. This means that Bob uses $Pu_{Alice}$ to encrypt $M_{Bob}$ before sending the message to Alice.
3.  Let's assume that we have an eavesdropper, X, who is using {$Pr_X$, $Pu_X$}. The attacker is able to intercept the public key exchanges between Bob and Alice and replace them with its own public certificate.
4.  Bob sends $M_{Bob}$ to Alice, encrypting it with $Pu_X$ instead of $Pu_{Alice}$, wrongfully thinking that this is Alice's public certificate. Eavesdropper X intercepts the communication. It intercepts the $M_{Bob}$ message and decrypts it using $Pr_{Bob}$.

This MITM attack is shown in the following diagram:

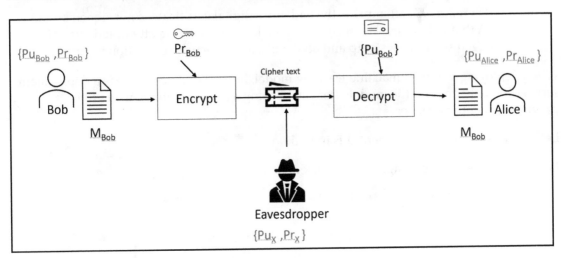

Now, let's look at how we can prevent MITM attacks.

# How to prevent MITM attacks

Let's explore how we can prevent MITM attacks by introducing a CA to the organization. Let's say the name of this CA is myTrustCA. The digital certificate has its public key, named $Pu_{myTrustCA}$, embedded in it. myTrustCA is responsible for signing the certificates for all of the people in the organization, including Alice and Bob. This means that both Bob and Alice have their certificates signed by myTrustCA. When signing their certificates, myTrustCA verifies that they are indeed who they claim to be.

Now, with this new arrangement in place, let's revisit the sequential interaction between Bob and Alice:

1. Bob is using $\{Pr_{Bob}, Pu_{Bob}\}$ and Alice is using $\{Pr_{Alice}, Pu_{Alice}\}$. Both of their public keys are embedded into their digital certificates, signed by myTrustCA. Bob has created a message, $M_{Bob}$, and Alice has created a message, $M_{Alice}$. They want to exchange these messages with each other in a secure way.

2. They exchange their digital certificates, which contain their public keys. They will only accept the public keys if they are embedded in the certificates signed by the CA they trust. They need to exchange their public keys to establish a secure connection with each other. This means that Bob will use $Pu_{Alice}$ to encrypt $M_{Bob}$ before sending the message to Alice.

3. Let's assume that we have an eavesdropper, $X$, who is using $\{Pr_X, Pu_X\}$. The attacker is able to intercept the public key exchanges between Bob and Alice and replace them with its own public certificate, $Pu_X$.

4. Bob rejects $X$'s attempt, as the bad guy's digital certificate is not signed by the CA that Bob trusts. The secure handshake is aborted, the attempted attack is logged with a timestamp and all details, and a security exception is raised.

When deploying a trained machine learning model, instead of Alice, there is a deployment server. Bob only deploys the model after establishing a secure channel, using the previously mentioned steps.

Let us see how we can implement this in Python.

First let us import the packages that are needed.

```
from xmlrpc.client import SafeTransport, ServerProxy
import ssl
```

Now let us create a class that can verify the certirficate.

```
class CertVerify(SafeTransport):
    def __init__(self, cafile, certfile=None, keyfile=None):
        SafeTransport.__init__(self)
        self._ssl_context = ssl.SSLContext(ssl.PROTOCOL_TLSv1)
        self._ssl_context.load_verify_locations(cafile)
        if cert:
            self._ssl_context.load_cert_chain(certfile, keyfile)
        self._ssl_context.verify_mode = ssl.CERT_REQUIRED

def make_connection(self, host):
    s = super().make_connection((host, {'context': self._ssl_context}))
    return s

# Create the client proxy
s = ServerProxy('https://cloudanum.com:15000',
transport=VerifyCertSafeTransport('server_cert.pem'), allow_none=True)
```

Let us look into other vulnerabilities that our deployed model can face.

# Avoiding Masquerading

Attacker X pretends to be an authorized user, Bob, and gains access to sensitive data, which is the trained model, in this case. We need to protect the model against any unauthorized changes.

One way of protecting our trained model against masquerading is by encrypting the model with an authorized user's private key. Once encrypted, anyone can read and utilize the model by decrypting it through the public key of the authorized user, which is found in their digital certificate. No one can make any unauthorized changes to the model.

# Data and Model Encrpytion

Once the model is deployed, the real-time unlabeled data that is provided as input to the model can also be tampered with. The trained model is used for inference and provides a label to this data. To protect data against tampering, we need to protect the data at rest and in communication. To protect the data at rest, symmetric encryption can be used to encode it. To transfer the data, SSL/TLS-based secure channels can be established to provide a secure tunnel. This secure tunnel can be used to transfer the symmetric key and the data can be decrypted on the server before it is provided to the trained model.

This is one of the more efficient and foolproof ways to protect data against tampering.

Symmetric encryption can also be used to encrypt a model when it has been trained, before deploying it to a server. This will prevent any unauthorized access to the model before it is deployed.

Let's see how we can encrypt a trained model at the source, using symmetric encryption with the help of the following steps, and then decrypt it at the destination before using it:

1. Let's first train a simple model using the Iris dataset:

```
import cryptography as crypt
from sklearn.linear_model
import LogisticRegression
from cryptography.fernet
import Fernet from sklearn.model_selection
import train_test_split
from sklearn.datasets import load_iris
iris = load_iris()

X = iris.data
y = iris.target
X_train, X_test, y_train, y_test = train_test_split(X, y)
model = LogisticRegression()
model.fit(X_train, y_train)
```

2. Now, let's define the names of the files that will store the model:

```
filename_source = 'myModel_source.sav'
filename_destination = "myModel_destination.sav"
filename_sec = "myModel_sec.sav"
```

Note that `filename_source` is the file that will store the trained unencrypted model at the source. `filename_destination` is the file that will store the trained unencrypted model at the destination, and `filename_sec` is the encrypted trained model.

3. We will use `pickle` to store the trained model in a file:

```
from pickle import dump dump(model, open(filename_source, 'wb'))
```

4. Let's define a function named `write_key()` that will generate a symmetric key and store it in a file named `key.key`:

```
def write_key():
    key = Fernet.generate_key()
    with open("key.key", "wb") as key_file:
        key_file.write(key)
```

5. Now, let's define a function named `load_key()` that can read the stored key from the `key.key` file:

```
def load_key():
    return open("key.key", "rb").read()
```

6. Next, let's define an `encrypt()` function that can encrypt and train the model, and store it in a file named `filename_sec`:

```
def encrypt(filename, key):
    f = Fernet(key)
    with open(filename_source,"rb") as file:
        file_data = file.read()
    encrypted_data = f.encrypt(file_data)
    with open(filename_sec,"wb") as file:
        file.write(encrypted_data)
```

7. We will use these functions to generate a symmetric key and store it in a file. Then, we will read this key and use it to store our trained model in a file named `filename_sec`:

```
write_key()
encrypt(filename_source,load_key())
```

Now the model is encrypted. It will be transferred to the destination where it will be used for prediction:

1. First, we will define a function named `decrypt()` that we can use to decrypt the model from `filename_sec` to `filename_destination` using the key stored in the `key.key` file:

```
def decrypt(filename, key):
    f = Fernet(key)
    with open(filename_sec, "rb") as file:
        encrypted_data = file.read()
    decrypted_data = f.decrypt(encrypted_data)
    with open(filename_destination, "wb") as file:
        file.write(decrypted_data)
```

2. Now let's use this function to decrypt the model and store it in a file named `filename_destination`:

```
decrypt(filename_sec,load_key())
```

3. Now let's use this unencrypted file to load the model and use it for predictions:

```
In [21]:  loaded_model = pickle.load(open(filename_destination, 'rb'))
          result = loaded_model.score(X_test, y_test)
          print(result)

          0.9473684210526315
```

Note that we have used symmetric encryption to encode the model. The same technique can be used to encrypt data as well, if needed.

# Summary

In this chapter, we learned about cryptographic algorithms. We started by identifying the security goals of a problem. We then discussed various cryptographic techniques and also looked at the details of the PKI infrastructure. Finally, we looked at the different ways of protecting a trained machine learning model against common attacks. Now, you should be able to understand the fundamentals of security algorithms used to protect modern IT infrastructures.

In the next chapter, we will look at designing large-scale algorithms. We will study the challenges and trade-offs involved in designing and selecting large algorithms. We will also look at the use of a GPU and clusters to solve complex problems.

# 13
# Large-Scale Algorithms

Large-scale algorithms are designed to solve gigantic complex problems. The characterizing feature of large-scale algorithms is their need to have more than one execution engine due to the scale of their data and processing requirements. This chapter starts by discussing what types of algorithms are best suited to be run in parallel. Then, it discusses the issues related to parallelizing algorithms. Next, it presents the **Compute Unified Device Architecture (CUDA)** architecture and discusses how a single **graphics processing unit (GPU)** or an array of GPUs can be used to accelerate the algorithms. It also discusses what changes need to be made to the algorithm to effectively utilize the power of the GPU. Finally, this chapter discusses cluster computing and discusses how Apache Spark creates **Resilient Distributed Datasets (RDDs)** to create an extremely fast parallel implementation of standard algorithms.

By the end of this chapter, you will be able to understand the basic strategies related to the design of large-scale algorithms.

The following topics are covered in this chapter:

- Introduction to large-scale algorithms
- The design of parallel algorithms
- Algorithms to utilize the GPU
- Understanding algorithms utilizing cluster computing
- How to use the GPU to run large-scale algorithms
- How to use the power of clusters to run large-scale algorithms

Let's start with the introduction.

# Introduction to large-scale algorithms

Human beings like to be challenged. For centuries, various human innovations have allowed us to solve really complex problems in different ways. From predicting the next target area of a locust attack to calculating the largest prime number, the methods to provide answers for complex problems around us kept on evolving. With the advent of the computer, we found a powerful new way to solve complex algorithms.

# Defining a well-designed, large-scale algorithm

A well-designed, large-scale algorithm has the following two characteristics:

- It is designed to handle a huge amount of data and processing requirements using an available pool of resources optimally.
- It is scalable. As the problem becomes more complex, it can handle the complexity simply by provisioning more resources.

One of the most practical ways of implementing large-scale algorithms is by using the divide and conquer strategy, that is, divide the larger problem into smaller problems that can be solved independently of each other.

# Terminology

Let's look into some of the terminology that can be used to quantify the quality of large-scale algorithms.

# Latency

Latency is the end-to-end time taken to perform a single computation. If $Compute_1$ represents a single computation that starts at $t_1$ and ends at $t_2$, then we can say the following:

$Latency = t_2 - t_1$

# Throughput

In the context of parallel computing, throughput is the number of single computations that can be performed simultaneously. For example, if, at $t_1$, we can perform four simultaneous computations, $C_1$, $C_2$, $C_3$, and $C_4$, then the throughput is four.

# Network bisection bandwidth

The bandwidth between two equal parts of a network is called the **network bisection bandwidth**. For distributed computing to work efficiently, this is the most important parameter to consider. If we do not have enough network bisection bandwidth, the benefits gained by the availability of multiple execution engines in distributed computing will be overshadowed by slow communication links.

# Elasticity

The ability of the infrastructure to react to a sudden increase in processing requirements by provisioning more resources is called elasticity.

> The three cloud computing giants, Google, Amazon, and Microsoft can provide highly elastic infrastructures. Due to the gigantic size of their shared resource pools, there are very few companies that have the potential to match the elasticity of infrastructure of these three companies.

If the infrastructure is elastic, it can create a scalable solution to the problem.

# The design of parallel algorithms

It is important to note that parallel algorithms are not a silver bullet. Even the best designed parallel architectures may not give the performance that we may expect. One law that is widely used to design parallel algorithms is Amdahl's law.

# Amdahl's law

Gene Amdahl was one of the first people who studied parallel processing in the 1960s. He proposed Amdahl's law, which is still applicable today and can become a basis to understand the various trade-offs involved when designing a parallel computing solution. Amdahl's law can be explained as follows:

It is based on the concept that in any computing process, not all of the processes can be executed in parallel. There will be a sequential portion of the process that cannot be parallelized.

Let's look at a particular example. Assume that we want to read a large number of files stored on a computer and want to train a machine learning model using the data found in these files.

This whole process is called P. It is obvious that P can be divided into the following two subprocesses:

- *P1*: Scan the files in the directory, create a list of filenames that matches the input file, and pass it on.
- *P2*: Read the files, create the data processing pipeline, process the files, and train the model.

# Conducting sequential process analysis

The time to run *P* is represented by $T_{seq}(P)$. The times to run *P1* and *P2* are represented by $T_{seq}(P1)$ and $T_{seq}(P2)$. It is obvious that, when running on a single node, we can observe two things:

- *P2* cannot start running before P1 is complete. This is represented by *P1 --> P2*
- $T_{seq}(P) = T_{seq}(P1) + T_{seq}(P2)$

Let's assume that P overall takes 10 minutes to run on a single node. Out of these 10 minutes, P1 takes 2 minutes to run and P2 takes 8 minutes to run on a single node. This is shown in the following diagram:

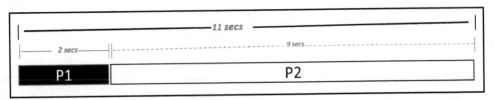

Now the important thing to note is that *P1* is sequential in nature. We cannot make it faster by making it parallel. On the other hand, *P2* can easily be split into parallel subtasks that can run in parallel. So, we can make it run faster by running it in parallel.

> The major benefit of using cloud computing is the availability of a large pool of resources and many of them are used in parallel. The plan to use these resources for a given problem is called an execution plan. Amdahl's law is used comprehensively to identify the bottlenecks for a given problem and a pool of resources.

## Conducting parallel execution analysis

If we want to use more than one node to speed up P, it will only affect P2 by a factor of *s>1*:

$$T_{par}(P) = T_{seq}(P1) + \frac{1}{s}T_{seq}(P2)$$

The speedup of the process P can be easily calculated as follows:

$$S(P) = \frac{T_{seq}(P)}{T_{par}(P)}$$

The ratio of the parallelizable portion of a process to its total is represented by *b* and is calculated as follows:

$$b = \frac{T_{seq}(P2)}{T_{seq}(P)}$$

For example, in the preceding scenario, *b* = 8/10 = 0.8.

Simplifying these equations will give us Amdahl's law:

$$S(P) = \frac{1}{1 - b + \frac{b}{s}}$$

Here, we have the following:

- *P* is the overall process.
- *b* is the ratio of the parallelizable portion of *P*.
- *s* is the speedup achieved in the parallelizable portion of *P*.

Let's assume that we plan to run the process P on three parallel nodes:

- *P1* is the sequential portion and cannot be reduced by using parallel nodes. It will remain at 2 seconds.
- *P2* now takes 3 seconds instead of 9 seconds.

So, the total time taken by process *P* is reduced to 5 seconds, as shown in the following diagram:

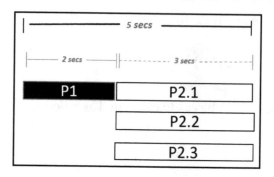

In the preceding example, we can calculate the following:

- $n_p$ = the number of processors = 3
- *b* = the parallel portion = 9/11 = 81.81%
- *s* = the speedup = 3

Now, let's look at a typical graph that explains Amdahl's law:

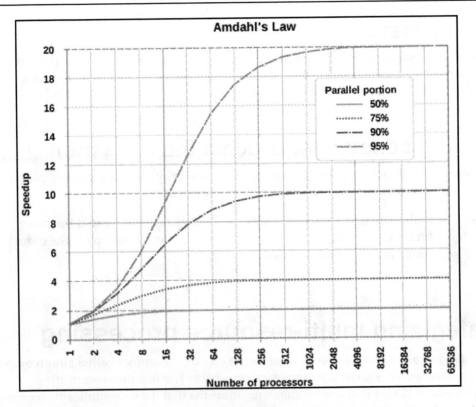

In the preceding diagram, we draw the graph between $s$ and $n_p$ for different values of $b$.

# Understanding task granularity

When we parallelize an algorithm, a larger job is divided into multiple parallel tasks. It is not always straightforward to find the optimal number of parallel tasks into which a job should be divided. If there are too few parallel tasks, we will not get much benefit from parallel computing. If there are too many tasks, then it will generate too much overhead. This is a challenge also termed as task granularity.

# Load balancing

In parallel computing, a scheduler is responsible for selecting the resources to execute the tasks. Optimal load balancing is a difficult thing to achieve, in the absence of which, the resources are not fully utilized.

# Locality issues

In parallel processing, the movement of data should be discouraged. Whenever possible, instead of moving data, it should be processed locally on the node where it resides, otherwise, it reduces the quality of the parallelization.

# Enabling concurrent processing in Python

The easiest way to enable parallel processing in Python is by cloning a current process that will start a new concurrent process called the **child process**.

 Python programmers, although not biologists, have created their own process of cloning. Just like a cloned sheep, the clone copy is the exact copy of the original process.

# Strategizing multi-resource processing

Initially, large-scale algorithms were used to run on huge machines called **supercomputers**. These supercomputers shared the same memory space. The resources were all local—physically placed in the same machine. It means that the communications between the various processors were very fast and they were able to share the same variable through the common memory space. As the systems evolved and the need to run large-scale algorithms grew, the supercomputers evolved into **Distributed Shared Memory** (**DSM**) where each processing node used to own a portion of the physical memory. Eventually, clusters were developed, which are loosely coupled and rely on message passing among processing nodes. For large-scale algorithms, we need to find more than one execution engines running in parallel to solve a complex problem:

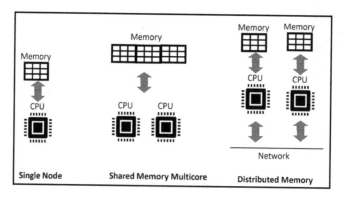

There are three strategies to have more than one execution engine:

- **Look within**: Exploit the resources already on the computer. Use the hundreds of cores of the GPU to run a large-scale algorithm.
- **Look outside**: Use distributed computing to find more computing resources that can be collectively used to solve the large-scale problem at hand.
- **Hybrid strategy**: Use distributed computing and, on each of the nodes, use the GPU or an array of GPUs to expedite the running of the algorithm.

# Introducing CUDA

GPUs have been designed originally for graphic processing. They have been designed to suit the needs of optimization dealing with the multimedia data of a typical computer. To do so, they have developed certain characteristics that differentiate them from CPUs. For example, they have thousands of cores as compared to the limited number of CPU cores. Their clock speed is much slower than a CPU. A GPU has its own DRAM. For example, Nvidia's RTX 2080 has 8GB of RAM. Note that GPUs are specialized processing devices and do not have general processing unit features, including interrupts or means of addressing devices, for example, a keyboard and mouse. Here is the architecture of GPUs:

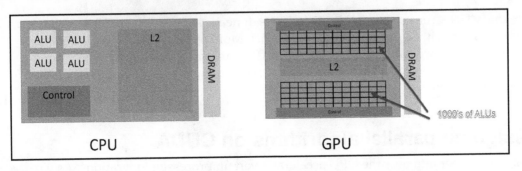

Soon after GPUs became mainstream, data scientists started exploring GPUs for their potential to efficiently perform parallel operations. As a typical GPU has thousands of ALUs, it has the potential to spawn 1,000s concurrent processes. This makes GPUs the architecture optimized for data-parallel computation. Hence, algorithms that can perform parallel computations are best suited for GPUs. For example, an object search in a video is known to be at least 20 times faster in GPUs, compared to CPUs. Graph algorithms, which were discussed in `Chapter 5`, *Graph Algorithms*, are known to run much faster on GPUs than on CPUs.

To realize the dreams of data scientists to fully utilize GPUs for algorithms, in 2007, Nvidia created an open source framework called CUDA, which stands for Compute Unified Device Architecture. CUDA abstracts the working of the CPU and GPU as a host and device respectively. The host, that is, the CPU, is responsible for calling the device, which is the GPU. The CUDA architecture has various layers of abstractions that can be presented as follows:

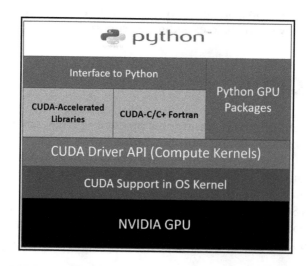

Note that CUDA runs on top of Nvidia's GPUs. It needs support in the OS kernel. CUDA initially started with support in the Linux kernel. More recently, Windows is now fully supported. Then, we have the CUDA Driver API that acts as a bridge between the programming language API and the CUDA driver. On the top layer, we have support for C, C+, and Python.

# Designing parallel algorithms on CUDA

Let's look deeper into how the GPU accelerates certain processing operations. As we know, CPUs are designed for the sequential execution of data that results in significant running time for certain classes of applications. Let's look into the example of processing an image of a size of 1,920 x 1,200. It can be calculated that there are 2,204,000 pixels to process. Sequential processing means that it will take a long time to process them on a traditional CPU. Modern GPUs such as Nvidia's Tesla are capable of spawning this unbelievable amount of 2,204,000 parallel threads to process the pixels. For most multimedia applications, the pixels can be processed independently of each other and will achieve a significant speedup. If we map each pixel with a thread, they can all be processed in $O(1)$ constant time.

But image processing is not the only application where we can use data parallelism to speed up the process. Data parallelism can be used in preparing data for machine learning libraries. In fact, the GPU can massively reduce the execution time of parallelizable algorithms, which include the following:

- Mining money for bitcoins
- Large-scale simulations
- DNA analysis
- Video and photos analysis

GPUs are not designed for **Single Program, Multiple Data** (**SPMD**). For example, if we want to calculate the hash for a block of data, it is a single program that cannot run in parallel. GPUs will perform slower in such scenarios.

 The code that we want to run on the GPU is marked with special CUDA keywords called **kernels**. These kernels are used to mark the functions that we intend to run on GPUs for parallel processing. Based on the kernels, the GPU compiler separates which code needs to run on the GPU and the CPU.

## Using GPUs for data processing in Python

GPUs are great for data processing in a multidimensional data structure. These data structures are inherently parallelizable. Let's see how we can use the GPU for multidimensional data processing in Python:

1. First, let's import the Python packages that are needed:

```
import numpy as np
import cupy as cp
import time
```

2. We will be using a multidimensional array in NumPy, which is a traditional Python package that uses the CPU.

3. Then, we create a multidimensional array using a CuPy array, which uses the GPU. Then, we will compare the timings:

```
### Running at CPU using Numpy
start_time = time.time()
myvar_cpu = np.ones((800,800,800))
end_time = time.time()
print(end_time - start_time)

### Running at GPU using CuPy
start_time = time.time()
myvar_gpu = cp.ones((800,800,800))
cp.cuda.Stream.null.synchronize()
end_time = time.time()
print(end_time - start_time)
```

If we will run this code, it will generate the following output:

```
1.130657434463501
0.012250661849975586
```

Note that it took around 1.13 seconds to create this array in NumPy and around 0.012 in CuPy, which makes the initialization of this array 92 times faster in the GPU.

# Cluster computing

Cluster computing is one of the ways of implementing parallel processing for large-scale algorithms. In cluster computing, we have multiple nodes connected via a very high-speed network. Large-scale algorithms are submitted as jobs. Each job is divided into various tasks and each task is run on a separate node.

Apache Spark is one of the most popular ways of implementing cluster computing. In Apache Spark, the data is converted into distributed fault-tolerant datasets, which are called **Resilient Distributed Datasets (RDDs)**. RDDs are the core Apache Spark abstraction. They are immutable collections of elements that can be operated in parallel. They are split into partitions and are distributed across the nodes, as shown here:

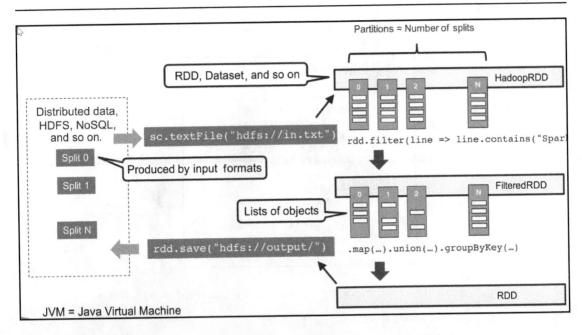

Through this parallel data structure, we can run algorithms in parallel.

# Implementing data processing in Apache Spark

Let's see how we can create an RDD in Apache Spark and run distributed processing on it across the cluster:

1. For this, first, we need to create a new Spark session, as follows:

```
from pyspark.sql import SparkSession
spark = SparkSession.builder.appName('cloudanum').getOrCreate()
```

2. Once we have created a Spark session, we use a CSV file for the source of the RDD. Then, we will run the following function—it will create an RDD that is abstracted as a DataFrame called df. The ability to abstract an RDD as a DataFrame was added in Spark 2.0 and this makes it easier to process the data:

```
df = spark.read.csv('taxi2.csv',inferSchema=True,header=True)
```

Let's look into the columns of the DataFrame:

```
In [3]:  df.columns

Out[3]:  ['pickup_datetime',
          'dropoff_datetime',
          'pickup_longitude',
          'pickup_latitude',
          'dropoff_longitude',
          'dropoff_latitude',
          'passenger_count',
          'trip_distance',
          'payment_type',
          'fare_amount',
          'tip_amount',
          'tolls_amount',
          'total_amount']
```

3. Next, we can create a temporary table from the DataFrame, as follows:

```
df.createOrReplaceTempView("main")
```

4. Once the temporary table is created, we can run SQL statements to process the data:

```
In [9]:  data=spark.sql("SELECT payment_type,Count(*) AS COUNT,AVG(fare_amount),
                AVG(tip_amount) AS AverageFare from main GROUP BY payment_type")
         data.show()

+------------+-----+--------------------+-----------------+
|payment_type|COUNT|    avg(fare_amount)|      AverageFare|
+------------+-----+--------------------+-----------------+
|         CRD|10000|  32.384988999999784|  7.61713200000006|
|         Cas| 3080|   34.64730519480518|7.497457792207749|
+------------+-----+--------------------+-----------------+
```

An important point to note is that although it looks like a regular DataFrame, it is just a high-level data structure. Under the hood, it is the RDD that spreads data across the cluster. Similarly, when we run SQL functions, under the hood, they are converted into parallel transformer and reducers and they fully use the power of the cluster to process the code.

# The hybrid strategy

Increasingly, cloud computing is becoming more and more popular to run large-scale algorithms. This provides us with the opportunity to combine *look outside* and *look within* strategies. This can be done by provisioning one or more GPUs in multiple virtual machines, as shown in the following screenshot:

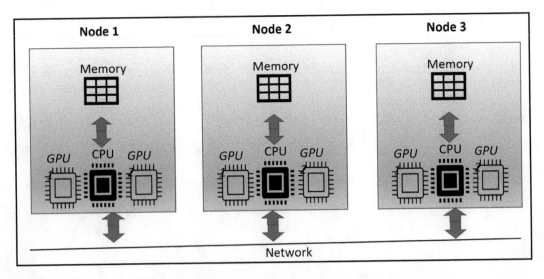

Making the best use of hybrid architecture is a non-trivial task. This is approached by first dividing the data into multiple partitions. Compute-intensive tasks that require less data are parallelized within each node at the GPUs.

# Summary

In this chapter, we looked into the design of parallel algorithms and the design issues of large-scale algorithms. We looked into using parallel computing and GPUs to implement large-scale algorithms. We also looked into how we can use Spark clusters to implement large-scale algorithms.

In this chapter, we learned about issues related to large-scale algorithms. We looked into the issues related to parallelizing algorithms and the potential bottlenecks created in the process.

In the next chapter, we will look at some practical aspects of implementing algorithms.

# 14
# Practical Considerations

There are a bunch of algorithms presented in this book that can be used to solve real-world problems. This chapter is about some practical considerations the algorithms presented in this book.

This chapter is organized as follows. We will start with an introduction. Then, we will present the important topic of the explainability of an algorithm, which is the degree to which the internal mechanics of an algorithm can be explained in understandable terms. Then, we will present the ethics of using an algorithm and the possibility of creating biases when implementing them. Next, the techniques for handling NP-hard problems are discussed. Finally, we will look into factors that should be considered before choosing an algorithm.

By the end of this chapter, you will have learned about the practical considerations that are important to keep in mind when using algorithms.

In this chapter, we will cover the following topics:

- Introducing practical considerations
- The explainability of an algorithm
- Understanding ethics and algorithms
- Reducing bias in models
- Tackling NP-hard problems
- When to use algorithms

Let's start with the introduction,

# Introducing practical considerations

In addition to designing, developing, and testing an algorithm, in many cases, it is important to consider certain practical aspects of starting to rely on a machine to solve a real-world problem as this makes the solution more useful. For certain algorithms, we may need to consider ways to reliably incorporate new important information that is expected to keep changing even after we have deployed our algorithm. Will incorporating this new information change the quality of our well-tested algorithm in any way? If so, how does our design handle it? And then, for some algorithms that use global patterns, we may need to keep an eye on real-time parameters that capture changes in the global geopolitical situation. Also, in some use cases, we may need to consider regulatory polices enforced at the time of use for the solution to be useful.

 When we are using algorithms to solve a real-world problem, we are, in a way, relying on machines for problem solving. Even the most sophisticated algorithms are based on simplification and assumptions and cannot handle surprises. We are still not even close to fully handing over critical decision making to our own designed algorithms.

For example, Google's designed recommendation engine algorithms have recently faced the European Union's regulatory restrictions due to privacy concerns. These algorithms may be some of the most advanced in their field. But if banned, these algorithms may actually turn out to be useless as they cannot be used to solve the problems they were supposed to tackle.

The truth of the matter is that, unfortunately, the practical considerations of an algorithm are still afterthoughts that are not usually considered at the initial design phase. For many use cases, once an algorithm is deployed and the short-term excitement of providing the solution is over, the practical aspects and implications of using an algorithm will be discovered over time and will define the success or failure of the project.

Let's look into a practical example where not paying attention to the practical consideration failed a high-profile project designed by one of the best IT companies in the world.

# The sad story of an AI Twitter Bot

Let's present the classical example of Tay, which was presented as the first-ever AI Twitter bot created by Microsoft in 2016. Being operated by an AI algorithm, Tay was supposed to learn from the environment and keep on improving itself. Unfortunately, after living in cyberspace for a couple of days, Tay started learning from the racism and rudeness of ongoing tweets. It soon started writing offensive tweets of its own. Although it exhibited intelligence and quickly learned how to create customized tweets based on real-time events, as designed, at the same time, it seriously offended people. Microsoft took it offline and tried to re-tool it, but that did not work. Microsoft had to eventually kill the project. That was the sad end of an ambitious project.

Note that although the intelligence built into it by Microsoft was impressive, the company ignored the practical implications of deploying a self-learning Twitter bot. The NLP and machine learning algorithms may have been the best in the class but due to the obvious shortcomings, it was practically a useless project. Today, Tay has become a textbook example of a failure due to ignoring the practical implications of allowing algorithms to learn on the fly. The lessons learned by the failure of Tay definitely influenced the AI projects of later years. Data scientists also started paying more attention to the transparency of algorithms. That brings us to the next topic, which explores the need and ways to make algorithms transparent.

# The explainability of an algorithm

A black box algorithm is one whose logic of is not interpretable by humans either due to its complexity or due to its logic being represented in a convoluted manner. On the other hand, a white box algorithm is one whose logic is visible and understandable for a human. In other words, explainability helps the human brain to understand why an algorithm is giving specific results. The degree of explainability is the measure to which a particular algorithm is understandable for the human brain. Many classes of algorithms, especially those related to machine learning, are classified as black box. If the algorithms are used for critical decision-making, it may be important to understand the reasons behind the results generated by the algorithm. Converting black box algorithms into white box ones also provides better insights into the inner workings of the model. An explainable algorithm will guide doctors as to which features were actually used to classify patients as sick or not. If the doctor has any doubts about the results, they can go back and double-check those particular features for accuracy.

# Machine learning algorithms and explainability

The explainability of an algorithm has special importance for machine learning algorithms. In many applications of machine learning, users are asked to trust a model to help them to make decisions. Explainability provides transparency when needed in such use cases.

Let's look deeper at a specific example. Let's assume that we want to use machine learning to predict the prices of houses in the Boston area based on their characteristics. Let's also assume that local city regulations will allow us to use machine learning algorithms only if we can provide detailed information for the justification of any predictions whenever needed. This information is needed for audit purposes to make sure that certain segments of the housing market are not artificially manipulated. Making our trained model explainable will provide this additional information.

Let's look into different options that are available for implementing the explainability of our trained model.

# Presenting strategies for explainability

For machine learning, there are fundamentally two strategies to provide explainability to algorithms:

- **A global explainability strategy:** This is to provide the details of the formulation of a model as a whole.
- **A local explainability strategy:** This is to provide the rationale for one or more individual predictions made by our trained model.

For global explainability, we have techniques such as **Testing with Concept Activation Vectors (TCAV)**, which is used for providing explainability for image classification models. TCAV depends on calculating directional derivatives to quantify the degree of the relationship between a user-defined concept and the classification of pictures. For example, it will quantify how sensitive a prediction of classifying a person as male is to the presence of facial hair in the picture. There are other global explainability strategies such as **partial dependence plots** and calculating the **permutation importance**, which can help to explain the formulations in our trained model. Both global and local explainability strategies can either be model-specific or model-agnostic. Model-specific strategies apply to certain types of models, whereas model-agnostic strategies can be applied to a wide variety of models.

The following diagram summarizes the different strategies available for machine learning explainability:

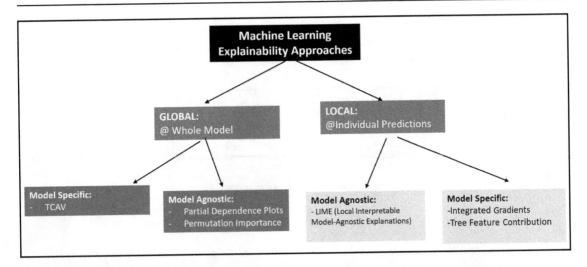

Now, let's look at how we can implement explainability using one of these strategies.

## Implementing explainability

**Local Interpretable Model-Agnostic Explanations** (**LIME**) is a model-agnostic approach that can explain individual predictions made by a trained model. Being model-agnostic, it can explain the predictions of most types of trained machine learning models.

LIME explains decisions by inducing small changes to the input for each instance. It can gather the effects on the local decision boundary for that instance. It iterates over the loop to provide details for each variable. Looking at the output, we can see which variable has the most influence on that instance.

Let's see how we can use LIME to make the individual predictions of our house price model explainable:

1. If you have never used LIME before, you need to install the package using `pip`:

   ```
   !pip install lime
   ```

2. Then, let's import the Python packages that we need:

   ```
   import sklearn as sk
   import numpy as np
   from lime.lime_tabular import LimeTabularExplainer as ex
   ```

3. We will train a model that can predict housing prices in a particular city. For that we will first import the dataset that is stored in the `housing.pkl` file. Then, we will explore the features it has:

```
In [2]:  pkl_file = open("housing.pkl","rb")
         housing = pickle.load(pkl_file)
         pkl_file.close()
         housing['feature_names']

Out[2]:  array(['crime_per_capita', 'zoning_prop', 'industrial_prop',
                'nitrogen_oxide', 'number_of_rooms', 'old_home_prop',
                'distance_from_city_center', 'high_way_access',
                'property_tax_rate', 'pupil_teacher_ratio', 'low_income_prop',
                'lower_status_prop', 'median_price_in_area'], dtype='<U25')
```

Based on these features we need to predict the price of a home.

4. Now, let's train the model. We will be using a random forest regressor to train the model. First we divide the data into testing and training partitions and then we using it to train the model:

```
from sklearn.ensemble import RandomForestRegressor
X_train, X_test, y_train, y_test =
sklearn.model_selection.train_test_split(
    housing.data, housing.target)

regressor = RandomForestRegressor()
regressor.fit(X_train, y_train)
```

5. Next, let us identify the category columns:

```
cat_col = [i for i, col in enumerate(housing.data.T)
                    if np.unique(col).size < 10]
```

6. Now, let's instantiate the LIME explainer with the required configuration parameters. Note that we are specifying that our label is `'price'`, representing the prices of houses in Boston:

```
myexplainer = ex(X_train,
    feature_names=housing.feature_names,
    class_names=['price'],
    categorical_features=cat_col,
    mode='regression')
```

7. Let us try to look into the details of predictions. For that first let us import the pyplot as the plotter from matplotlib

```
exp = myexplainer.explain_instance(X_test[25], regressor.predict,
        num_features=10)
```

```
exp.as_pyplot_figure()
from matplotlib import pyplot as plt
plt.tight_layout()
```

8. As the LIME explainer works on individual predictions, we need to choose the predictions we want to analyze. We have asked the explainer for its justification of the predictions indexed as 1 and 35:

```
In [9]:  for i in [1, 35]:
             exp = myexplainer.explain_instance(X_test[i], regressor.predict,
                 num_features=10)
             exp.as_pyplot_figure()
             plt.tight_layout()
```

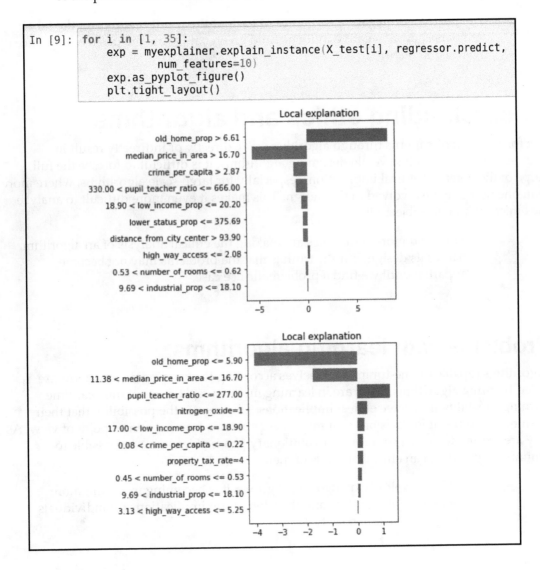

Let's try to analyze the preceding explanation by LIME, which tells us the following:

- **The list of features used in the individual predictions**: They are indicated on the *y*-axis in the preceding screenshot.
- **The relative importance of the features in determining the decision**: The larger the bar line, the greater the importance is. The value of the number is on the *x*-axis.
- **The positive or negative influence of each of the input features on the label**: Red bars show a negative influence and green bars show the positive influence of a particular feature.

# Understanding ethics and algorithms

The formulation of patterns through algorithms may directly or indirectly result in unethical decision making. While designing algorithms, it is difficult to foresee the full scope of the potential ethical implications, especially for large-scale algorithms, where more than one user may be involved in the design. This makes it even more difficult to analyze the effects of human subjectivity.

More and more companies are making the ethical analysis of an algorithm part of its design. But the truth is that the problems may not become apparent until we find a problematic use case.

# Problems with learning algorithms

Algorithms capable of fine-tuning themselves according to changing data patterns are called **learning algorithms**. They are in learning mode in real time, but this real-time learning capability may have ethical implications. This creates the possibility that their learning could result in decisions that may have problems from an ethical point of view. As they are created to be in a continuous evolutionary phase, it is almost impossible to continuously perform an ethical analysis of them.

As the complexity of algorithms grows, it is becoming more and more difficult to fully understand their long-term implications for individuals and groups within society.

# Understanding ethical considerations

Algorithmic solutions are mathematical formulations without hearts. It is the responsibility of the people responsible for developing algorithms to ensure that they conform to ethical sensitivities around the problem we are trying to solve. These ethical considerations of algorithms depend on the type of the algorithm.

For example, let's look into the following algorithms and their ethical considerations. Some examples of powerful algorithms for which careful ethical considerations are needed are as follows:

- Classification algorithms, when used on society, determine how individuals and groups are shaped and managed.
- Algorithms, when used in recommendation engines, can match resumes to job seekers, both individuals and groups.
- Data mining algorithms are used to mine information from users and are provided to decision-makers and governments.
- Machine learning algorithms are starting to be used by governments to grant or deny visas to applicants.

Hence, the ethical consideration, of algorithms will depend on the use case and the entities they directly or indirectly affect. Careful analysis is needed from an ethical point of view before starting to use an algorithm for critical decision-making. In the upcoming sections, we shall see the factors that we should keep in mind while performing a careful analysis of algorithms.

# Inconclusive evidence

The data that is used to train a machine learning algorithm may not have conclusive evidence. For example, in clinical trials, the effectiveness of a drug may not be proven due to the limited available evidence. Similarly, there may be limited inconclusive evidence that a certain postal code in a certain city is more likely to be involved in fraud. We should be careful when we are judging our decision-making based on the mathematical patterns found through algorithms using this limited data.

 Decisions that are based on inconclusive evidence are prone to lead to unjustified actions.

# Traceability

The disconnection between the training phase and the testing phase in machine learning algorithms means that if there is some harm caused by an algorithm, it is very hard to trace and debug. Also, when a problem is found in an algorithm, it is difficult to actually determine the people who were affected by it.

# Misguided evidence

Algorithms are data-driven formulations. The **Garbage-in, Garbage-out** (**GIGO**) principle means that results from algorithms can only be as reliable as the data on which they are based. If there are biases in the data, they will be reflected in the algorithms as well.

# Unfair outcomes

The use of algorithms may result in harming vulnerable communities and groups that are already at a disadvantage.

Additionally, the use of algorithms to distribute research funding has been proven on more than one occasion to be biased toward the male population. Algorithms used for granting immigration are sometimes unintentionally biased toward vulnerable population groups.

Despite using high-quality data and complex mathematical formulations, if the result is an unfair outcome, the whole effort may bring more harm than benefit.

# Reducing bias in models

In the current world, there are known, well-documented general biases based on gender, race, and sexual orientation. It means that the data we collect is expected to exhibit those biases unless we are dealing with an environment where an effort has been made to remove these biases before collecting the data.

All bias in algorithms is, directly or indirectly, due to human bias. Human bias can be reflected either in data used by the algorithm or in the formulation of the algorithm itself. For a typical machine learning project following the **CRISP-DM** (short for **Cross-Industry Standard Process**) lifecycle, which was explained in `Chapter 5`, *Graph Algorithms*, the bias looks like the following:

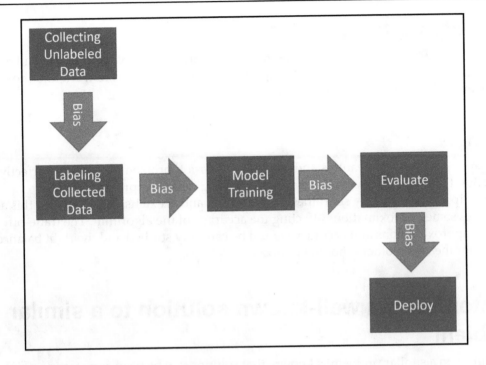

The trickiest part of reducing bias is to first identify and locate unconscious bias.

# Tackling NP-hard problems

NP-hard problems were extensively discussed in `Chapter 4`, *Designing Algorithms*. Some NP-hard problems are important and we need to design algorithms to solve them.

If finding the solution for an NP-hard problem seems out of reach due to its complexity or the limitations of the available resources, we can take one of these approaches:

- Simplifying the problem
- Customizing a well-known solution to a similar problem
- Using a probabilistic method

Let's look into them one by one.

# Simplifying the problem

We can simplify the problem based on certain assumptions. The solved problem still gives a solution that is not perfect but is still insightful and useful. For this to work, the chosen assumptions should be as non- restrictive as possible.

## Example

The relationship between features and labels in regression problems is seldom perfectly linear. But it may be linear within our usual operating range. Approximating the relationship as linear greatly simplifies the algorithm and is extensively used. But this also introduces some approximations affecting the accuracy of the algorithm. The trade-off between approximations and accuracy should be carefully studied and the right balance suitable for the stakeholders should be chosen.

# Customizing a well-known solution to a similar problem

If a solution to a similar problem is known, that solution can be used as a starting point. It can be customized to solve the problem we were looking for. The concept of **Transfer Learning (TL)** in machine learning is based on this principle. The idea is to use the inference of already pre-trained models as the starting point for training the algorithm.

## Example

Let's assume that we want to train a binary classifier that can differentiate between Apple and Windows laptops based on real-time video feed using computer vision during corporate training. From the video feed, the first phase of model development would be to detect different objects and identify which of the objects are laptops. Once done, we can move to the second phase of formulating rules that can differentiate between Apple and Windows laptops.

Now, there are already well-trained, well-tested open source models that can deal with the first phase of this model training. Why not use them as a starting point and use the inference toward the second phase, which is to differentiate between Windows and Apple laptops? This will give us a jump start and the solution will be less error-prone as phase 1 is already well tested.

# Using a probabilistic method

We use a probabilistic method to get a reasonably good solution that is workable, but not optimal. When we used decision tree algorithms in Chapter 7, *Traditional Supervised Learning Algorithms*, to solve the given problem, the solution was based on the probabilistic method. We did not prove that it is an optimal solution, but it was a reasonably good solution to give us a useful answer to the problem that we were trying to solve within the constraints defined in the requirements.

# Example

Many machine learning algorithms start from a random solution and then iteratively improve the solution. The final solution might be efficient but we cannot prove that it is the best one. This method is used in complex problems to solve them in a reasonable timeframe. That is why, for many machine learning algorithms, the only way to get repeatable results is to use the same sequence of random numbers by using the same seed.

# When to use algorithms

Algorithms are like tools in a practitioner's toolbox. First, we need to understand which tool is the best one to use under the given circumstances. Sometimes, we need to ask ourselves whether we even have a solution for the problem we are trying to solve and when the right time to deploy our solution is. We need to determine whether the use of an algorithm can provide a solution to a real problem that is actually useful, rather than the alternative. We need to analyze the effect of using the algorithm in terms of three aspects:

- **Cost**: Can use justify the cost related to the effort of implementing the algorithm?
- **Time**: Does our solution make the overall process more efficient than simpler alternatives?
- **Accuracy**: Does our solution produce more accurate results than simpler alternatives?

To choose the right algorithm, we need to find the answers to the following questions:

- Can we simplify the problem by making assumptions?
- How will we evaluate our algorithm? What are the key metrics?
- How will it be deployed and used?
- Does it need to be explainable?

- Do we understand the three important non-functional requirements—security, performance, and availability?
- Is there any expected deadline?

# A practical example – black swan events

Algorithms input data, process and formulate it, and solve a problem. What if the data gathered is about an extremely impactful and very rare event? How can we use algorithms with the data generated by that event and the events that may have led to that Big Bang? Let's look into this aspect in this section.

Such extremely rare events were represented by the *black swan events* metaphor by Nassim Taleb in his book, *Fooled by Randomness*, in 2001.

 Before black swans were first discovered in the wild, for centuries, they were used to represent something that cannot happen. After their discovery, the term remained popular but there was a change in what it represents. It now represents something so rare that it cannot be predicted.

Taleb provided these four criteria to classify an event as a black swan event.

# Four criteria to classify an event as a black swan event

It is a bit tricky to decide whether a rare event should be classified as a black swan event or not. In general, in order to be classified as a black swan, it should meet the following four criteria.

1. First, once the event has happened, for observers it must be a mind-blowing surprise, for example, dropping the atom bomb on Hiroshima.
2. The event should be a blockbuster—a disruptor and a major one, such as the outbreak of the Spanish Flu.
3. Once the event has happened and the dust has settled, data scientists who were part of the observer group should realize that actually it was not that much of a surprise. Observers never paid attention to some important clues. Had they the capacity and initiative, the black swan event could have been predicted. For example, the Spanish Flu outbreak had some leads that were known to be ignored before it became a global outbreak. Also, the Manhattan Project was run for years before the atomic bomb was actually dropped on Hiroshima. People in the observer group just could not connect the dots.

4. When it happened, while the observers of the black swan event got the surprise of their lifetime, there may be some people for whom it may not have been a surprise at all. For example, for scientists working for years to develop the atomic bomb, the use of atomic power was never a surprise but an expected event.

# Applying algorithms to black swan events

There are majors aspects of black swan events that are related to algorithms:

- There are many sophisticated forecasting algorithms available. But if we hope to use standard forecasting techniques to predict a black swan event as a precaution, it will not work. Using such forecasting algorithms will only offer false security.
- Once the black swan event has happened, predicting its exact implications on broader areas of society including the economy, the public, and governmental issues is not usually possible. First, being a rare event, we do not have the right data to feed to the algorithms, and we do not have a grasp of the correlation and interactions between broader areas of society that we may have never explored and understood.
- An important thing to note is that black swan events are not random events. We just did not have the capacity to pay attention to the complex events that eventually led to these events. This is an area where algorithms can play an important role. We should make sure that, in the future, we have a strategy to predict and detect these minor events, which combined over time to generate the black swan event.

 The COVID-19 outbreak of early 2020 is the best example of a black swan event of our times.

The preceding example shows how important it is to first consider and understand the details of the problem we are trying to solve and then come up with the areas where we can contribute toward a solution by implementing an algorithm-based solution. Without a comprehensive analysis, as presented earlier, the use of algorithms may only solve part of a complex problem, falling short of expectations.

# Summary

In this chapter, we learned about the practical aspects that should be considered while designing algorithms. We looked into the concept of algorithmic explainability and the various ways we can provide it at different levels. We also looked into the potential ethical issues in algorithms. Finally, we described which factors to consider while choosing an algorithm.

Algorithms are engines in the new automated world that we are witnessing today. It is important to learn about, experiment with, and understand the implications of using algorithms. Understanding their strengths and limitations and the ethical implications of using algorithms will go a long way in making this world a better place to live in. And this book is an effort to achieve this important goal in this ever-changing and evolving world.

# Other Books You May Enjoy

If you enjoyed this book, you may be interested in these other books by Packt:

**Modern Computer Architecture and Organization**
Jim Ledin

ISBN: 978-1-83898-439-7

- Get to grips with transistor technology and digital circuit principles
- Discover the functional elements of computer processors
- Understand pipelining and superscalar execution
- Work with floating-point data formats
- Understand the purpose and operation of the supervisor mode
- Implement a complete RISC-V processor in a low-cost FPGA
- Explore the techniques used in virtual machine implementation
- Write a quantum computing program and run it on a quantum computer

## Mastering Machine Learning Algorithms - Second Edition
Giuseppe Bonaccorso

ISBN: 978-1-83882-029-9

- Understand the characteristics of a machine learning algorithm
- Implement algorithms from supervised, semi-supervised, unsupervised, and RL domains
- Learn how regression works in time-series analysis and risk prediction
- Create, model, and train complex probabilistic models
- Cluster high-dimensional data and evaluate model accuracy
- Discover how artificial neural networks work – train, optimize, and validate them
- Work with autoencoders, Hebbian networks, and GANs

# Leave a review - let other readers know what you think

Please share your thoughts on this book with others by leaving a review on the site that you bought it from. If you purchased the book from Amazon, please leave us an honest review on this book's Amazon page. This is vital so that other potential readers can see and use your unbiased opinion to make purchasing decisions, we can understand what our customers think about our products, and our authors can see your feedback on the title that they have worked with Packt to create. It will only take a few minutes of your time, but is valuable to other potential customers, our authors, and Packt. Thank you!

# Index

# O

obscurity 294
optimal solution 87
ordered tree 58

# P

packages, SciPy ecosystem
  iPython 19
  Matplotlib 19
  NumPy 19
  pandas 19
  Python programs, executing 19
  scikit-learn 19
  Seaborn 19
PageRank algorithm
  about 95
  Eigenvector centrality 115
  implementing 95
  presenting 97, 98
  problem definition 95
pandas
  URL 19
parallel algorithms
  concurrent processing, enabling in Python 324
  design 319
  designing, on CUDA 326
  load balancing 323
  locality issues 324
  parallel execution analysis, conducting 321, 322
  sequential process analysis, conducting 320
  task granularity 323
parametric ReLU 230
partial dependence plots 336
passes 61
perfect tree 58
Personally Identifiable Information (PII) 295
phases 134
plain text 295
polynomial algorithm 80
Polynominal 81
pop operation 55
practical considerations
  about 334
  AI Twitter Bot 335

precision 183
prediction 173
principal component analysis (PCA)
  about 152, 154
  limitations 155
  using 151
processing pipeline, designing
  data, importing 178
  dataset, dividing 180
  feature selection 179
  features and label, specifying 180
  features, scaling 181
  one-hot encoding 179
pseudocode
  about 14
  example 15, 16
Public Key Infrastructure (PKI) 309
push operation 55
Python packages
  about 18, 19
  SciPy ecosystem 19
Python
  data structures 36
  GPUs, using for data processing 327
  implementing, via Jupyter Notebook 20, 21
  URL 18
  used, for calculating centrality metrics 115
  variable values, swapping 60

# Q

queue data structure 119
queues
  about 55
  front end 53
  implementing 54
  rear end 53
  using 55

# R

random forest algorithm
  about 192
  from ensemble boosting 193
  training 192
  using, for classifiers challenge 193, 194
  using, for predictions 192, 193

## W

watchtower fraud analytics methodology, limitations
- degree of suspicion (DOS) 128, 130
- negative outcomes, scoring 128

weakest link
- significance 294

weather prediction example 213, 214, 215

whitebox models 189

word embedding
- about 254
- neighborhood 255
- properties 255, 256

## X

XGBoost algorithm
- used, for implementing gradient boosting 191, 192

CPSIA information can be obtained
at www.ICGtesting.com
Printed in the USA
FSHW010725180820
73002FS